Palgrave Macmillan Memory Studies

Series Editors
Andrew Hoskins
University of Glasgow
Glasgow, UK

John Sutton
Department of Cognitive Science
Macquarie University
Macquarie, Australia

The nascent field of Memory Studies emerges from contemporary trends that include a shift from concern with historical knowledge of events to that of memory, from 'what we know' to 'how we remember it'; changes in generational memory; the rapid advance of technologies of memory; panics over declining powers of memory, which mirror our fascination with the possibilities of memory enhancement; and the development of trauma narratives in reshaping the past. These factors have contributed to an intensification of public discourses on our past over the last thirty years. Technological, political, interpersonal, social and cultural shifts affect what, how and why people and societies remember and forget. This groundbreaking new series tackles questions such as: What is 'memory' under these conditions? What are its prospects, and also the prospects for its interdisciplinary and systematic study? What are the conceptual, theoretical and methodological tools for its investigation and illumination?

More information about this series at
http://www.palgrave.com/gp/series/14682

Sandra Garrido • Jane W. Davidson

Music, Nostalgia and Memory

Historical and Psychological Perspectives

palgrave
macmillan

Sandra Garrido
MARCS Institute for Brain, Behaviour
& Development
Western Sydney University
Milperra, NSW, Australia

Jane W. Davidson
Associate Dean Research, Deputy
Director ARC Centre of Excellence for
the History of Emotions
Faculty of Fine Arts & Music
The University of Melbourne
Melbourne, VIC, Australia

Palgrave Macmillan Memory Studies
ISBN 978-3-030-02555-7   ISBN 978-3-030-02556-4   (eBook)
https://doi.org/10.1007/978-3-030-02556-4

Library of Congress Control Number: 2019931332

Cover illustration: Claudio Tebaldi / EyeEm / Getty images
Cover design: Samantha Johnson

This Palgrave Macmillan imprint is published by the registered company Springer Nature
Switzerland AG.
The registered company address is: Gewerbestrasse 11, 6330 Cham, Switzerland

CONTENTS

1	**Introduction**	1
	Music as a Soundtrack to Our Lives	1
	The Conceptual Framework of This Book	4
	The Methodological Approach to This Research	10
	Systematic Narrative Review of Historical and Cross-Cultural Sources	11
	Analysis of Musical Works: Texts and Musical Settings	13
	Empirical Survey of Modern-Day Listeners and Case-Studies of Individual Listeners	17
	The Structure of This Volume	20
	References	21
Part I	**Personal and Contextual Variables Influencing Music Listening Choices**	27
2	**Longing for the Past and Music Listening Preferences**	29
	Nostalgia in History	29
	Personal Nostalgia	32
	Historical Nostalgia	37
	Case Study: Nostalgia and Classical Music	40
	Summarising Music and Nostalgia	43
	References	43

3 Desire for Family Connections: Family History and Cultural Context   49
The Influence of Family   49
Race and Culture   52
Cultural Displacement   56
Conclusions   60
References   61

4 Personality, Gender, and Education   65
Personality   65
Gender   69
Social Class and Education   71
Conclusions   74
References   75

5 Setting the Mood: Throughout History and in the Modern Day   79
Affective Regulation Using Music Throughout History   81
   The Ancients   81
   Medieval Period   84
   The Renaissance and Elizabethan Era   88
   Baroque Period, Classicism and the Enlightenment   89
Mood Altering and Self-Medicating with Music in Modern Times   91
References   95

6 Music Throughout the Life Span   99
First Memories   102
Case Studies: Andrew and Simonne   106
Music in Identities   107
Case Study: Hreimur Choir, Iceland   109
Case Study: Choirs to Celebrate and Embrace Old Age   111
On Performance and Performers Across the Lifespan   116
Case Study: Music, Activism, Memory and Emotion   117
Conclusion   118
References   119

Part II   Historical and Psychological Variables Reflected in Music Choices for Key Life Events   125

7   Birth   127
Historical and Cross-Cultural Practices   127
   Music for Labour and Childbirth   129
   Announcing the Birth   131
   Re-integration into the Community and Celebrations of the Birth   133
Modern Day Playlists   136
   Music for Labour and Childbirth   136
   Celebrations of the Birth   140
The Trajectory from the Past to the Modern Day   141
References   146

8   Childhood   151
Introduction   151
Historical and Cross-Cultural Practices   153
   Lullabies   154
   Play Songs   155
   Social and Psychological Functions   156
Modern Day Playlists   158
A Case Study: Emma   162
The Trajectory from the Past to the Modern Day   164
   Changing Cultural Values   164
   Functions of Singing to Children   167
References   169

9   Coming of Age and Birthdays   173
Historical and Cross-Cultural Practices   173
Modern Day Playlists   177
Case Study: Joy's Birthday   181
The Trajectory from the Past to the Modern Day   183
References   187

10   Love and Heartbreak   189
Historical and Cross-Cultural Practices   189
   Love in Songs of Ancient Times   189
   The Medieval and Early Modern Periods   191
   After the Renaissance   196
Modern-Day Playlists   199
   Songs for Romance   200
   Songs of Heartbreak   203
The Trajectory from the Past to the Modern Day   210
References   213

11   Weddings   217
Historical and Cross-Cultural Practices   217
   Common Formats and Phases of Wedding Rituals   221
   Processions and Preparations for the Marriage   221
   The Ceremony   226
   Recessional and Post-ceremonial Celebrations   227
Modern-Day Playlists   229
   Traditional Versus Personal: Two Case Studies   232
The Trajectory from the Past to the Modern Day   234
References   237

12   Funerals and Mourning Rituals   241
Historical and Cross-Cultural Practices   243
   Georgian Laments   243
   Little Angels   244
   The Jazz Funeral   245
   Mourning, Bells and English Early Modern History 247
Modern Day Playlists: Australian Funerals Today   250
   MLAP Funeral Studies   251
   Diana, Princess of Wales (1 July 1961–31 August 1997)   254
   Philippa Maddern (24 August 1952–17 June 2014)   257
   Benjamin Patrick Leske (11 September 1980–7 March
   2018)   258
The Trajectory from the Past to the Modern Day   260
References   261

13   Towards a New Contextual Psychology of Music and
     Emotion   265
     References   275

Index   277

List of Figures

Fig. 5.1   Bi-directional relationship between memories and emotions   80
Fig. 13.1   Model of a contextual psychology of music and emotion   271
Fig. 13.2   A contextual psychological approach to music and emotion
research   274

LIST OF TABLES

Table 1.1	Documents reviewed in systematic narrative reviews	13
Table 1.2	Primary musical works analysed by topic	15
Table 1.3	Survey instruments used	19
Table 8.1	Sleep songs and play songs selected for lyrical analysis	161
Table 9.1	Top 15 most frequently used words in birthday lyrics	179
Table 10.1	Frequently nominated songs for a first date	201
Table 10.2	Frequently nominated songs for heartbreak	204
Table 11.1	Frequently nominated songs for a wedding	230

CHAPTER 1

Introduction

Music as a Soundtrack to Our Lives

Since the beginning of recorded human history music has created a sense of the sacred around key life events such as birth, marriage and death, heightening the experience of these peak moments. The ancient Greeks used music in all kinds of rituals to the gods, such as rain-making rituals (Haland, 2001). In Plato's *Laws* (Fourth to fifth century BC), he spoke at length about the use of music and dance in rituals to the gods. Terracotta figures found in Ibiza, Spain which date from the fifth to third centuries BC, depict women playing musical instruments and were likely used in funerary marches or fertility rituals (Lopez-Bertran & Garcia-Ventura, 2012). Similarly in ancient Egypt, music was used to appease the gods, and musicians often held religious titles (Lopez-Bertran & Garcia-Ventura, 2012). The Chinese Xunzi (ca. 312-230 BC) also discussed the attainment of perfection in ritual through music (Knoblock, 1994).

There is evidence of music use even in pre-human times. The Divje Babe flute, found in a Slovenian cave, is believed by many to be the earliest found example of a musical instrument, being over 40,000 years old and possibly manufactured by Neanderthal man (Tuniz et al., 2012). The Hohle Fels flute is also an example of a musical instrument dating from the paleolithic era (Conard, Malina, & Muenzel, 2009). The finding of a female figurine on the same site as the Hohle Fels flute, probably used as

© The Author(s) 2019
S. Garrido, J. W. Davidson, *Music, Nostalgia and Memory*, Palgrave Macmillan Memory Studies,
https://doi.org/10.1007/978-3-030-02556-4_1

a symbol of fertility, suggests that the two items were linked and may have been used together for ceremonial purposes (Conard et al., 2009).

While the functions and uses of these prehistoric musical instruments can only be speculated upon at this stage, it is likely that early rituals involving music and dancing served as ways of binding communities together in a common purpose. To our evolutionary ancestors, cooperation between members of the group was important in terms of survival. Not only are groups more effective at defending against predators—picture the lone zebra being attacked by a lion as opposed to a herd of zebra stampeding away—but they are also more effective at obtaining precious resources such as food. One theory about the evolutionary origins of music therefore suggests that music was a form of 'vocal grooming' that developed when social groups amongst our ancestors became too large for physical grooming to be a practical way of bonding between individuals (Dunbar, 1998). Music may therefore have become a way of improving group cohesiveness and cooperation.

There is no doubt that even today music has a binding function between individuals in a group. In live performance venues, hundreds of people may move in unison together, sing in unison, and experience the emotional highs and lows of the music as one. One of the most powerful mechanisms believed to trigger emotional responses to music is that of emotional contagion, in which, through a process involving empathy, mimicry and mirror neurons, the listener begins to feel the very emotions being expressed in the music (Molnar-Szakacs & Overy, 2006). In a group listening situation this contagion is compounded when the people around also begin to express emotional responses to the music, in much the same way that the impact of a film viewed in a crowded cinema may be heightened by the emotions of those around us (Garrido & Macritchie, 2018). In fact, research suggests that the situation in which music is heard can have a profound impact on both the functions music serves and how we respond to it (Greb, Schlotz, & Steffens, 2017).

However, while music has evidently been a powerful force for binding communities and groups together from prehistoric times until today, increasingly in the modern world it also provides a way of isolating an individual from the world around them. The advent of recording technology was the first step in shifting music from being a communal activity to something that could be enjoyed in private.

The invention of the phonograph enabled people to listen to music in solitude in the comfort of their own homes rather than in a concert hall.

As digital technology advances, music is becoming ever more portable. Listeners can now carry hundreds of tracks of music on small devices that can be taken wherever they go. The use of headphones means that even while walking on a crowded city street or sitting in a cram-packed train at peak hour, an individual can create a sense of personal space, a bubble of isolation from those around them (Garrido & Schubert, 2011). Thus, music in the modern world is playing an increasingly important role in our inner lives as individuals. We use it on a daily basis to create atmosphere, shape our moods, to aid us in the fulfillment of personal goals, to express personal values and emotions, and to delineate personal and cultural boundaries. Our daily lives are accompanied by a musical soundtrack that is sometimes of our own creation and sometimes not, with the key moments of our existence as humans being marked by music in striking ways.

One of the primary ways by which music is able to take on such significance in our inner world is by the way it interacts with memory. Memories associated with important emotions tend to be more deeply embedded in our memory than other events. Emotional memories are more likely to be vividly remembered (Kensinger & Corkin, 2003) and are more likely to be recalled with the passing of time than neutral memories (Sharot & Phelps, 2004). Since music can be extremely emotionally evocative, key life events can be emotionally heightened by the presence of music, ensuring that memories of the event become deeply encoded. Retrieval of those memories is then enhanced by contextual effects, in which a recreation of a similar context to that in which the memories were encoded can facilitate its retrieval. Thus, re-hearing the same music associated with the event can activate intensely vivid memories of the event. Memory is therefore closely intertwined with how our musical preferences develop and the personal significance that music holds in our individual lives, and will be a key theme considered throughout this volume.

Globally, music listening is now the predominant musical experience enjoyed by most people, with statistics revealing that sales of recorded music worldwide are massive: US$17.3 billion in 2017 (IFPI, 2018). At other points in history, prior to recorded sound and the mass production of recorded music, musical enjoyment was contingent on active participation. Many people had skills that facilitated communal musical activities ranging from barns dances to sing-alongs in pubs. The notion of music listening as a rarefied experience was not imaginable. There is thus no doubt that the recording revolution in the availability of recorded music has changed the way people use music. Questions remain about the degree to which this has changed our very perception of music.

While the ways in which we engage with music have changed dramatically in the last century—with an inevitable flow-on effect to the functions that music serves—in some ways music still fulfills fundamental purposes that have ensured its prominence in human society since the beginning of recorded history. One of the primary aims of this volume is to examine the twists and turns in the flow of music use throughout history, with a view to generating a better understanding of the role it serves both socially and psychologically in our lives today.

The Conceptual Framework of This Book

How are our personal soundtracks of life devised? What makes some pieces of music more meaningful to us than others? The answer is that a complex interaction of variables takes place to shape our musical tastes and preferences. Our personality, our family background, the music of our peers and our parents, the culture and the history of that culture in which our lives are situated, the daily experiences which shape our moods, and many other things act together in creating the personal soundtracks of our lives.

However, many music and emotion studies typically consider the interaction of only one or two variables. For example, some studies have considered the correlations between personality and genre preferences (Delsing, Ter Bogt, Engels, & Meeus, 2008; Litle & Zuckerman, 1986) or between mental health and genre preferences (Martin, Clarke, & Colby, 1993) without considering the influence of the social, cultural, or historical meanings of such genre choices. However, as acknowledged by McCrae and colleagues (2000), formulators of the Five-Factor model of personality, "trait manifestations must fit within a cultural context" (p. 175). Other discussions have focused on the cognitive mechanisms by which emotional responses are induced (Juslin & Vastfjall, 2008) without considering the contextual variables which may influence the different emotional outcomes produced.

Similarly, discussions of music and emotion rarely consider the historical context of the music itself, nor the way the listener's response to it is shaped by historical and cultural factors. This has led to two divergent streams of research on music and emotion, one led by the universalist premises of cognitive psychology, and the other based on the constructionist perspectives of cultural anthropology and contextualism (Reddy,

2001). Thus, historians of emotion argue that while emotions may have a biological basis, they are both shaped and expressed in varying ways in different historical and cultural contexts (Matt, 2011; Rosenwein, 2002). Psychology and other sciences, on the other hand, often focus on the biological underpinnings of emotion or the cognitive mechanisms by which it is evoked.

However, the two viewpoints are not necessarily mutually exclusive. As emotions historian Rosenwein states: "social constructionism and biological approaches to emotions have opposite tendencies. But their differences are not insuperable" (p. 9). Indeed, psychological theories of emotion include appraisal theories, some models of which suggest that while the biophysical manifestations of emotions may be similar from one individual to another, an individuals' evaluation of the situation giving rise to the emotional response are what determine the 'label' or value the emotion is given (Scherer, Shorr, & Johnstone, 2001). Thus, historical studies find ample evidence of embodied emotional responses even in contexts in which conventions for the expression of emotion differed from conventions in Western cultures today (see for example McGillivray, 2013).

Similarly, studies in music psychology indicate that while some emotions seem to be cross-culturally recognizable in music, others rely on culturally-specific conventions for their expression (Balkwill & Thompson, 1999) and are strongly affected by cultural influences on our perception of emotion. Appraisal theories of emotion posit that since physiological symptoms of numerous emotions can be similar, it is our appraisal of an event that determines the emotion we will experience in response to an event. Anthropological studies provide much evidence for appraisal theories, such as the work of Levy (1973) who reported that when people in Tahiti experienced psychological symptoms in situations of loss that we would call sadness or grief, they attributed these symptoms to other causes, having no concept of sadness or grief in their language. This illustrates how both biological mechanisms and social constructs interact to create an emotional response.

In relation to art appreciation, Bullot and Reber (2013) therefore propose a "psycho-historical framework" (p. 123) in which psychological responses toward art must be understood in the light of the unique historical context in which the artworks were created. In fact, any comprehensive approach to the psychology of music and emotion must consider the fact that biological and contextual factors such as culture and historical influences have profound interactions with each other in creating our emotional response to music. This volume therefore aims to draw together these divergent perspectives to create a new framework for understanding music and emotion. The starting point for our framework is therefore individual differences psychology and the belief that individual experiences with music are all vastly different. In order to understand the human experience of music, we must take multiple variables into consideration, including the influence of history on shaping musical perspectives. Neglecting to consider this point has meant that many philosophical discussions of emotional response to music and the emotional meaning of music have become mired in discussing the merits of various viewpoints without considering the fact that multiple points of view may actually be valid.

Take the question of whether people experience 'real' emotions when listening to music. Philosophers of different camps variously argue that when listening to music we experience real emotions (Krumhansl, 1997), a special set of aesthetic emotions (Levinson, 1996), or that we only experience 'aesthetic awe' which we then mistake for the emotions we perceive being expressed by the music (Kivy, 1989). However, it has been argued elsewhere that all these viewpoints may be true (Garrido & Schubert, 2010). Some people may experience emotions with all the physiological manifestations and subjective feelings of emotions evoked by real-life events, while others may experience a more detached emotion tempered by the knowledge that the situation contains no real-life implications. Still others may feel only awe at the beauty of the music.

Similarly, conflict exists over the issue of whether or not 'problem music' genres such as rap/hip-hop, heavy metal or rock are to blame for various incidences of violence or suicide. Proponents of Drive Reduction Theory would argue that music provides an outlet for people experiencing negative emotions that reduces the likelihood of them expressing their feelings in less appropriate contexts (Berkowitz, 1962). On the other hand, advocates of Social Learning Theory would argue that the presence of media which displays certain attitudes or behaviours encourages belief that such behaviour is socially acceptable (Bandura, Ross, & Ross, 1961). There is empirical evidence supporting each theory (for a summary see Davidson & Garrido, 2014; McFerran, Garrido, & Saarikallio, 2013). It is therefore possible that both lines of argument are valid and that in fact for some people rap music or heavy metal, for example, might provide a useful outlet for their feelings of aggression, while for others it might encourage them to feel that violence and aggression in public is acceptable behavior.

The basic fact is, that to untangle the various ways that music has an emotional impact on people, we must consider the individual differences in the ways people respond to and use music. To a large degree this may include personality. Several large-scale studies have demonstrated the relationships between music preferences and certain personality traits (Dunn, Ruyter, & Bouwhuis, 2012; North, Hargreaves, & Hargreaves, 2004; Rentfrow & Gosling, 2006). Thus, the research outlined in this volume takes individual differences psychology as a basis for examining emotional response to music and music preferences.

However, in addition to personality are the strategies for mood management that people have learned throughout their lives. Thus a second theoretical approach that forms an important part of the discussions in this book is mood management theory. Mood management theory in its various modifications argues that a basic motivation for music choices—at least in the modern day world—is mood improvement, i.e. people will choose music that either improves their mood or helps them to sustain a previously good mood (Knobloch & Zillmann, 2002). Empirical evidence supports this, demonstrating that people do rate mood regulation as one of their primary motivations for music listening (Saarikallio & Erkkila, 2007). People learn strategies for affect and mood regulation throughout the course of their lives, although they tend to be largely formed in childhood and adolescence (Cole, Michel, & O'Donnell Teti, 1994). Since mood modification is such a large part of modern music use, logically, these learned strategies play an important role in shaping personal music use and the effectiveness of those strategies in terms of moderating mood.

A third premise behind the arguments and research outlined in this book is the idea of context shaping emotional response to music. The term "contextual psychology" is sometimes used to refer to forms of therapy derived from the philosophy of contextualism (Stolorow, 2000). While we do not necessarily advocate some of the more radical aspects of contextualism such as the philosophically controversial argument that 'truth' only has meaning relevant to a specific context, in this volume we do argue that a complete understanding of emotional response to music cannot be achieved without examining the context in which it occurs.

Both cultural and historical context, and personal situational variables are important to such an understanding. An individual's personal history and experiences play a large role in their emotional response to music. Personal memories become entangled with particular pieces of music to the extent that we can't hear a particular piece of music without thinking of a certain person, a certain place or a certain event. In fact, music is one of the strongest triggers of nostalgic remembrance (Barrett et al., 2010; Zentner, Grandjean, & Scherer, 2008). Therefore our personal need to connect with the past—whether it be our own personal past, or a historical past—also influences the music we listen to.

Music is laden with cultural associations, forming a language of expression that is, at least in part, closely associated with the culture one has grown up in (Gorbman, 1987). However, this is an aspect that is seldom considered in literature about music preferences. Take for example the Javanese pelog scale. It contains intervals that are slightly larger or smaller than intervals from Western scales, which tend to be based on regular measurements of a semitone (Kunst, 1973). Lynch and colleagues (1991) found that the more musical exposure their participants had had to Western music, the more they perceived Javanese intervals as being a result of mis-tuning, illustrating how acculturation shapes our perception of what is pleasant or unpleasant.

Many musically informed people in Western cultures also believe strongly that specific keys are linked to particular moods (Powell & Dibben, 2005). They may believe, for example, that the key of D major expresses joy, while the key of E flat is more mellow or melancholy. These beliefs stemmed from seventeenth and eighteenth century philosophies which derive from the time when mean-tone tuning systems meant that there were some minor differences between intervals in different keys (Powell & Dibben, 2005). However, the belief has remained in the cultural lexicon despite the fact that equal tempering has been used on keyboard instruments for several centuries now.

Similarly, in Western art music, minor keys are usually perceived as sad. However, numerous studies reveal that minor keys of themselves do not necessarily seem to evoke sadness in all listeners (Collier & Hubbard, 2001; Huron, 2008). Rather, its usual coupling with slow tempos and a low melodic pitch range may be why we often think of sad music as being in minor keys. However, one would never think that the well-known *Rondo alla Turca* by Mozart[1] is sad, despite the fact that it is in the key of A minor for much of the movement. There is some strength to the argument that we may even be biologically programmed to perceive some of these other features of the music such as tempo and pitch range as sad,

[1] See Track 1 (*Rondo alla Turca* by Mozart) of the Spotify playlist which accompanies this book at https://sandragarrido.weebly.com/hearing-memories%2D%2D-companion-page-to-the-book.html

because of the similarities with features of speech prosody that express sadness.

That a knowledge of the historical context of a work and the historical context of the listener is important to understanding emotional response, is further illustrated by the case of Elton John's "Goodbye England's Rose".[2] This piece, which the Guinness Book of World Record's of 2009 states is the highest selling single in the U.S. and U.K. since the charts began, is well-known to many as the re-versioning of Elton's "Candle in the Wind" as a tribute to the late Princess Diana. The emotional response of a teenage girl listening to this song in 2019 who may not have an intimate knowledge of the context of its creation would obviously differ from that of a young woman in the 1990s who may have felt personally impacted by the tragic death of a public figure. Thus emotional response to that particular song is influenced by both the context of the song's creation and the listener's relationship to that knowledge.

These examples highlight the fact that cultural history and cultural memory shape our perceptions of the present. Drawing connections between historical and modern day uses of music and emotional responses to music can help us to better understand the influence of heritage and the past on music's role in contemporary settings. Given the fact that so much of the world's population is displaced—an estimated 92.6 million people in 2012 (Worldwatch, 2013)—the impact of historical influences becomes even more tangled. Tastes and preferences become coloured by the cultural conventions of the place of residence. However, people continue to have an emotional investment in their culture of origin even several generations after the displacement occurs. We therefore have a variety of personal and cultural histories to consider when examining the shaping of music preferences and emotional responses to music in Western societies in modern times. Insight from history thus informs our understanding of the present and provides a context for modern-day responses to music.

This volume therefore takes a novel approach by attempting to draw together historical evidence and evidence from a large-scale study of music choices in the modern day in order to provide a comprehensive model of music preferences and emotional response. Although we will touch on beliefs in ancient civilizations and the classical era, the historical focus of this book will be on the Medieval and Early Modern periods. This was a period in Western European history when education levels were rising,

---

[2] See Track 2 of the accompanying Spotify playlist: Goodbye England's Rose/Candle in the Wind (1997).

movable type was invented resulting in the increased availability of printed reading materials, and in which both the Protestant Reformation and the Scientific Revolution occurred. It thus represents a period in which remarkable changes in thinking and world-views occurred, changes that still influence life in Western societies today. It is also the era in which the tradition of Western art music became solidified in much the same way that we still know it today. It thus provides a fascinating platform from which to view the music of today.

It is evident that the subject of how our music choices are shaped is multifaceted, entailing a detailed discussion of the reciprocal relationship between music and numerous variables. It therefore necessitates an integration of approaches from across the academic spectrum. Thus, in this book, these three conceptual premises—individual differences, mood management and history shaping the modern—converge to create a broad-reaching framework for understanding emotional responses to music and music preferences and the role of memory within them. Within this framework we set out to answer the following questions:

1. What is the role of cultural memory and historical nostalgia in shaping our music preferences and listening choices today?
2. How do modern day music choices reflect the societal beliefs and values that have occurred over time?
3. Why are some people still attracted to music of the past despite the vast transformations to our viewpoints and ways of life in the last century?
4. How do personal, psychological, historical and social factors interact with our hard-wired biological make-up in creating emotional response to music?

These questions were examined in this research by examining both cultural and historical contexts, personal variables and situational variables.

THE METHODOLOGICAL APPROACH TO THIS RESEARCH

The research reported in this volume was a large-scale project conducted over a period of more than four years within the Australian Research Council's Centre of Excellence for the History of Emotions. Ethics approval was granted for the project from the University of Western Australia's Human Ethics Committee. Given our aim to draw together historical and cross-cultural information along with empirical data from the modern-day, the research reported in this volume utilizes a variety of methods—methods that are often viewed as irreconcilably different—but which complement the cross-disciplinary perspective taken in this volume. Overall, our methods derive from the fields of musicology, history of emotions research, and music psychology. Three overall methodological strategies were utilized:

1. *Systematic narrative review of both primary and secondary documents relating to historical and cross-cultural uses of music*
2. *Analysis of musical works—their texts and musical settings*
3. *Large-scale empirical surveys of modern-day listeners using psychometric measures.*

For some topic areas we also supplemented our understanding of how modern-day listeners use music by conducting interviews with several individuals. This enabled us to look at some of the individual variations in music use that occurred within the patterns revealed by the large-scale quantitative data.

Systematic Narrative Review of Historical and Cross-Cultural Sources

Given the breadth of the topics being considered in this project—one of which could alone provide enough material for an entire career's worth of study—it was not our intention to conduct in-depth historical analyses of any of the subject areas covered in this volume. Rather our intention was to draw on the work of other expert historians in these areas and to perhaps draw new insights from our unique cross-disciplinary perspectives. Thus our consideration of each key topic area—birth, childhood, coming of age, love and heartbreak, weddings, and funerals—thus began with a systematic review of the literature which led us to identify a number of primary historical documents for closer examination.

Our approach here differed from many systematic reviews in that the purpose was to consider historical practices and theories rather than to conduct a meta-analysis of the results of clinical studies and interventions. The process thus resembled the techniques of narrative synthesis, drawing on principles of historical analysis. Narrative synthesis can be described as an approach to the synthesis of evidence that relies primarily on the use of words and text to 'tell the story' of the literature that has been reviewed (Bender, 2002; Popay et al., 2006). It is therefore a method applicable to a wide range of questions not just those relating to the effectiveness of particular interventions. Historical comparative analysis is a method used in social science research which is defined as having "a concern with causal analysis, an emphasis on processes over time, and the use of systematic contextualized comparison" (Mahoney & Rueshemeyer, 2003, p. 6). We thus drew on the methodological principles of these traditions in the current study in order to compile narratives of music use at key life moments in a variety of contexts.

The first step in our investigation was to undertake a comprehensive search of online databases such as Informit, Ingenta Connect, and JSTOR for any mention of our topic area in relation to music. For example, for the section on music and birth, search terms such as Music* AND Birth* (or other related terms) were used. Similar search methods were used for each topic area of consideration. Any relevant beliefs, theories, anecdotes, texts or historical figures that were mentioned in these texts were noted and an effort made to trace the information back to its original source.

While primary sources were of principal interest, secondary sources were also reviewed in line with the methods of historical comparative analysis. This was done because of their potential to help situate the primary texts within their historical context and to determine how the information found within the primary sources had shaped later perspectives. In addition, where primary texts and/or their translations were not accessible, secondary sources were used as evidence of their content.

The quality of the literature that was reviewed was assessed in several ways. In the case of primary sources, evidence of the historicity of the texts was gleaned from historians who have studied the texts in detail. It was not considered necessary to ascertain the veracity of each anecdote contained in such texts, as anecdotes themselves provide evidence as to the beliefs and theories held at the time, whether the events described actually occurred or not. In the case of secondary sources, quality was assessed according to the scholarship displayed in their writings as well as the frequency with which they were cited by other scholars.

Table 1.1 displays the number of documents included in the review, the number and type of primary sources examined in relation to the key topic areas of the research covered in this volume. Primary sources included medical and philosophical texts as well as treatises on music theory. Each topic considered texts from a wide variety of time periods, depending on the sources available, ranging from transcriptions of ancient texts from the

Table 1.1 Documents reviewed in systematic narrative reviews

Topic	Documents reviewed	Number of primary documents	Document sources	Date range of primary texts
Birth	57	13	Medical, religious texts, ethnographies	1098–2013
Childhood	40	12	Song collections, ethnographies, literary works, transcripts of blackletter broadsides and historical artefacts	4000 BC–1999
Coming of age	24	5	Ethnographies	1952–2013
Love & heartbreak	50	13	Transcripts of blackletter broadsides and historical artefacts; song collections	1300 BC– nineteenth century
Weddings	45	19	Newspapers; paintings; biographies; ethnographic texts	Eighth century BC–2013
Funerals	71	12	Newspapers; Letters; Ethnographic texts	1475–2013

pre-Christian era to modern day ethnographic records or song texts from the twenty-first century.

As a second step in the review process the data was organized chronologically and preliminary syntheses of key theories, beliefs or practices were formulated in relation to each topic. Data from both primary and secondary sources were then coded and thematic analysis was conducted in order to search for patterns of thinking and recurrent concepts across different time periods and cultural contexts (Arai, Britten, Roberts, Petticrew, & Sowden, 2007). Given the breadth of material and subjects covered in this volume, only a sample of the texts examined could be cited. Decisions were made about the documents to cite based on their power to illustrate the themes and patterns that were identified.

Analysis of Musical Works: Texts and Musical Settings

History of emotions research is concerned with the role of emotions in history and how they are shaped by the contextual and historical time-periods in which they exist (Matt, 2011). Sources for history of emotions research are usually written texts such as books and letters, or other material representations of emotions. The written word is of course limited in what it can express compared to the spoken word. When reading a text one is not able to draw on the non-linguistic aspects of speech in interpreting the meaning of the words, such as tone of voice, facial expressions or gestures.

However, music provides a unique way to explore the non-linguistic aspects of emotional expression, above and beyond the words of a written text. Indeed, music can lend *expression* to a written text, conveying emotions where none seem to be apparent in the text itself. For example, the text of the Latin mass was set to music by many composers across the centuries. While the text itself remains relatively stable from composer to composer, the messages expressed in the musical settings differ greatly between, say William Byrd's Mass for Five Voices for instance—written for use in clandestine Catholic services during a time of Catholic persecution under Queen Elizabeth—and Bach's Mass in B Minor, written for use in the Lutheran service in Leipzig 150 years later. Both composers used musical devices to emphasize certain parts of the text and to convey their own personal spiritual messages (Tomita, Leaver, & Smaczny, 2013).

Written music can therefore provide a material representation of emotional nuances similar to speech prosody, which can be re-created and re-experienced in the modern day. Many composers further oblige us by publishing texts explaining the affective purpose of some of the musical techniques they utilized in their compositions. Other treatises on musical theory can further help us to understand the affective intentions of the composers. Thus the synergistic conjoining of historical texts and musical devices to express emotions provides a particularly illuminating area of consideration in history of emotions research.

In the research reported in this volume, our survey of historical material was supplemented by in-depth analyses of particular musical works and the circumstances of their composition which served as musical illustrations of the topics under examination. Table 1.2 lists a number of musical works that we paid particular attention to. Our purpose in examining these works was to explore the imagery and emotional vocabulary of texts and how composers used musical devices to express differing cultural and historical viewpoints in their settings of these texts.

In our analysis we drew on several key concepts from history of emotions research as theoretical lenses through which to view the musical texts and the compositional techniques used to set them. One of these concepts is Barbara Rosenwein's notion of "emotional communities" (2002).

Table 1.2   Primary musical works analysed by topic

Birth
Nursery Suite, by Edward Elgar[a]
Blessed Jesu! Here we Stand[b]
Childhood
Lavender's Blue (and song family)[c]
Stay Awake (from Mary Poppins)[d]
Coming of age
Stevie Wonder's *Happy Birthday*[e] *(+ more than 1000 songs were analyzed in linguistic software)*
The Vandals, "Happy Birthday to Me"[f]
Love and heartbreak
Scarborough Fair (and song family)[g]
Weddings
Wedding Cantata, by J. S. Bach
Funerals
'Cantos de angeles' of Chile
'Goodbye England's Rose', by Elton John

---

[a]Tracks 3–7: Nursery Suite, Edward Elgar/London Symphony Orchestra
[b]Track 8: Blessed Jesu! Here we Stand, Choir of the Chapel Royal & Huw Williams
[c]Track 9: Lavender's Blue, The Rainbow Collections
[d]Track 10: Stay Awake (from Mary Poppins), Julie Andrews
[e]Track 11: Happy Birthday, Stevie Wonder
[f]Track 12: Happy Birthday to Me, The Vandals
[g]Track 13: Scarborough Fair, Greta Bradman

'Emotional communities', as described by Rosenwein, are formed when individuals become aligned with certain individuals and against others by their emotions. Members of an emotional community come to use a common emotional language which may differ from the language used by another community. For example, a peasant woman living in Europe in the Medieval period might use a very different language around the subject of love to a middle-class English woman in the Victorian era.

Related to the concept of emotional communities, is William Reddy's idea of "emotional regimes" (2001). 'Emotional regimes' refers to the dominant mode for acceptable emotional thought and expression as created and enforced by governments or societies. To go back to our previous example, emotions expressed on the subject of love by a middle-class English woman in the Victorian era would likely reflect the ideals of passive, chaste femininity that were predominant at the time as embodied by Queen Victoria herself. This emotional regime was created and imposed in order to ensure the prosperity of both the family unit and the British empire. Nevertheless, it was in this era that the seeds of the feminist movement were beginning to take root, and more 'subversive' expressions of emotion are also evident in historical documents (Mendus & Rendall, 2002).

A further concept that provided a useful framework for our analyses was that of "cognitive ecologies". An idea arising from the work of anthropologist Edwin Hutchins (2010), 'cognitive ecologies' can be defined as "the multidimensional contexts in which we remember, feel, think, sense, communicate, imagine and act, often collaboratively, on the fly, and in rich ongoing interaction with our environments" (Tribble & Sutton, 2011, p. 94). This concept highlights the fact that a number of interconnected elements operate together as a system in influencing our thoughts, memories and emotions at any one time in a particular cultural setting, including internal cognitive mechanisms, external artifacts, and the social environment, and that the interactions between these elements is continually shifting.[3] Tribble and Sutton applied the concept in their examination of Shakespearean theatre, demonstrating how audience attention to a performance is influenced not only by biological mechanisms of vision and cognitive mechanisms of perception and attention, but are also shaped by social knowledge, and mediated by the skills of the performers, and the technology available to them. Thus in its dual focus on both context and internal mechanisms, the concept of cognitive ecologies provides a useful model for our own investigations into how cultural and historical context interact with both biological and psychological processes to influence our engagement with music.

These three key theoretical lenses thus formed the basis for our examination of the musical examples presented in this research and the texts on which they were based, as well as some of the other primary historical documents that formed part of our investigations. In particular, the use of the concepts prompted us to develop a set of questions that we used as the basis for our analyses:

---

[3] Although many think of cognition as being a form of rational thought that excludes affect, Hutchins and Andy Clark use the term broadly in a way that does not exclude emotion or limit the term to thinking alone.

1. What do the texts and musical settings reveal about the composer's own emotional community or about the dominant emotional regime of the day?
2. How does the composer reveal information about what he/she viewed as valuable or harmful?
3. What emotions are avoided or undermined in the texts and their musical settings?
4. What differences exist between the emotional expressions in the musical work under examination and similar works from other time periods or other cultural contexts?
5. What factors, such as biological mechanisms as well as context-specific knowledge and situational performance settings, may have influenced response to the musical work at the time of its composition?

The written score and, where possible, the text of the musical examples we considered were studied in the light of these questions, drawing on additional texts that further illuminated contextual information about compositional techniques or social meanings at the time of composition.

Empirical Survey of Modern-Day Listeners and Case-Studies of Individual Listeners

The research relating to modern-day uses of music reported in this volume is the culmination of a large-scale study of the music choices of over 1000 participants. Developed in collaboration with the Australian Broadcasting Corporation (ABC), the research project known as "My Life as a Playlist" (hereafter referred to as "MLAP") involved the creation of an interactive website that enabled participants to create personalized playlists for various occasions and to answer questions about their choices. Participants were recruited via advertising on ABC radio stations, in print media and in bulk emails.

Data was collected by means of online surveys over a period of one year. Several surveys were running concurrently on the site. Five short surveys related specifically to the themes of birth/birthdays, childhood, love and heartbreak, weddings, funerals. Within these surveys, participants were asked to indicate a piece of music that was important to them or that they would select to use at a future time to celebrate or mark that key event in their life. They further answered a number of questions in relation to their reasons for their choice. In addition, participants listened to an excerpt of a piece of music that represented a historical example of music relevant to the theme under consideration. For example, under the topic of funerals, participants were played an excerpt of Mozart's *Requiem Mass* and asked whether they would use it for their own funeral and to give reasons for their answer.

Three additional surveys collected information about personality, coping style, and general music preferences using predominantly pre-established psychometric instruments or scales that we developed ourselves and tested in pilot projects (see Table 1.3). Demographic information was collected as part of the general sign-in to the website, and survey data by a single participant could be linked across the various surveys by means of a system-generated ID number that created a unique identifier for each participant on the website.

Since recruitment was largely achieved by advertising by our partner organization, the ABC, and, given the musical nature of the topics under investigation, it is no surprise that the greatest number of people who responded to our surveys were people to whom music has a great importance. Therefore, the findings reported herein, necessarily reflect the interests and preferences of a musically oriented Australian sample. However, other than this bias towards people with an interest in music, little response bias would be expected given that participants were largely unaware of the purpose of the surveys other than that it was to examine how people use music at key events in their lives. Response bias was also limited since the radio stations through whom participants were recruited were widely divergent, ranging from a classical music station, to local news and talk-back stations, as well as Triple J, a station intended to appeal to young listeners. Therefore our participants covered a broad demographic in terms of age, ethnicity, and socio-economic status, ranging in age from 12 to 88 years, and coming from 32 different racial backgrounds. The demographics of participants who responded to each survey section will be reported separately in the relevant chapters.

In order to look more closely at how individuals used music in each of the settings examined in this volume, we also report on multiple case studies from each of the 6 topics covered in the second part of this volume. Some of these case studies were drawn from data we have published elsewhere, with the published sources acknowledged where that is the case. Several of the case studies consider publically available information, such

Table 1.3   Survey instruments used

Survey section	Psychometric instruments used	Reliability scores (Cronbach's alpha)	Number of survey completers
Birth/ birthdays	Questions developed by authors	N/A	801
Childhood	Questions developed by authors	N/A	594
Love	Questions developed by authors	N/A	780
Weddings	Questions developed by authors	N/A	525
Funerals	Questions developed by authors	N/A	469
Personality and mood	Rumination Reflection Questionnaire (Trapnell & Campbell, 1999)	0.91	784
	Beck Depression Inventory (Beck, Ward, Mendelson, Mock, & Erbaugh, 1961)	0.86	784
	Like Sad Music Scale (Garrido & Schubert, 2013)	0.80	784
	Coping Orientation to Problems Experienced (Carver, Scheier, & Weintraub, 1989)	>0.77 (except for Mental Disengagement subscale which was excluded)	784
	Big Five Inventory (Rammstedt & John, 2007)	>0.76	784
	Implicit Positive and Negative Affect Test (Quirin, Kazen, & Kuhl, 2009)	0.77	784
Nostalgia	Batcho Nostalgia Inventory (Batcho, 1995)	0.89	787
	Southampton Nostalgia Scale (Sedikides, Wildschut, Arndt, & Routledge, 2008)	0.74	787
	Experienced Effect of Nostalgic Listening— Negative Subscale (Garrido, 2018)	0.75	787
	Holbrook Historical Nostalgia Scale (Holbrook, 1993)	0.70	787

as the discussion of music used as the funeral of Diana Princess of Wales contained in Chap. 12. However, the majority are based on short interviews conducted especially for this volume to illustrate the variability inherent in how people use music in the modern day that is not immediately apparent from the survey data. Participants were recruited for these interviews through advertisements on social media and other websites or through word of mouth. Interviewees were asked a number of questions relating to their music selections at particular key events in their lives and the reasons for those choices. Answers were provided either in writing or verbally in short face-to-face interviews or over the phone. The case study data reported in this volume uses pseudonyms to protect the privacy of our participants with the exception of the case studies presented in Chap. 12 on Funerals. These participants were personally known to the authors of this volume and permission was obtained from their next of kin to use their real names in the text as a tribute to the individuals concerned. The key themes were drawn from the transcripts of these interviews using standard techniques for qualitative data analysis and are presented in a narrative form in the relevant chapters.

The three methodological approaches used in this research enabled us to take a 'broad brush' approach to each topic, sketching a picture of music use from antiquity, through the Medieval and Early Modern periods, and into the twenty-first century. Tracing threads of evidence derived from these multiple sources, a final synthesis of findings across a variety of temporal and cultural settings including the modern day was able to be developed, drawing together information about music use in multiple contexts and contemporary perspectives.

THE STRUCTURE OF THIS VOLUME

In Part I of this volume we will first outline and discuss a number of the personal and contextual variables that come together to influence our music listening choices and the reasons particular pieces of music take on personal significance. Chapter 2 begins by considering the topic of nostalgia and memory as a whole and the key role this plays in forming our relationship with music. Chapter 3 follows this up by considering the formative influence of family history and upbringing. Then in Chap. 4 we look at differences in music preferences relating to personality, education levels, gender and cultural context. Chapter 5 further considers how mood and mood regulation strategies affect the music that is meaningful to us. Chapter 6 concludes Part I by considering how the factors discussed in the previous chapter develop and change across the lifespan. Part I thus sets the scene for understanding how history, culture, personality, memory and other factors merge together to form our musical preferences and listening behaviours.

Part II of the book illustrates how these influences merge in shaping listening choices by focusing specifically on the role of music in six peak life events: birth (Chap. 7), childhood (Chap. 8), coming of age (Chap. 9), love and heartbreak (Chap. 10), weddings (Chap. 11) and funerals (Chap. 12). Under each of these headings we first consider the involvement of music in rituals surrounding these events throughout history and in diverse cultural contexts. We then present the unique findings about modern-day music choices gleaned from our MLAP research, drawing on case studies to illustrate the findings in more detail. Each chapter in Part II compares and contrasts the way music has been used in key rituals in different temporal and geographical contexts, demonstrating the trajectory from historical uses of music to modern day perspectives.

In a final chapter (Chap. 13) we draw together the multi-disciplinary perspectives considered in the volume to articulate a new theory of music, emotion and memory that build on the results of our historical survey and empirical studies. The text is supplemented by Spotify Playlist or a collection of musical examples which illustrate the findings and arguments presented in this volume. These sound files were often drawn from the MLAP data itself, providing examples of songs nominated by real-life participants in our research. Footnotes are used throughout the text to indicate when a musical example is available to accompany the written text and links to the tracks can be accessed at https://sandragarrido.weebly.com/hearing-memories%2D%2D-companion-pageto-the-book.html.

REFERENCES

Arai, L., Britten, N., Roberts, H., Petticrew, M., & Sowden, A. (2007). Testing Methodological Developments in the Conduct of Narrative Synthesis: A Demonstration Review of Research on the Implementation of Smoke Alarm Interventions. *Evidence and Policy, 3*(3), 361–383.

Balkwill, L.-L., & Thompson, W. F. (1999). A Cross-Cultural Investigation of the Perception of Emotion in Music: Psychophysical and Cultural Cues. *Music Perception, 17*(1), 43–64.

Bandura, A., Ross, D., & Ross, S. A. (1961). Transmission of Aggression Through Imitation of Aggressive Models. *Journal of Abnormal and Social Psychology, 63*, 575–582.

Barrett, F. S., Grimm, K. J., Robins, R. W., Wildschut, T., Sedikides, C., & Janata, P. (2010). Music-Evoked Nostalgia: Affect, Memory, and Personality. *Emotion, 10*(3), 390–403.

Batcho, K. I. (1995). Nostalgia: A Psychological Perspective. *Perceptual and Motor Skills, 80*, 131–143.

Beck, A. T., Ward, C. H., Mendelson, M., Mock, J., & Erbaugh, J. (1961). An Inventory for Measuring Depression. *Archives of General Psychiatry, 4*, 561–571.

Bender, T. (2002). Strategies of Narrative Synthesis in American History. *The American Historical Review, 107*(1), 129–153.

Berkowitz, L. (1962). *Aggression: A Social Psychological Analysis*. New York: McGraw-Hill Book Company Inc.

Bullot, N. J., & Reber, R. (2013). The Artful Mind Meets Art History: Toward a Psycho-Historical Framework for the Science of Art Appreciation. *Behavioral and Brain Sciences, 36*(2), 123–137. https://doi.org/10.1017/S0140525X12000489

Carver, C. S., Scheier, M. F., & Weintraub, J. K. (1989). Assessing Coping Strategies: A Theoretically Based Approach. *Journal of Personality and Social Psychology, 56*, 267–283.

Cole, P. M., Michel, M. K., & O'Donnell Teti, L. (1994). The Development of Emotion Regulation and Dysregulation: A Clinical Perspective. *Monographs of the Society for Research in Child Development, 59*(2–3), 73–102.

Collier, W. G., & Hubbard, T. L. (2001). Musical Scales and Evaluations of Happiness and Awkwardness: Effects of Pitch, Direction, and Scale Mode. *American Journal of Psychology, 114*(3), 355–375.

Conard, N. J., Malina, M., & Muenzel, S. C. (2009). New Flutes Document the Earliest Musical Tradition in Southwestern Germany. *Nature, 460*, 737–740.

Davidson, J., & Garrido, S. (2014). *My Life as a Playlist*. Perth: University of Western Australia Publishing.

Delsing, M. J. M. H., Ter Bogt, T. F. M., Engels, R. C. M., & Meeus, W. H. J. (2008). Adolescents' Music Preferences and Personality Characteristics. *European Journal of Personality, 22*, 109–130.

Dunbar, R. (1998). *Grooming, Gossip, and the Evolution of Language*. Harvard University Press.

Dunn, P. G., Ruyter, B. d., & Bouwhuis, D. G. (2012). Toward a Better Understanding of the Relation Between Music Preference, Listening Behavior, and Personality. *Psychology of Music, 40*(4), 411–428.

Garrido, S. (2018). The Influence of Personality and Coping Style on the Affective Outcomes of Nostalgia: Is Nostalgia a Healthy Coping Mechanism or Rumination? *Personality and Individual Differences, 120*, 259–264. https://doi.org/10.1016/j.paid.2016.07.021

Garrido, S., & Macritchie, J. (2018). Audience Engagement with Community Music Performances: Emotional Contagion in Audiences of a 'Pro-Am' Orchestra in Suburban Sydney. *Musicae Scientiae.* https://doi.org/10.1177/1029864918783027

Garrido, S., & Schubert, E. (2010). Imagination, Empathy, and Dissociation in Individual Response to Negative Emotions in Music. *Musica Humana, 2*(1), 55–80.

Garrido, S., & Schubert, E. (2011). Negative Emotion in Music: What Is the Attraction? A Qualitative Study. *Empirical Musicology Review, 6*(4), 214–230.

Garrido, S., & Schubert, E. (2013). Adaptive and Maladaptive Attraction to Negative Emotion in Music. *Musicae Scientiae, 17*(2), 145–164. https://doi.org/10.1177/1029864913478305

Gorbman, C. (1987). *Unheard Melodies: Narrative Film Music.* Bloomington: Indiana University Press.

Greb, F., Schlotz, W., & Steffens, J. (2017). Personal and Situational Influences on the Functions of Music Listening. *Psychology of Music.* https://doi.org/10.1177/0305735617724883

Haland, E. J. (2001). Rituals of Magical Rain-Making in Modern and Ancient Greece: A Comparative Approach. *Cosmos, 17,* 197–251.

Holbrook, M. B. (1993). Nostalgia and Consumption Preferences: Some Emerging Patterns of Consumer Tastes. *Journal of Consumer Research, 20,* 245–256.

Huron, D. (2008). A Comparison of Average Pitch Height and Interval Size in Major- and Minor-Key Themes: Evidence Consistent with Affect-Related Pitch Prosody. *Empirical Musicology Review, 3*(2), 60–63.

Hutchins, E. (2010). Cognitive Ecology. *Topics in Cognitive Science, 2,* 705–715.

IFPI. (2018). *IFPI Global Music Report 2018.* London, UK. Retrieved from https://www.ifpi.org/news/IFPI-GLOBAL-MUSIC-REPORT-2018

Juslin, P. N., & Vastfjall, D. (2008). Emotional Response to Music: The Need to Consider Underlying Mechanisms. *Behavioral and Brain Sciences, 31,* 559–621.

Kensinger, E. A., & Corkin, S. (2003). Memory Enhancement for Emotional Words: Are Emotional Words More Vividly Remembered than Neutral Words? *Memory and Cognition, 31,* 1169–1180.

Kivy, P. (1989). *Sound Sentiment.* Princeton University Press.

Knobloch, S., & Zillmann, D. (2002). Mood Management Via the Digital Jukebox. *Journal of Communication, 52*(2), 351–366.

Knoblock, J. (1994). *Xunzi: A Translation and Study of the Complete Words.* Stanford: Stanford University Press.

Krumhansl, C. L. (1997). An Exploratory Study of Musical Emotions and Psychophysiology. *Canadian Journal of Experimental Psychology, 51*(4), 336–352.

Kunst, J. (1973). *Music in Java: Its History, Its Theory and Its Technique.* The Hague: Martinus Nijhoff.

Levinson, J. (1996). Emotional Response to Art: A Survey of the Terrain. In M. Hjort & S. Laver (Eds.), *The Pleasures of Aesthetics: Philosophical Essays*. New York: Cornell University Press.

Levy, R. I. (1973). *Tahitians: Mind and Experience in the Society Islands*. Chicago: University of Chicago Press.

Litle, P., & Zuckerman, M. (1986). Sensation Seeking and Music Preferences. *Personality and Individual Differences, 7*(4), 575–578.

Lopez-Bertran, M., & Garcia-Ventura, A. (2012). Music, Gender and Rituals in the Ancient Mediterranean: Revisiting the Punic Evidence. *World Archaeology, 44*(3), 393–408.

Lynch, M. P., Eilers, R. E., Oller, K. D., Urbano, R. C., & Wilson, P. (1991). Influences of Acculturation and Musical Sophistication on Perception of Musical Interval Patterns. *Journal of Experimental Psychology: Human Perception and Performance, 17*(4), 967–975.

Mahoney, J., & Rueshemeyer, D. (2003). *Comparative Historical Analysis in the Social Sciences*. Cambridge: Cambridge University Press.

Martin, G., Clarke, M., & Colby, P. (1993). Adolescent Suicide: Music Preference as an Indicator of Vulnerability. *Journal of the American Academy of Child & Adolescent Psychiatry, 32*(3), 530–535.

Matt, S. (2011). Current Emotion Research in History: Or, Doing History from the Inside Out. *Emotion Review, 3*(1), 117–124.

McCrae, R. R., Costa, P. T. J., Ostendor, F., Angleitner, A., Hrebickova, M., Jesus Sanz, M. D. A., … Smith, P. B. (2000). Nature Over Nurture: Temperament, Personality, and Life Span Development. *Journal of Personality and Social Psychology, 78*(1), 173–186.

McFerran, K., Garrido, S., & Saarikallio, S. (2013). A Critical Interpretive Synthesis of the Literature Linking Music and Adolescent Mental Health. *Youth & Society*. https://doi.org/10.1177/0044118X13501343

McGillivray, G. (2013). Motions of the Mind: Transacting Emotions on the Eighteenth-Century Stage. *Restoration and Eighteenth-Century Theatre Research, 28*(2), 5–129.

Mendus, S., & Rendall, J. (2002). *Sexuality and Subordination: Interdisciplinary Studies of Gender in the Nineteenth Century*. Routledge.

Molnar-Szakacs, I., & Overy, K. (2006). Music and Mirror Neurons: From Motion to 'E'motion. *SCAN, 1*, 235–241.

North, A. C., Hargreaves, D. J., & Hargreaves, J. J. (2004). Uses of Music in Everyday Life. *Music Perception, 22*(1), 41–77.

Popay, J., Roberts, H., Sowden, A., Petticrew, M., Arai, L., Rodgers, M., … Duffy, S. (2006). *Guidance on the Conduct of Narrative Synthesis in Systematic Reviews: A Product from the ESRC Methods Programme*. Version 1. Retrieved from http://www.lancs.ac.uk/shm/research/nssr/research/dissemination/ppublications/NS_Synthesis_Guidance_v1.pdf

Powell, J., & Dibben, N. (2005). Key-Mood Association: A Self Perpetuating Myth. *Musicae Scientiae, 9*(2), 289–311.

Quirin, M., Kazen, M., & Kuhl, J. (2009). Nonsense Sounds Happy or Helpless: The Implicit Positive and Negative Affect Test (IPANAT). *Journal of Personality and Social Psychology, 97*(3), 500–516.

Rammstedt, B., & John, O. P. (2007). Measuring Personality in One Minute or Less: A 10-item Short Version of the Big Five Inventory in English and German. *Journal of Research in Personality, 41*, 203–212.

Reddy, W. M. (2001). *The Navigation of Feeling: A Framework for the History of Emotions*. Cambridge and New York: Cambridge University Press.

Rentfrow, P. J., & Gosling, S. D. (2006). Message in a Ballad – The Role of Music Preferences in Interpersonal Perception. *Psychological Science, 17*(3), 236–242.

Rosenwein, B. H. (2002). Worrying About Emotions in History. *The American Historical Review, 107*(3), 821–845.

Saarikallio, S., & Erkkila, J. (2007). The Role of Music in Adolescents' Mood Regulation. *Psychology of Music, 35*(1), 88–109.

Scherer, K. R., Shorr, A., & Johnstone, T. (2001). *Appraisal Processes in Emotion: Theory, Methods, Research*. Canary, NC: Oxford University Press.

Sedikides, C., Wildschut, T., Arndt, J., & Routledge, C. (2008). Nostalgia: Past, Present and Future. *Current Directions in Psychological Science, 17*(5), 304–307.

Sharot, T., & Phelps, E. A. (2004). How Arousal Modulates Memory: Disentangling the Effects of Attention and Retention. *Cognitive, Affective & Behavioral Neuroscience, 4*(3), 294–306.

Stolorow, R. D. (2000). From Isolated Minds to Experiential Worlds: An Intersubjective Space Odyssey. *American Journal of Psychotherapy, 54*(2), 149–151.

Tomita, Y., Leaver, R. A., & Smaczny, J. (Eds.). (2013). *Exploring Bach's B-Minor Mass*. Cambridge: Cambridge University Press.

Trapnell, P. D., & Campbell, J. D. (1999). Private Self-Consciousness and the Five-Factor Model of Personality: Distinguishing Rumination from Reflection. *Journal of Personality and Social Psychology, 76*(2), 284–304.

Tribble, E., & Sutton, J. (2011). Cognitive Ecology as a Framework for Shakespearean Studies. *Shakespeare Studies, 39*, 94–103.

Tuniz, C., Bernardini, F., Turk, I., Dimkaroski, L., Mancini, L., & Dreossi, D. (2012). Did Neanderthals Play Music? X-ray Computed Micro-Tomography of the Divje Babe 'flute'. *Archaeometry, 54*(3), 581–590.

Worldwatch. (2013). *Global Number of Displaced People Surges*. Retrieved from http://www.worldwatch.org/global-number-displaced-people-surges

Zentner, M., Grandjean, D., & Scherer, K. R. (2008). Emotions Evoked by the Sound of Music: Characterization, Classification and Measurement. *Emotion, 8*, 494–521.

PART I

Personal and Contextual Variables Influencing Music Listening Choices

Longing for the Past and Music Listening Preferences

Nostalgia in History

Nostalgia is defined in *The New Oxford Dictionary of English* (1998) as 'a sentimental longing or wistful affection for the past'. It is found in young and old across many cultural contexts (Sedikides, Wildschut, Arndt, & Routledge, 2008), and is typically described as a 'bittersweet' emotion that combines both the pleasure of reconnecting with the past with a sense of loss at its passing.

Interestingly, while nostalgia today is largely viewed as an ordinary, everyday experience for many people, originally, nostalgia was believed to be a serious pathological disorder (Dickinson & Erben, 2006). It was first documented by the Swiss physician Johannes Hofer (1934, originally 1678) who reported its effects in soldiers fighting far from their homeland who developed severe and debilitating symptoms of melancholy and homesickness.

Nostalgia was also documented in the nineteenth century in cases of children taken from their mothers to live with wet-nurses. This was a relatively common custom among the middle-class in Europe (Roth, 1991). Medical records from this time period describe cases in which children suffered first the separation from their mother at a very young age, and then their subsequent separation from the wet-nurse by whom they had effectively been raised. Michael Roth explains that among

S. Garrido, J. W. Davidson, *Music, Nostalgia and Memory*, Palgrave Macmillan Memory Studies, https://doi.org/10.1007/978-3-030-02556-4_2

the French medical profession in the 1800s, nostalgia was believed to be "potentially fatal" and "contagious" (p. 7).

English physicians described the condition as resulting from being transplanted into an environment differing from that amidst which the affected person had passed his or her early days. In a rather startling description in the medical journal *The Lancet* of June 24, 1899 it was claimed that one's vulnerability to the condition was influenced by race, education and temperament. It was argued that phlegmatic individuals were more likely to experience the condition than their sanguine counter-parts: "A tendency to despond without sufficient cause undoubtedly sub-serves towards nostalgia" (p. 1727). It was also argued that education would make one more immune to the condition, while "the deeper the ignorance" of an individual, the greater the probability that nostalgia would occur. Anglo-Saxons and Celtics, it was claimed, were less likely to suffer from the affliction than other races. In harsh terms nostalgia is described as "querulous repining", "a cat's complaining, a purely selfish disorder", which no self-respecting Englishman would "give in" to despite a deep love of country.

In fact, the concepts of 'place', connection to the environment, and displacement were central to the idea of nostalgia in medical treatises of the nineteenth century. Early in the twentieth century, psychoanalytic approaches began to regard cases of nostalgia as being associated with the loss of the mother's breast or as an expression of the oedipal complex (Kaplan, 1987).

However, from the 1880s onwards the use of the term outside of the medical profession also began to increase. It was increasingly found in literature of the time and began to take on a less specific and clinical con-notation in its popular usage. As Lisa Gabrielle O'Sullivan (2006) puts it: "at the start of the nineteenth century nostalgia was a purely clinical term … by the century's end it was a vague and sentimental desire, the province of poets and philosophers" (p. 22). As the meaning of the term evolved at the very time that clinical approaches to medicinal research were on the rise, nostalgia was seen less and less as a medical condition.

According to O'Sullivan, nostalgia has now also come to be less about place than about time. Some scholars describe nostalgia as a yearning for an idealised version of the past, one to which the reality of the present moment can never match up (Hirsch, 1992). This yearning for the ideal of the past can be a longing to return to past, happier stages of one's own life—known as personal nostalgia—or even for historical periods or contexts which the individual has not personally experienced—known as historical nostalgia (Holbrook, 1993; Marchegiani & Phau, 2013).

Thus in its modern understanding, nostalgia is no longer a pathological condition, but an experience that is commonly reported in people of all ages, with over 80% of British undergraduate students reporting incidents of nostalgic remembering at least once per week (Wildschut, Sedikides, Arndt, & Routledge, 2006). In this modern sense, nostalgia is often associated with a discontent with the present, "a rebellion against the modern idea of time, the time of history and progress … the mourning of displacement and temporal irreversibility" (Boym, 2007, pp. 8–10). Some argue that there is in effect, a global epidemic of nostalgia in the twenty-first century, in which many people find themselves displaced from their countries of origin (Boym, 2007).

Geographical displacement is not the only factor which has contributed to this epidemic. Svetlana Boym argues that nostalgia has often appeared in the aftermath of political upheaval, such as after the French Revolution of 1789, or as the Russian armies were venturing into Germany in 1733. Boym further argues that the accelerated pace of industrialization and modernization in this century and the last, have led to an increased longing for the slower paced-life of the past and thus a longing for tradition as a way to preserve continuity. Thus in the mid-nineteenth century during which the industrial revolution was gaining sway, there was an increase in the institutionalization of nostalgic remembering through the establishment of museums, and other monuments to the past (Nora, 1989). Stephanie Koontz (2016) similarly notes that rapidly changing gender roles has led to a tendency for present day relationships to be viewed through the 'foggy lens' of nostalgia, which is more an ideal of relationships than an accurate understanding of the past. Thus, nostalgia is often conceptualised as a response to the challenges and uncertainties of the rapid changes that occur in the modern world (Pickering & Keightley, 2006).

The psychological literature agrees that nostalgia can be triggered by feelings of loneliness and depression, discontent with the present, and discontinuity in one's life path. Tim Wildschut and colleagues (2006), for example, found that their study participants were more prone to nostalgia when in a negative mood than when they were experiencing a positive or neutral mood. Nostalgia proneness has also been found to be associated with the Sadness dimension of the Affective Neuroscience Personality Scale and with Neuroticism from the Big Five Personality Index (Barrett et al., 2010). Other studies have found that experimentally inducing a sense of meaninglessness leads to increased feelings of nostalgia (Routledge et al., 2011), and that existential threat of death can also be a trigger for nostalgic remembering (Juhl, Routledge, Arndt, Sedikides, & Wildschut, 2010). The need to belong is also associated with nostalgia (Seehusen et al., 2013).

PERSONAL NOSTALGIA

Music is one of the most powerful triggers of nostalgia (Barrett et al., 2010; Zentner, Grandjean, & Scherer, 2008). Just a few bars of a tune can be powerfully evocative of another time, another place, and the events and people associated with them. In fact, it has been found that nostalgia is triggered more often by music than other stimuli (Juslin, Liliestrom, Västfjäll, Barradas, & Silva, 2008). Music's power to evoke memories may come largely from the way music expresses emotion. Bower (1981) has argued for a semantic associative network model of memory, in which emotion nodes are linked to other forms of memory. Thus, when emotions associated with particular memories are evoked— as they so powerfully are by music—the associated memories can be more easily retrieved.

There appear to be two primary factors that affect whether or not a particular piece of music will trigger nostalgic remembering or not: the dispositional level of nostalgia proneness of the listener, and the autobiographical salience of the music for that individual (Barrett et al., 2010). While various scales have been designed to measure 'nostalgia proneness', in the sense that we use it here, nostalgia proneness can be understood to include a combination of both the capacity to imagine or remember oneself in another time or place, and a tendency to engage frequently in such imagining or remembering. Thus people who frequently engage in nostalgia must not only have the capacity to be transported vividly back to another time and place but have the desire and habit of engaging in these kinds of thought processes. For people who can be described as prone to nostalgia, music that describes situations that are biographically similar to those experienced by an individual or that holds particular connections with the past in an individual's mind, is most likely to induce nostalgia. Other studies have demonstrated that music that is more arousing and evokes more negative affect is also more likely to be nostalgic for the listener (Michels-Ratliff & Ennis, 2016).

Listening to music that induces nostalgia can serve several psychological functions. For example, nostalgic remembering can help people to process and reinterpret past events (Cassia, 2000; De Nora, 2000), and to construct identity (Khorsandi & Saarikallio, 2013). It also serves important social functions in that it can satisfy a need to belong by reconnecting an individual with people from their past (Loveland, Smeesters, & Mandel, 2010), as well as helping to forge social connections in the present between people with a shared past. This is borne out by studies in which content analyses of nostalgic memories have been shown to typically involve important interactions with people who have been meaningful in an individual's life (Wildschut et al., 2006). Descriptions of nostalgic memories may also contain more first-person plural pronouns such as "we" and "ours", and words about other people than ordinary autobiographical descriptions (Robertson, 2013). Thus, nostalgia appears to be a resource that is accessed as a psychological buffer in times of distress, and that can be associated with several positive coping strategies and increased positive affect in some people (Batcho, 2013; Wildschut et al., 2006).

Does nostalgia proneness influence one's musical preferences? We first examined this in a study involving 85 males and 128 females in which participants answered several measures of nostalgia proneness and answered questions about music preferences (Davidson & Garrido, 2014). Two different measures of nostalgia proneness were used: the Southampton Nostalgia Scale (SNS, Routledge, Arndt, Sedikides, & Wildschut, 2008) and the Batcho Nostalgia Inventory (BNI, Batcho, 1995). These scales are distinct in that the SNS asks participants questions relating to the frequency with which they experience nostalgia, while the BNI assesses the extent to which people miss people, objects and activities from their past.

We found that there were distinct patterns between nostalgia proneness and musical preferences. People who liked heavy metal music, for example, were more likely to show high scores in nostalgia proneness (BNI), while those who preferred new age music were the least likely of all groups to enjoy nostalgic remembering. Heavy metal has been described as a "subculture of alienation" (Arnett, 1993), or one that is socially exclusionary and marginalized from mainstream society (Weinstein, 2009). People who are attracted to heavy metal often report a strong sense of social alienation (Lacourse, Claes, & Villeneuve, 2001), social nonconformity (Schwartz & Fouts, 2003) or psychological distress (McFerran, Garrido, O'Grady, Grocke, & Sawyer, 2014). Studies reveal that heavy metal users often use music in dealing with negative emotions. Since, as previously discussed, nostalgic remembering is often triggered by a loneliness, depression or disconnection and can in fact foster a sense of social connectedness, it is not entirely surprising that heavy metal users may also be particularly nostalgia prone.

Our results in our larger-scale MLAP sample were similar. We found that people that selected RNB or hard rock for their significant life moments showed higher scores in nostalgia proneness (or were more likely to miss things from their past) (BNI) while those who selected world music and instrumental music were the least nostalgia-prone. However, when questioned about their general genre preferences rather than song choices for particular occasions, results were slightly different. People who liked jazz music had the highest scores on the BNI, indicating that they were the most likely to report missing things in their past, while people who preferred rock music had the lowest scores. Some further questions revealed further differences related to the type of nostalgic experiences people were prone to have. For example, people who listened to classical music were the least likely to report that remembering the past was painful, while people who preferred alternative genres reported nostalgia as a more painful experience that they tended to avoid. Alternatively, people who preferred pop music were more likely to engage in pleasant nostalgic remembering, such as remembering happy times, using nostalgia as an escape from the present, or as a cathartic release that made them feel better, while people who listened to classical or jazz tended to report these benefits less.

We also found that people with high scores in the BNI who tend to miss the past were more likely to indicate having been attracted to their preferred genre because their parents or grandparents listened to it and less likely to listen to music because their friends liked it. They also reported generally having a high liking for music that their parents or grandparents listened to. People who were not currently residing in the country they were born in also had higher scores on the BNI. In other words, migrants— who have suffered geographical and cultural displacement—tend to be more nostalgic and to miss the past more strongly than other people.

These results suggest that people who tend to miss the past were less likely to report pleasant experiences with nostalgic listening. These individuals were more likely to listen to jazz music than others, although they tended to select RNB and hard rock for their key life moments. On the other hand, people who listened to classical music generally did not find nostalgic remembering painful, while people who prefer pop music reported more positive benefits to nostalgic remembering than others. Interestingly, there was little relationship between music preferences and the frequency with which one indulged in nostalgic remembering (as measured by the SNS) in our studies. This suggests that although many people may engage in nostalgic remembering frequently, those who do so with a sense of loss or longing are more likely to also be attracted to music that represents the past to them.

Other studies support the idea that nostalgic remembering can be more painful for people who feel a strong sense of loss over the past or who are discontented with the present (Garrido, 2018). Jazz music can be deeply reflective and nostalgic, having originated among African Americans with roots in blues music. Thus it is not surprising that people who particularly yearn for previous times might prefer to listen to jazz music. Pop music, on the other hand, as we will learn more about in Chap. 4, is often the type of music preferred by people with high scores in the personality traits of extraversion and agreeableness, and low in neuroticism (Delsing, Ter Bogt, Engels, & Meeus, 2008), and therefore could be expected to be popular with people who tend to use music for positive psychological ends.

However, a distinction can be made between the use of nostalgia as a healthy coping mechanism and a more extreme effect in which an individual may become stuck in a past-oriented way of thinking. In complicated grief, for example, obsession with the loss of the idealized past can worsen depression (Nolen-Hoeksema, Parker, & Larson, 1994). In some forms of schizophrenia the sufferer can become completely lost within a delusional system of idealized memories (Moritz, Woodward, Cuttler, & Whitman, 2004). Even in non-pathological situations, excessive nostalgia can make it difficult for individuals to move forward with their lives. Migrants who cling to an idealized past, for example, may fail to become adjusted to their new surroundings, resulting in increased feelings of isolation (Lijtmaer, 2001).

Other studies similarly report differing outcomes of nostalgia. Sedikides and colleagues (Sedikides, Wildschut, Gaertner, Routledge, & Arndt, 2010), for example, found that nostalgia effectively contributed to a sense of self-continuity in people who were happy but did not for those who were unhappy. They state that "when happiness is low, engaging in nostalgic reverie about the past may make the present seem particularly bleak by comparison" (p. 234). Other studies have shown that nostalgia can also increase anxiety and depression in people who are habitual worriers

(Verplanken, 2012). Frederick Barrett and colleagues (Barrett et al., 2010) therefore argued that two distinct types of nostalgia exists: reminiscing conducted in a brooding and ruminative way, and a reflective remembering from which an individual derives solace, comfort and understanding of one's past.

In fact, the distinction here mentioned between rumination and reflection is an interesting one for understanding the effects of nostalgia better. Rumination is an involuntary focus on negative and pessimistic thoughts (Joorman, 2005) which is highly predictive of depression (Nolen-Hoeksema, 1991). Reflection, on the other hand, is a form of self-analysis that is highly adaptive and psychologically helpful.

This involvement between rumination and nostalgia was explored further in a two-part study conducted by the first author of this volume (Garrido, 2018). The first study found that rumination was correlated both with a tendency to miss the past, and with the frequent engagement in nostalgic remembering. It was also found that the relationship between depression and nostalgia proneness was partially mediated by rumination. Studies have found that rumination is associated with negatively biased memory recall (Lyubomirsky, Caldwell, & Nolen-Hoeksema, 1998) and a tendency to interpret stimuli as negative (Raes, Hermans, & Williams, 2006). This suggests that ruminative people may tend to focus more on negative memories, view the past in a more negative light, or compare the present more unfavourably with the past, and therefore may be more likely to experience negative mood outcomes from nostalgic remembering.

However, since the effects of listening to nostalgic music had not been specifically studied in that first study, in her second study, Garrido (2018) looked more closely at affective results. The study involving 715 participants found that the majority of participants experienced positive mood effects from listening to self-selected nostalgic music. However, it was also found that a negative affective outcome from listening to nostalgic music was predicted by rumination and several other maladaptive coping styles such as denial, and emotion-focused coping. In addition, it was found that the degree to which one missed the past was also predictive of a negative mood outcome from listening to nostalgic music. This confirmed that ruminative people who may be more likely to feel a strong feeling of longing for the past and discontent with the present, are more likely to experience a worsened mood from engaging in nostalgic remembering.

The mechanisms behind this have been further clarified in a study in which 177 students kept a diary of the effect of listening to various pieces of music over a 4-week period (Garrido, Bangert, & Schubert, 2016). The authors of that study found that people who reported that the music had triggered negative memories or an intense longing for the past were more likely to have experienced negative mood outcomes from listening to music. For some, nostalgia increased feelings of homesickness or longing for people from who they were currently separated. One participant said "I experienced a profound melancholy, not because I'm yearning for that moment to return, but because of the sheer finality and irrevocability of these moments" (p. 50). Nevertheless, some people chose to continue to listen to music that was intensifying their feelings of loneliness and home-sickness despite the effects.

These studies and the research reviewed herein demonstrate that nostalgia for previous times in our lives has a big role in determining both what music we will select to figure in our key life moments, as well as the influence that music will have on our affective state. Our mental health, our capacity to re-visualise the past, our social situation, as well as our learned coping style, will all have a shaping influence on our music preferences and the ways we use music in daily life.

But what about that less specific yearning for past ways of life or imagined ideals of life described above as 'historical nostalgia'?

HISTORICAL NOSTALGIA

In addition to music's power to trigger personal memories and feelings of nostalgia, culturally acquired associations mean that music can prompt 'memories' and a longing for time periods or places that we only know about second-hand. In Chap. 10 we will report in more detail on the response of our study participants reported to the song "Scarborough Fair" sung by Paul Simon and Art Garfunkel. In brief, our participants reported that the music invoked images of pastoral scenes in the English countryside, and medieval maidens and their knightly suitors. For many participants this would have been images they had only seen in films and paintings for example, not experienced first-hand. However the music conjured up for them a nostalgia for an ideal of chivalric love and simple rustic lifestyles that they may never have personally experienced. This brief example illustrates how music can evoke a nostalgic yearning for eras and lifestyles never personally lived through by the listener.

This attraction to previous time periods and lifestyles—known as historical nostalgia—is a widely accepted phenomenon in the marketing industry, and one that is effectively capitalised upon in advertising strategies (Marchegiani & Phau, 2011). Research indicates that consumers are more likely to buy products that are associated with nostalgia. For example, in one study (Bambauer-Sachse & Gierl, 2009) participants were shown a printed advertisement that was either nostalgic or non-nostalgic. The results showed that people were more likely to experience positive emotions in response to the nostalgic advertisement than the non-nostalgic one and that those emotions had a significant effect on attitudes of consumers towards purchasing the product.

Historical nostalgia is also widely used in tourism. Known as heritage tourism, this form of tourism appeals to the desire to experience the cultural traditions of a region in an 'authentic' way. Although in actual fact many cultural events are staged in a way that is designed to attract tourists rather than being authentic re-enactments of activities conducted in past eras, some scholars argue that this consumption of images from the past both appeals to and feeds nostalgic desires (Kim, 2005).

The appeal and prevalence of historical nostalgia can also be seen in the fashion industry, with a resurgence in popularity of vintage fashion and clothing from the 1940s and 1950s, an event which some scholars argue embodies a desire to explore other times in a performative way (Jenß, 2013). Others posit that consumers are seeking to escape the perfectionism and loss of uniqueness inherent in a world where most fashion is mass-produced in a factory, and that vintage fashion also enables women to re-invent and express identity through creative 'remembering' and imagining (Economou, 2015).

Historical nostalgia is also evident in the popularity of period films and costume dramas such as *Downton Abbey* (Baena & Byker, 2015). This period drama written by Julian Fellowes and first released in 2010, portrays a very idealized version of Englishness in its depiction of a sumptuous country estate presided over by the Earl of Grantham. As such it appeals to a collective nostalgia for an English past that has been "idealized through memory and desire" (Baena & Byker, 2015, p. 261), a past of nobility and the gentry, exquisite landscapes and refined social manners. As Rosalia Baena and Christa Byker argue, this vision of Englishness is one that is perhaps more appealing to the English at a time where the country currently experiences less cultural unity than they have had in the past. However, the drama is estimated to have been viewed by more than 120 million viewers worldwide in the year 2013 alone, including in South Korea, Cambodia, Singapore, Denmark, Russia and the Middle East—countries where

English manners are hardly a matter of national identity. Nevertheless, the issues of wealth, class, and the romantic aesthetic depicted in the drama seem to appeal to the nostalgia of people from many cultural backgrounds, given the almost global demise of an aristocratic class after World War I.

Music can also remind people of a previous age or a different cultural context and stir longings for ideals and lifestyles that have come to be associated with those times and places in the popular memory. For example, iconic songs of the 1960s and 70s such as John Lennon's *Imagine*[1] have come to represent the era of free love and the peace movement, with the memorial to John Lennon in Central Park in New York City becoming a place of pilgrimage for people from around the world. To many the song represents a longing for the ideals of unity and equality, classlessness and gender-free boundaries, which has taken on iconic meaning in the years since 9/11 (Kruse, 2003). Nicholas Russo (2015) thus argues that use of particular "sonic markers" (p. 38) that represent certain time periods in collective cultural memory can be used to evoke nostalgia for a past outside of one's own lived experience.

What influence does historical nostalgia therefore have on the music choices of individuals? We first explored this in an early study (Davidson & Garrido, 2014) using Holbrook's measure of historical nostalgia (Holbrook, 1993), which was designed to measure the extent to which people feel that the past was 'better' or 'preferable' to the present or the future. We also asked a series of questions of our own design about how much participants like things which represent the past, present or future such as fashion, art, literature, films and music. Our results demonstrated that people with low scores in historical nostalgia and people with low levels of attraction to things representing the past tended to also prefer newly released music as compared to music from other time periods.

We explored this in more detail with the MLAP sample. We found that people with high scores on Holbrook's historical nostalgia scale were more likely to have selected traditional song choices for their key life moments. This was particularly so for wedding music, about which we will read more in Chap. 11. It may be that this represents a nostalgia for traditional relationship structures and gender roles and some level of discontent with modern relationship dynamics. Otnes and Pleck (2003), for example, argue that the frequent selection of Elvis Presley's rendition of "Can't Help Falling in Love" for weddings in the 1990s represented a

---

[1] Track 14: Imagine, John Lennon.

nostalgia for the relationship values of the 1950s in which Elvis's song was recorded.

The relationship between nostalgia and music choices was also reflected in general genre preferences reported by our MLAP sample as well. We found significant differences on both Holbrook's scale and on our own measure of a liking for historically representative items. Interestingly, although listening to jazz music had been closely related to personal nostalgia, people who preferred jazz music were less likely to have high scores on historical nostalgia, while people who preferred popular music reported higher scores in historical nostalgia on Holbrook's scale. People who liked classical music had higher scores on our historical nostalgia items which reflected a liking for historically representative items. This suggests that popular music lovers may often feel that past eras were better, while classical music lovers tend to value historical items such as fashion, art and drama more than other people. People with high scores in historical nostalgia were also more likely to report that their preferred genre had been preferred by their parents or grandparents too, and were less likely to select music based on its general popularity. People who valued historically representative items in general further reported thinking that music from their parents and grandparents time was better than the music of today.

In addition, we found that people who valued historically representative items were attracted to Latin music but not to fusion genres in the World music category. This may be due to the fact that Latin music represents an exotic and romantic world for many listeners (Waxer, 2002), while fusion genres tend to be a more modern representation of multicultural values. For those with high scores in historical nostalgia world music preferences were often due to the fact that a genre represented the individual's own cultural origins, because it brought up images of attractive and exotic lifestyles, or because it represented values missing in their own culture. A liking for features of the music itself was the least likely reason given for world music preferences by people with high scores in historical nostalgia, suggesting that what the music represents is of greater importance in the minds of nostalgic listeners than the music itself.

CASE STUDY: NOSTALGIA AND CLASSICAL MUSIC

While music of virtually any era can be representative of the past from one decade ago to several centuries ago, 'classical music' is often what many people think of when they think of music of the past. Of course, what is popularly known as classical music encompasses in itself several eras of musical composition from the 'early music' of the medieval period and the Renaissance, to the Baroque period of the seventeenth and eighteenth centuries, the Romantic music of the nineteenth and early twentieth century traditions, and more modern instrumental compositions from the twentieth and twenty-first centuries. The classical music tradition itself has experienced periods of self-conscious nostalgia in which there were attempts to re-invoke the music of the past. Max Bruch's *Odysseus*, for example, which as composed in 1872 during a turbulent period of German history, draws on many historically German works by Handel, Bach and other composers. Bruch deliberately intended to evoke in his German listeners a shared cultural heritage and national pride. The nationalist movement that swept the music of Europe in the early twentieth century also was designed to evoke a nostalgia for cultural traditions of the past.

There are many reasons why people do and do not like classical music. For many people classical music represents snobbish elitism or is quite simply boring and inaccessible, despite the fact that it likely accompanies many pivotal scenes in their favourite movies. For others, classical music provides a more absorbing emotional journey than popular music, and deep scope for the imagination. However, for some, classical music represents something stable and permanent, a musical tradition that has outlasted all others.

In order to explore this more closely, we looked at a number of online classical music blogs, forums and discussion boards for the reasons that people give for listening to classical music. For some people, classical music represented a family tradition and what they were largely exposed to in their early years. One person said: "I discovered classical music when I was very young, due to the fact that it was what my parents would listen to", and another: "I grew up in a 100% classical musical family" ("Talk Classical," 2007). Daniel Handler, also known as the author Lemony Snicket who wrote several children's books including *A Series of Unfortunate Events*, told *The Guardian* that he was barely aware that there was any music other than classical until he was around 11 years old. His books were largely written to the accompaniment of classical music such as Shostakovich's string quartets (Handler, 2016). For others, the discovery of classical music occurred through learning a musical instrument and developing a gradual appreciation for it.

For many though, exposure to classical music came about through film and television such as from the Looney Tunes cartoons, or films like Disney's *Fantasia*. For several people posting on these classical music websites, their discoveries came later and were often unexpected: being taken by a friend to a concert, an accidental discovery of a particular piece of music that moved them which led to further explorations in the genre, or becoming intrigued with sound tracks to films such as the *Star Wars* series or films by Stanley Kubrick which also spurred explorations into classical music.

In fact, film music is largely indebted to the world of classical music, and film may in fact be the primary way that many people are exposed to classical music in the twenty-first century. Techniques developed by composers some centuries ago to express particular emotions persist in film music today. Monteverdi for example, used a series of rapid semiquaver repetitions on a single note to accompany scenes of war and bravery. This was in effect the antecedent of the 'tremolo', a device that has been a staple of film-score composers in the twentieth and twenty-first centuries to build fear and create tension in dramatic scenes and horror films (Bellano, 2011). Many other techniques in modern film music composition draw directly on the traditions of the Romantic composers. One example of this is the use of particular themes for specific characters as in *The Lord of the Rings* film series, which draws on Richard Wagner's leitmotif technique in which a particular musical theme came to represent a single character, emotion or event.

On the other hand, some of the most well-known classical themes today are recognised largely because of their use in film. For example, Richard Strauss's *Also Sprach Zarathustra* is most widely recognised today for its use in the film *2001: A Space Odyssey* (1968, dir Stanley Kubrick). Similarly Samuel Barber's *Adagio for Strings* is widely known today because of its use in the film *Platoon* (1986, dir Oliver Stone). The use of classical music in film and the use of particular musical techniques in film music writing means that many of the thoughts and memories evoked by classical music will be flavoured by the context in which it has been used in film and advertising. In this case we see that particular pieces of music can likely conjure up a nostalgic yearning not only for a previous time in one's own life or a period in history which the music seems to represent, but for the more amorphous images and ideals associated with the various fictional settings in which we have previously encountered it, and for the meanings that have become associated with various compositional devices throughout years of connection with story-telling.

SUMMARISING MUSIC AND NOSTALGIA

Music is one of the strongest ways to evoke memories of previous places and times, whether those memories are of our own past, or of a nebulous and romanticized version of the past outside of our own experience. Our studies revealed that music preferences are closely aligned to the degree to which one misses things from the past. People with strong tendencies to miss past phases of their own lives were more likely to listen to genres such as heavy metal, RNB, or hard rock—genres often associated with negative emotions or psychological distress—as well as genres or styles that might have been representative of music listened to by one's parents or grandparents such as jazz. People with low scores in personal nostalgia proneness, on the other hand, were more likely to listen to modern music genres such as new age, rock or popular music. As revealed in this chapter and as will be discussed further in Chap. 5, much of these choices appear to be reflective of individual coping style, which also appears to influence the relative pleasantness or unpleasantness of nostalgic remembering for the listener.

Historical nostalgia is another way that music feeds a desire for the past—albeit a version of the past that may be largely built upon fictitious concepts. Of note here, was our findings that people who like historically representative items such as art, fashion and film, may also prefer the music their parents and grandparents listened to, historical genres such as classical, or more exotic world music genres such as Latin. In many, their music preferences may reflect an attachment to their culture of origin, even if only experienced through the memories of family and the collective diaspora. For others, music can represent ideals that have been lost in the present world, such as those surrounding relationships and gender roles, or broader social circumstances.

This chapter has begun to paint a picture of how the interaction between music, emotion and memory underpins much of our music preferences and listening selections. In the next chapter we explore this in greater detail in relation to family connections.

REFERENCES

Arnett, J. (1993). Three Profiles of Heavy Metal Fans: A Taste for Sensation and a Subculture of Alienation. *Qualitative Sociology, 16*(4), 423–443.

Baena, R., & Byker, C. (2015). Dialects of Nostalgia: *Downton Abbey* and English Identity. *National Identities, 17*(3), 259–269.

Bambauer-Sachse, S., & Gierl, H. (2009). Effects of Nostalgic Advertising Through Emotions and the Intensity of the Evoked Mental Images. *Advances in Consumer Research, 36*, 391–398.

Barrett, F. S., Grimm, K. J., Robins, R. W., Wildschut, T., Sedikides, C., & Janata, P. (2010). Music-Evoked Nostalgia: Affect, Memory, and Personality. *Emotion, 10*(3), 390–403.

Batcho, K. I. (1995). Nostalgia: A Psychological Perspective. *Perceptual and Motor Skills, 80*, 131–143.

Batcho, K. I. (2013). Nostalgia: Retreat or Support in Difficult Times? *The American Journal of Psychology, 126*(3), 355–367.

Bellano, M. (2011). I Fear What I Hear: The Expression of Horror in Film Music. In L. Baxter & P. Braescu (Eds.), *Fear Within Melting Boundaries* (pp. 69–78). Oxford: Inter-Disciplinary Press.

Bower, G. H. (1981). Mood and Memory. *American Psychologist, 36*, 129–148.

Boym, S. (2007). Nostalgia and Its Discontents. *The Hedgehog Review, 9*(2), 7–18.

Cassia, P. S. (2000). Exoticizing Discoveries and Extraordinary Experiences: "Traditional" Music, Modernity, and Nostalgia in Malta and Other Mediterranean Societies. *Ethnomusicology, 44*(2), 281–301.

Davidson, J., & Garrido, S. (2014). *My Life as a Playlist*. Perth: University of Western Australia Publishing.

De Nora, T. (2000). *Music in Everyday Life*. Cambridge: Cambridge University Press.

Delsing, M. J. M. H., Ter Bogt, T. F. M., Engels, R. C. M., & Meeus, W. H. J. (2008). Adolescents' Music Preferences and Personality Characteristics. *European Journal of Personality, 22*, 109–130.

Dickinson, H., & Erben, M. (2006). Nostalgia and Autobiography: The Past in the Present. *Auto/Biography, 14*, 223–244.

Economou, I. (2015). "Remembering" and Imagining: Women's Nostalgic Engagement with Vintage Fashion. *South African Journal of Art History, 30*(3), 56–73.

Garrido, S. (2018). The Influence of Personality and Coping Style on the Affective Outcomes of Nostalgia: Is Nostalgia a Healthy Coping Mechanism or Rumination? *Personality and Individual Differences, 120*, 259–264. https://doi.org/10.1016/j.paid.2016.07.021

Garrido, S., Bangert, D., & Schubert, E. (2016). Musical Prescriptions for Mood Improvements: A Mixed Methods Study. *The Arts in Psychotherapy, 51*, 46–53.

Handler, D. (2016). *Lemony Snicket: The Trouble with Being Interested in Classical Music Is That People Look at You Funny/Interviewer: I. Tilden*. UK: The Guardian.

Hirsch, A. R. (1992). Nostalgia: A Neuropsychiatric Understanding. *Advances in Consumer Research, 19*, 390–395.

Hofer, J. (1934, originally 1678). Medical Dissertation of Nostalgia. *Bulletin of Historical Medicine, 2*, 376–391.

Holbrook, M. B. (1993). Nostalgia and Consumption Preferences: Some Emerging Patterns of Consumer Tastes. *Journal of Consumer Research, 20*, 245–256.

Jenß, H. (2013). Cross-Temporal Explorations: Notes on Fashion and Nostalgia. *Critical Studies in Fashion & Beauty, 4*(1–2), 107–124.

Joorman, J. (2005). Inhibition, Rumination and Mood Regulation in Depression. In R. W. Engle, G. Sedek, U. V. Hecker, & D. N. McIntosh (Eds.), *Cognitive Limitations in Aging and Psychopathology: Attention, Working Memory, and Executive Functions* (pp. 275–312). New York: Cambridge University Press.

Juhl, J., Routledge, C., Arndt, J., Sedikides, C., & Wildschut, T. (2010). Fighting the Future with the Past: Nostalgia Buffers Existential Threat. *Journal of Research in Personality, 44*, 309–314.

Juslin, P. N., Liliestrom, S., Västfjäll, D., Barradas, G., & Silva, A. (2008). An Experience Sampling Study of Emotional Reactions to Music: Listener, Music, and Situation. *Emotion, 8*, 668–683.

Kaplan, H. A. (1987). The Psychopathology of Nostalgia. *Psychoanalytic Review, 74*(4), 465–486.

Khorsandi, A., & Saarikallio, S. (2013). *Music-Related Nostalgic Experiences of Young Migrants*. Paper Presented at the 3rd International Conference on Music & Emotion (ICME3), Jyväskylä, Finland.

Kim, H. (2005). Research Note: Nostalgia and Tourism. *Tourism Analysis, 10*, 85–88.

Koontz, S. (2016). *The Way We Never Were: American Families and the Nostalgia Trap*. UK: Hachette.

Kruse, R. J. (2003). Imagining Strawberry Fields as a Place of Pilgrimage. *Area, 35*(2), 154–162.

Lacourse, E., Claes, M., & Villeneuve, M. (2001). Heavy Metal Music and Adolescent Suicidal Risk. *Journal of Youth and Adolescence, 30*(3), 321–332.

Lijtmaer, R. M. (2001). Splitting and Nostalgia in Recent Immigrants: Psychodynamic Considerations. *Journal of the American Academy of Psychoanalysis, 29*(3), 427–438.

Loveland, K. E., Smeesters, D., & Mandel, N. (2010). Still Preoccupied with 1995: The Need to Belong and Preference for Nostalgic Products. *Journal of Consumer Research, 37*, 393–408.

Lyubomirsky, S., Caldwell, N. D., & Nolen-Hoeksema, S. (1998). Effects of Ruminative and Distractive Responses to Depressed Mood on Retrieval of Autobiographical Memories. *Journal of Personality and Social Psychology, 75*(1), 166–177.

Marchegiani, C., & Phau, I. (2011). The Value of Historical Nostalgia for Marketing Management. *Marketing Intelligence and Planning, 29*(2), 108–122.

Marchegiani, C., & Phau, I. (2013). Personal and Historical Nostalgia – A Comparison of Common Emotions. *Journal of Global Marketing, 26*(3), 137–146.

McFerran, K., Garrido, S., O'Grady, L., Grocke, D., & Sawyer, S. M. (2014). Examining the Relationship Between Self-Reported Mood Management and Music Preferences in Australian Teenagers. *Nordic Journal of Music Therapy, 24*(3), 1–17. https://doi.org/10.1080/08098131.2014.908942

Michels-Ratliff, E., & Ennis, M. (2016). This Is Your Song: Using Participants' Music Selections to Evoke Nostalgic and Autobiographical Memories Efficiently. *Psychomusicology, 26*(4), 379–384.

Moritz, S., Woodward, T. S., Cuttler, C., & Whitman, J. C. (2004). False Memories in Schizophrenia. *Neuropsychology, 18*(2), 276–283.

Nolen-Hoeksema, S. (1991). Responses to Depression and Their Effects on the Duration of Depressive Episodes. *Journal of Abnormal Psychology, 100*(4), 569–582.

Nolen-Hoeksema, S., Parker, L. E., & Larson, J. (1994). Ruminative Coping with Depressed Mood Following Loss. *Journal of Personality and Social Psychology, 67*(1), 92–104.

Nora, P. (1989). Between Memory and History: *Les Lieux de Memoire. Representations, 26*, 7–24.

O'Sullivan, L. G. (2006). *Dying for Home: The Medicine and Politics of Nostalgia in Nineteenth-Century France* (PhD). London: Queen Mary University.

Otnes, C. C., & Pleck, E. H. (2003). *Cinderella Dreams: The Allure of the Lavish Wedding.* University of California Press.

Pickering, M., & Keightley, E. (2006). The Modalities of Nostalgia. *Current Sociology, 54*, 919–941.

Raes, F., Hermans, D., & Williams, J. M. G. (2006). Negative Bias in the Perception of Others' Facial Emotional Expressions in Major Depression: The Role of Depressive Rumination. *Journal of Nervous and Mental Disease, 194*(10), 796–799.

Robertson, S. (2013). *Nostalgia and Wellbeing Across the Lifespan* (PhD). University of Southampton.

Roth, M. S. (1991). Dying of the Past: Medical Studies of Nostalgia in Nineteenth Century France. *History and Memory, 3*(1), 5–29.

Routledge, C., Arndt, J., Sedikides, C., & Wildschut, T. (2008). A Blast from the Past: The Terror Management Function of Nostalgia. *Journal of Experimental Social Psychology, 44*, 132–140.

Routledge, C., Arndt, J., Wildschut, T., Sedikides, C., Hart, C. M., Juhl, J., … Schlotz, W. (2011). The Past Makes the Present Meaningful: Nostalgia as an Existential Resource. *Journal of Personality and Social Psychology, 101*(3), 638–652.

Russo, N. (2015). *'Feels Like We Only Go Backwards': Nostalgia and Contemporary Retro Rock Music* (Doctor of Philosophy). Wollongong: University of Wollongong. Retrieved from http://ro.uow.edu.au/theses/4786

Schwartz, K. D., & Fouts, G. T. (2003). Music Preferences, Personality Style, and Developmental Issues of Adolescents. *Journal of Youth and Adolescence, 32*(3), 205–213.

Sedikides, C., Wildschut, T., Arndt, J., & Routledge, C. (2008). Nostalgia: Past, Present and Future. *Current Directions in Psychological Science, 17*(5), 304–307.

Sedikides, C., Wildschut, T., Gaertner, L., Routledge, C., & Arndt, J. (2010). Nostalgia as Enabler of Self-Continuity. In F. Sani (Ed.), *Self Continuity: Individual and Collective Perspectives*. Psychology Press.

Seehusen, J., Cordaro, F., Wildschut, T., Sedikides, C., Routledge, C., Blackhart, G. C., ... Vingerhoets, A. J. J. M. (2013). Individual Differences in Nostalgia Proneness: The Integrating Role of the Need to Belong. *Personality and Individual Differences, 55*, 904–908.

Talk Classical. (2007). Retrieved from https://www.talkclassical.com/2422-how-did-you-discover.html

Verplanken, B. (2012). When Bittersweet Turns Sour: Adverse Effects of Nostalgia on Habitual Worriers. *European Journal of Social Psychology, 42*, 285–289.

Waxer, L. (2002). *Situation Global Markets and Local Meanings in Latin Popular Music*. New York: Routledge.

Weinstein, D. (2009). *Heavy Metal: The Music and Its Culture*. Da Capo Press.

Wildschut, T., Sedikides, C., Arndt, J., & Routledge, C. (2006). Nostalgia: Content, Triggers, Functions. *Journal of Personality and Social Psychology, 91*(5), 975–993.

Zentner, M., Grandjean, D., & Scherer, K. R. (2008). Emotions Evoked by the Sound of Music: Characterization, Classification and Measurement. *Emotion, 8*, 494–521.

CHAPTER 3

Desire for Family Connections: Family History and Cultural Context

The music of any particular culture at a given point in time reflects the sounds of the environment in that place and time as well as idiosyncrasies of the local language such as prosodic and rhythmic elements (Patel & Daniele, 2003). In this chapter we consider how an individual's music choices are influenced by both family and culture. However, for many people, a tension can exist between family and the cultural environment in which they reside. This can particularly be so for people who live in a country other than the one in which they were born. Increasing globalization and mobility of the world's population means that this applies to a growing number of people in the twenty-first century. Taking Australia as a case study—a country with a high proportion of culturally displaced people—we will consider the tension and interactions that occur between family values and environment, particularly in cases of cultural displacement.

THE INFLUENCE OF FAMILY

Musical activities provide significant opportunities for social bonding (Selfhout, Branje, ter Bogt, & Meeus, 2009), as well as for expressing personal values and group identity (Tarrant, 2002). Family life is the context in which children experience their initial socializations as well as being the environment in which children are initially exposed to music. The two often go hand in hand, as music can play an important role in establishing

© The Author(s) 2019
S. Garrido, J. W. Davidson, *Music, Nostalgia and Memory*, Palgrave Macmillan Memory Studies,
https://doi.org/10.1007/978-3-030-02556-4_3

bonds with family members. As shall be discussed more deeply in Chap. 8, music is frequently used in very early infancy to establish and enhance bonds between caregiver and child, and this often continues throughout childhood. For example, one study of 10 families with three-year old children showed that families often use singing to create and maintain traditions and memories as well as to transform mundane everyday tasks into opportunities for connection and closeness between family members (Custodero, 2006). As Diane Boer and Amina Abubakar (2014) put it, music becomes part of "family identity, a way of transmitting family values, norms, and cultures, and enhancing family cohesion" (p. 3).

Some studies have found that parental influence can be greater than that which occurs in the educational environment (van Eijck & Knulst, 2005). The transfer of cultural values and tastes between family generations can be actively communicated in much the same way that parents seek to teach their children other behaviours and attitudes (Grusec & Davidov, 2007), such as by taking them to concerts, having them learn an instrument or otherwise deliberately exposing them to particular styles of music. It may also occur through much less conscious processes in that cultural behaviours and attitudes are modelled by parents, and children are exposed to this on a regular basis in the family home. It seems that mothers are particularly influential in transferring cultural practices and preferences in this way (Nagel & Ganzeboom, 2002).

Empirical evidence supports the idea that parental tastes have a strong influence on the developing musical tastes of children. Tom der Bogt and colleagues (ter Bogt, Diesling, van Zalk, & Christensen, 2011) surveyed 325 two-parent families from the Netherlands and found evidence of an intergenerational continuity of music preferences, with parental preferences being predictive of adolescent music choices. In particular, they found that parents preference for Pop or for 'Highbrow' music such as classical and jazz, was predictive of their children's preference for those genres as well.

Of course, adolescents will at some stage begin to develop their own autonomy and personal identity, and interests may diverge from the family to some degree in processes of individuation (Reis & Buhl, 2008). This tends to occur earlier in individualist cultures, with family retaining a greater influence over time in collectivist cultures which continue to put a high emphasis on family bonds (Dwairy, Achoui, Abouserie, & Farah, 2006).

However, there may be a genetic basis for the degree to which family influences musical preferences as well. One study found that the arginine vasopressin receptor 1A (AVPR1A) gene haplotypes—genes associated with communication and attachment—were positively associated with active current and lifelong listening to music, suggesting that music listening behaviours tend to correspond with attachment behaviours (Ukkola-Vuoti et al., 2011).

Given the role that music plays in cementing family relationships and traditions, it could be hypothesised that the structure of the household in which one was primarily raised could also have an influence on our musical tastes and the degree to which one values the music to which one was exposed in the family home. We explored this further in our MLAP sample. In our study, 50% of participants came from a family with 2 parents and 1–2 siblings, 22% came from a family with 2 parents and 3–5 siblings, 14% came from a single-parent family, 10% grew up in a home with two parents but no siblings, while the remainder grew up in a home with more than 5 siblings, were raised by extended family or were adopted.

We found no significant differences in genre choices based on the makeup of one's childhood home, although there were non-significant trends for people from single parent families to select hard-rock compared to other groups. Individuals who came from a 'traditional' family makeup, with 2 parents and 1–2 siblings, were more likely to select electronic music than people from other groups.

While there were no significant differences in genre choices, we did find significant differences on the reasons reported for song choices at key life moments. For example, people who reported selecting music because it was traditional were more likely to have been raised in a household with one parent, or to have been adopted. People who grew up primarily in a single parent household were also more likely to choose music that would have a positive mood impact, while people who were adopted were more likely to select music that validated their feelings. We also found that people who were primarily raised in non-traditional family structures such as adopted families or living with extended family rather than being raised by their own parents were more likely to report a high level of liking for the music of their parents and grandparents, while people raised in a household with 2 parents and 1–2 siblings were the least likely to report liking such music. However, people raised in single parent homes were least likely to report that listening to such music brought back memories or made them feel connected to family of previous generations.

Thus it seems that people that have experienced disruption to the family structure such as those finding themselves in single parent families or losing both parents and hence being adopted, may find it more important to develop strong traditions that support a sense of connection to culture than other groups. The tendency for people from single parent families to select music that has a positive mood impact also perhaps reflects the added resilience to stress that children of single parent families often develop (Kelly & Emery, 2003), or their increased reliability on music for emotional regulation in the absence of support from 2 parents.

On the other hand, people who made their music selections on the basis of how closely the music expressed their views were more likely to have been raised in a household with 2 parents and no siblings. People for whom music selections were designed to please someone else were more likely to have grown up in a household with 5 or more siblings. The same group was also more likely to rate their music selections as higher in arousal than people from single parent families. This likely reflects family dynamics as well, with people who are only children being more likely to have become used to expressions of individuality taking precedence, since such children are likely to have had more parental attention and interaction (Mancillas, 2006). On the other hand, children of families with a large number of siblings may have become more used to having to defer personal preferences to the tastes of others and thus are more likely to make choices designed to please others. Growing up in a family with a larger number of children may also have led to a higher threshold for arousal activation, and thus a tolerance for higher arousal music.

These results tend to confirm that music selections are related to family structure. The degree to which the family has experienced disruptions in the family structure appears to influence how deeply an individual feels the need to stay close to family traditions and to stay connected to family memories, how much they may come to rely on music for emotion regulation and support as opposed to other people, and how they make decisions about the music that will play a role in key moments of their lives.

RACE AND CULTURE

Chapter 4 will consider in more detail how music can communicate a great deal about personal values and social allegiances. Since music can differ so greatly from culture to culture it can also serve as a means of both preserving cultural memory and of articulating ideologies of belonging to or difference from particular cultural or racial groups. This function may be particularly valuable for groups who form a cultural minority in their country of residence, who suffer oppression by a more dominant cultural group, or who are in conflict with other groups.

As British musicologist Simon Frith (1996) puts it, social groups "get to know themselves as groups (as a particular organization of individual and social interests, of sameness and difference) through cultural activity, through aesthetic judgment" (p. 111). Frith goes on to recount several examples from the ethnomusicology literature in which music serves so as to articulate a shared value system within a cultural group. Thus music preferences communicate racial or cultural identity as well as personal identity.

This can be illustrated by looking at the patterns of popularity of some genres of music. Despite the fact that rock music, rap and country music all developed under the influence of a complex mix of cultures, traditions and styles, each has come to represent a particular cultural group in popular discourse and the media (Haynes, 2013). Radano and Bohlman (2000) state that in the U.S. at least, music "historically conjures racial meaning" (p. 1). Folk music, for example, became recognized as a primarily 'white' genre in the folk music revival of the 1960s (e.g., *Where have all the flowers gone* by Pete Seeger),[1] when African Americans (who were experiencing their own revival of the blues) were in the midst of a civil rights movement that sought to establish their place in a regime that white American youths were rejecting (Roy, 2002).

In the twentieth century, rap and hip-hop, on the other hand, have been described as fostering "a profound nationalism in the youth of Black America" even greater than that of the jazz music era in the 1920s (Henderson, 1996, p. 309). Rap developed and grew primarily through the work of DJs in the South Bronx of New York, where gang warfare abounded. One particular gang leader—Afrika Bambaataa—became a hip-hop legend. The messages of rap and hip-hop spring largely from shared perceptions of oppression by the dominant white culture, and aspirations by African and Hispanic Americans to improve their social standing. Rap's focus on the lyrics rather than melody and harmony make it a useful vehicle for expressing social and political messages (e.g., Afrika Bambaataa, *Planet Rock*).[2]

These features of rap and hip-hop have meant it has become a cultural tool for youths in many contexts all over the world to express their own

---

[1] Track 15: Where have all the flowers gone, Pete Seeger.
[2] Track 16: Planet Rock, by Afrika Bambaataa.

social meaning. In Australia, for example, where cultural and racial diversity continues to increase, ethnic and indigenous youths experience a variety of social disadvantages which are not necessarily expressed in the traditional music of their parents (Iveson, 1997). While other genres of Australian music such as 'Oz Rock' have tended to represent the values of 'white' youths in Australia, the subject matter of rap and hip-hop—addressing segregation, oppression and social disadvantage—have provided the materials for youths from minority groups to express their cross-cultural experiences. Music is thus used both to emphasize boundaries and to express solidarity within cultural or racial groups.

These cultural barriers between music genres still exist despite the appropriation of particular styles by other cultural groups. The blues, for example, has its roots in the music of African American slaves and their descendants in the South of the U.S. However, white American musicians such as Elvis Presley adopted these styles leading to the development of rock 'n' roll. Similarly, despite the origin of rap music among African and Hispanic youths in New York, it has been made popular among white youths as well through the work of rappers such as Vanilla Ice. Nevertheless, rap still tends to represent the gangland culture of youth minority groups in the popular imagination. The ongoing cultural divide between music genres was vividly illustrated when African-American hip-hop artist Kanye West stormed the stage of the MTV Music Video Awards in 2009 to protest the award to white country singer Taylor Swift, proclaiming that it should have been awarded to the African-American female artist Beyonce. These actions were widely interpreted as racially motivated in the media and in posts on social media and blogs.[3]

The idea that particular racial identities tend to prefer genres of music with which their culture is typically associated is also backed up by empirical research. Richard Zweigenhaft (2008) for example, found that in the U.S. coloured students gave higher ratings to religious music, to soulfunk and to gospel, music popular among African American people. On the other hand, Christine White (2001) reported that white participants in her study tended to be more omnivorous than African Americans, perhaps because of their lesser need to identify with particular genres.

The data from our MLAP research across all song categories also demonstrated significant differences in song selections between some cultural

---

[3] See for example http://www.avclub.com/article/daily-buzzkills-the-kanye-westtaylor-swift-inciden-32869; http://www.etonline.com/news/188048_kanye_west_says_closet_racism_was_to_blame_for_taylor_swift_s_2009_vma_win/

groups. For example participants of English-speaking origins were less likely to select songs from the RNB cluster (which included hip-hop and rap), or traditional songs than people of Asian origin. There were no significant differences between cultural groups on the reasons given for song selections or for the valence and arousal ratings of those selected songs.

While the majority of people currently living in Australia have British ancestry, people from Asia have lived in Australia since the gold-rushes of the mid nineteenth century. By the beginning of the twentieth century, however, settlers from Asia and the European Continent made up only about 2% of the population. However, after the repudiation of the 'white Australia' policy and the adoption of a non-discriminatory immigration policy in 1973, a large influx of migrants from Asia began to arrive in the country. Today, people of Asian origin make up 39.7% of the Australian population (Australian Bureau of Statistics, 2017).

While the Asian people in Australia come from a variety of places and backgrounds, including Taiwan, Hong Kong, Vietnam and Malaysia, many are of Chinese heritage or come from cultures that were strongly influenced by China. Thus, despite their varying countries of origin, many share, to some degree, values influenced by Confucian tradition in which family is paramount (Yee, 1989). Traditional Asian societies are highly collectivist in nature, in contrast to the individualist mentality of most Australians of European or English origin. While migrants to Australia may be influenced by the prevailing views in their new country and to some degree by globalization and modernization, the family and tradition continues to be a mainstay of many people of Asian heritage (Mak & Chan, 1995).

Culture also has an influence on the degree to which family and tradition will influence music use and preferences (see also Chap. 4). Diana Boer and Amina Abubaker (2014) surveyed 760 young people from two traditional/collectivist cultures (Kenya and the Philippines) and two secular/individualist cultures (New Zealand and Germany). They found that listening to music in family groups contributes to social cohesion across all the cultures they studied. However, their study also showed that participants from Kenya and the Philippines tended to put the greatest emphasis on the social and cultural functions of musical engagement—such as family bonding—among the cultural groups studied. People from Germany and Turkey were the least likely to experience family bonding through musical activities. Family listening rituals were found to only contribute to the well-being of individuals from traditional/collectivist cultures. Thus it is evident that differing life-views that are predominant within a specific culture can influence the extent to which family and tradition will be valued and thus the degree to which they will influence music choices.

CULTURAL DISPLACEMENT

For many people in the twenty-first century world-views do not fit simply into any particular cultural category. Music choices also, can reflect a tension between the need for continuity and tradition, and increasing pressures towards individualism. Cultural displacement—or the movement of people from their locality of origin into an environment in which they may be a marginalized minority—provides an interesting example of how these cultural pressures are changing in the modern world.

Australia's cultural diversity, and indeed increasing globalization and mobility of the world population, means that Australian music is influenced by a diverse range of cultural traditions introduced by a large migrant population. The percentage of Australians who were born in other countries was found to be at its highest point since the late 1800s in the 2016 census (ABS, 2016). Twenty-eight percent of Australians were not born in the country. An even higher percentage are first or second generation Australians, the children and grandchildren of people who arrived in the country as migrants and refugees. Thus many have experienced cultural displacement personally or may still feel the tug of the 'mother country' and the strain of sitting between two cultures despite having been born in Australia.

As was discussed in Chap. 2 in our examination of nostalgia, geographical and cultural displacement is often accompanied by a sense of loss and a psychological idealization of the homeland (Tummala-Narra, 2009), along with feelings of social exclusion and discontinuity of self. Music's strong capacity for eliciting autobiographical and episodic memory makes it a powerful way for migrants to retain a sense of connection with their culture of origin as well as to explore changing narratives of self as they emerge in a new cultural environment (Khorsandi & Saarikallio, 2013). Scholars such as Beatriz Ilari argue that a core part of dealing with the experience of migration is the ability to negotiate multiple identities, and that music can form a central part of resolving cultural differences (Ilari, 2017). Research suggests, for example, that musical activities centred on the music of one's cultural heritage can do much to bolster the self-esteem of children who experience geographical displacement as a result of violence (Zapata & Hargreaves, 2017).

Music has indeed been a large part of the lives of migrants in Australia since Europeans first settled on the land. Historical accounts in Australia from the nineteenth and early twentieth centuries contain evidence of a range of diverse musical cultures being performed in all parts of Australia, including Chinese opera in the Victorian gold fields, Japanese Shinju festivals in north-Western Australia, and Muslim celebrations of Ramadan involving singing and dancing in many parts of the country (Falk, 2016). Some cultural groups appear to cling to the traditions of their country of origin even some generations after migration. Others try to put their roots as far behind them as possible in order to assimilate. This can be influenced by a number of variables, including the fluctuating attitudes towards cultural diversity and migration in the country of residence, the conditions under which the migration took place (i.e. forced or voluntary, traumatic or relatively peaceful), and the degree to which family and tradition are valued by the individual and their associates. Migrants often experience the phenomenon of temporal displacement as well, in that the culture they remember from their country of origin no longer exists—it itself changes as time goes on (Baily & Collyer, 2006).

From a policy point of view, Tony Bennett (2001) argues that governmental policies on cultural diversity typically go through three stages. In the first, the focus may be on providing support for cultural minorities to sustain their ethnicity. In a second stage, the national culture may itself be viewed as a combination of diverse cultures in co-existence rather than having a dominant culture and numerous minorities, while in a third stage, culture may be viewed as being more dynamic and fluid, a construct which is continually changing and evolving as cultural mixes change. These stages can be discerned in the music of Australia, as well (Smith, 2009), although arguably they do not proceed in a strictly linear fashion or at the same pace for all cultural groups.

As Australia has come to be more economically reliant on a migrant population and on migration policies that support trade deals with important economic partners such as China or that align with international obligations to support refugees, themes of multiculturalism have become prominent in political rhetoric. Thus Australian governments of recent decades have chosen to represent Australia publically through "displays of difference" (Smith, 2009).

These changing policies have had differing effects on particular cultural groups residing in Australia due to the timing of their migration. For example, many Italians migrated to Australia in the post-war era of the 1950s and 1960s. At the time, Australians were predominantly of English background and had little interest in the preservation of the minority cultures that arrived on their shores. Thus, for many Italians the primary goal of assimilation meant that there was more focus on adopting Australian language and customs than there was on retaining the culture of their homeland. Thus, while some specifically Italian music may have continued to have been played in religious and other community events, the musical traditions were rarely enculturated in the children of those migrants (Barwick & Keller, 2012).

However, in the 1970s and 1980s, government policies of multiculturalism and the increasing acceptance of the concept by the public allowed second generation migrants to begin to explore musical identity in more diverse ways (Barwick & Keller, 2012). Fusion genres emerged, in which exotic sounds from non-Western music were combined with Australian folk or rock music. Groups of performers in this range were able to benefit from funding from the Australia Council—the body largely responsible for arts funding in Australia—because of their ability to support the political ideal of Australia as a cultural 'melting pot' (Smith, 2009).

For example, the popular music of countries such as Vietnam includes styles such as Tân cổ giao duyên that combines features of Western popular music with elements of traditional Vietnamese music. Vietnamese-Australian composers and song-writers similarly produce a type of fusion music. In many of these the vocal style remains typically Vietnamese while tonality, harmonies, rhythms and song structure resemble Western popular music (Hung, 2003). This may be the primary form of music listened to by Vietnamese people in Australia at home, at nightclubs and community events such as weddings or New Year celebrations. It serves the function not only of providing entertainment, but often also of disseminating political messages and preserving cultural pride (Hung, 2003). Other composers write in the Western classical tradition, but flavour their compositions through the use of Vietnamese folk melodies, modes or rhythmic structures, while still others experiment with combinations of traditional and non-traditional sounds.

In other cultural groups, musical ensembles, often made up of second-generation migrants, formed revival groups in Australia, and are active and popular among migrant populations, playing a role in keeping alive musical traditions from the mother countries of the populations they serve. As Graeme Smith argues (2009), for some musicians their personal identification with their culture of origin is a crucial part of their performances, while for many, "these are likely to be rediscovered or reemphasized cultural roots, rather than a simple expression of upbringing" (p. 12). Whether these cultural roots are in their original form or in a form that has been transformed by displacement, the sense of belonging to an identifiable cultural group—or to a group of similarly displaced individuals—creates a sense of personal empowerment in the members of the group through the shared overcoming of adversity (Travis, 2013).

For some migrant musicians commercial concerns can also become an issue shaping their use of music in their new cultural context. For example, Dan Bendrups (2011) discusses how Latin American migrants to Australia in the 1970s had to negotiate a line between their need for music to "articulate a shared sense of cultural identity" (p. 193) and the need to cater to broader, more global concepts of Latin music which provided commercial opportunities to Latin musicians. He argues that these two competing forces both limited the ability for musicians to create new music, and that it is really only since the beginning of the twenty-first century that the children of Latin American migrants who do not carry the same psychological burdens of exile as their parents, have been able to develop their own individual creative identity.

Music associated with particular rituals may play a particularly powerful link to the culture of one's country of origin and are in fact the songs that are least likely to change in importance in the lives of culturally displaced people (Baily & Collyer, 2006). Thus the data from MLAP which investigated the music people selected to celebrate and remember important life rituals such as weddings and funerals or the birth of their children, enabled us to explore whether there was any relationship between migrant status and the music selected for those occasions. While these rituals will be discussed in more detail in Part II of this volume, in a general sense, our results demonstrated that people who did not live in their country of birth were more likely to like soul music, spiritual music or world music than people who were born in their country of residence, while non-migrants were more likely to select electronica and instrumental music than migrants.

We also found that the reasons given for attraction to particular genres differed according to migrant status. People who were born in the country in which they currently reside were more likely to be attracted to a particular genre because it represented who they are, while migrants were more likely to be attracted to a particular genre because it is what their parents or grandparents listened to. Given that the majority of non-migrants in this sample would have been Australian born, this may reflect a clear differentiation between collectivist and individualist cultures, with native born Australians (an individualist country) more likely to select music for reasons of personal expression, and those born elsewhere (likely largely collectivist cultures) more likely to be attracted to music inherited from family. It could however, also reflect the greater need for people who have experienced cultural displacement to retain a connection to their culture of origin.

These differences were also found across racial orientations. People from Island cultures were more likely to be attracted to genres that were popular with their friends than people of Caucasian or Middle Eastern heritage. People from the Middle East were the least likely to listen to music genres that were popular with their parents or grandparents or other family members, while people of African origin were the most likely to be attracted to such music. Asian people were the most likely to listen to genres that were generally popular, compared to people of Caucasian or European origins.

CONCLUSIONS

Family plays an important role in musical preferences since the family provides the earliest exposures to music, and bonding between children and family members are often enhanced by musical experiences. Family traditions often revolve around music and thus autobiographical memories become closely entwined with concepts of family and heritage.

However, the degree to which family will continue to play a role in personal music tastes is largely influenced by the culture of origin, as well as the degree to which life circumstances work so as to enhance an individual's sense of attachment to tradition. Music expresses cultural boundaries and allegiances. However, people who experience discontinuity in their lives such as through disruptions to the family structure or cultural displacement may find that traditional music or music of one's parents or grandparents becomes of greater importance in enhancing a sense of connection to one's roots. These variables in turn interact with other environmental variables such as commercial circumstances and government policies on the preservation of migrant culture. To a large degree nostalgia for previous times and places underlies much of the influence that family and culture will have on musical preferences throughout the lifespan. However, there are other ways in which culture affects the music we are attracted to. These aspects along with the influence of personality and gender will be considered in the next chapter.

References

Australian Bureau of Statistics. (2017). *Census of Population and Housing: Reflecting Australian Stories from the Census, 2016.* Canberra: Australian Bureau of Statistics.

Baily, J., & Collyer, M. (2006). Introduction: Music and Migration. *Journal of Ethnic and Migration Studies, 32*(2), 167–182. https://doi.org/10.1080/13691830500487266

Barwick, L., & Keller, M. S. (2012). Transnational Perspectives on Italy in Australia's Musical Landscape. In L. Barwick & M. S. Keller (Eds.), *Italy in Australia's Musical Landscape* (pp. 3–12). Melbourne: Lyrebird Press.

Bendrups, D. (2011). Latin Down Under: Latin American Migrant Musicians in Australia and New Zealand. *Popular Music, 30*(2), 191–207.

Bennett, T. (2001). *Differing Diversities: Transversal Study on the Theme of Cultural Policy and Cultural Diversity.* Strasbourg: Council of Europe.

Boer, D., & Abubakar, A. (2014). Music Listening in Families and Peer Groups: Benefits for Young People's Social Cohesion and Emotional Well-Being Across Four Cultures. *Frontiers in Psychology, 5,* 392.

Custodero, L. A. (2006). Singing Practices in 10 Families with Young Children. *Journal of Research in Music Education, 54*(1), 37–56.

Dwairy, M., Achoui, M., Abouserie, R., & Farah, A. (2006). Parenting Styles, Individuation, and Mental Health of Arab Adolescents: A Third Cross-Regional Research Study. *Journal of Cross Cultural Psychology, 37,* 262–272.

Falk, C. (2016). Australia's Asian Songline. *Asian Currents.* Retrieved from http://asaa.asn.au/australias-asian-songline/

Frith, S. (1996). Music and Identity. In S. Hall & P. D. Gay (Eds.), *Questions of Cultural Identity* (pp. 108–150). SAGE Publication.

Grusec, J. E., & Davidov, M. (2007). Socialization in the Family: The Role of Parents. In J. E. Grusec & P. D. Hastings (Eds.), *Handbook of Socialization: Theory and Research.* Guilford Press.

Haynes, J. (2013). *Music, Difference and the Residue of Race.* New York: Routledge.

Henderson, E. A. (1996). Black Nationalism and Rap Music. *Journal of Black Studies, 26*(3), 308–339.

Hung, L. T. (2003). Vietnamese Traditions. In J. Whiteoak & A. Scott-Maxwell (Eds.), *Currency Companion to Music and Dance in Australia* (pp. 678–680). Sydney: Currency House.

Ilari, B. (2017). Children's Ethnic Identities, Cultural Diversity, and Music Education. In R. Macdonald, D. J. Hargreaves, & D. Miell (Eds.), *Handbook of Musical Identities*. Oxford, UK: Oxford University Press.

Iveson, K. (1997). Partying, Politics and Getting Paid – Hip Hop and National Identity in Australia. *Overland, 147*, 39–47.

Kelly, J. B., & Emery, R. E. (2003). Children's Adjustment Following Divorce: Risk and Resilience Perspectives. *Family Relations, 52*(4), 352–362.

Khorsandi, A., & Saarikallio, S. (2013). *Music-Related Nostalgic Experiences of Young Migrants*. Paper Presented at the 3rd International Conference on Music & Emotion (ICME3), Jyväskylä, Finland.

Mak, A. S., & Chan, H. (1995). Chinese Family Values in Australia. In R. Hartley (Ed.), *Families and Cultural Diversity in Australia*. Allen & Unwin.

Mancillas, A. (2006). Challenging the Stereotypes About Only Children: A Review of the Literature and Implications for Practice. *Journal of Counseling & Development, 84*(3), 268–275.

Nagel, I., & Ganzeboom, H. B. G. (2002). Participation in Legitimate Culture: Family and School Effects from Adolescence to Adulthood. *Netherlands Journal of Social Sciences, 38*(2), 102–120.

Patel, A. D., & Daniele, J. R. (2003). An Empirical Comparison of Rhythm in Language and Music. *Cognition, 87*(1), B35–B45.

Radano, R., & Bohlman, P. V. (Eds.). (2000). *Music and the Racial Imagination*. Chicago: University of Chicago Press.

Reis, O., & Buhl, H. M. (2008). Individual During Adolescence and Emerging Adulthood – Five German Studies. *International Journal of Behavioral Development, 32*(5), 412–421.

Roy, W. G. (2002). Aesthetic Identity, Race and American Folk Music. *Qualitative Sociology, 25*(3), 459.

Selfhout, M. H. W., Branje, S. J., Ter Bogt, T. F., & Meeus, W. H. J. (2009). The Role of Music Preferences in Early Adolescents' Friendship Formation and Stability. *Journal of Adolescence, 32*(1), 95–107.

Smith, G. (2009). Public Multicultural Music and the Australian State. *Music & Politics, III*(2). https://doi.org/10.3998/mp.9460447.0003.202

Tarrant, M. (2002). Adolescent Peer Groups and Social Identity. *Social Development, 11*, 110–123.

Ter Bogt, T. F., Diesling, M. J. W. H., van Zalk, M., & Christensen, P. G. (2011). Intergenerational Continuity of Taste: Parental and Adolescent Music Preferences. *Social Forces, 90*(1), 297–319.

Travis, R. (2013). Rap Music and the Empowerment of Today's Youth: Evidence in Everyday Music Listening, Music Therapy and Commercial Rap Music. *Child Adolescent Social Work Journal, 30*, 139–167. https://doi.org/10.1007/s10560-012-0285-x

Tummala-Narra, P. (2009). The Immigrant's Real and Imagined Return Home. *Psychoanalysis, Culture & Society, 14*(3), 237–252.

Ukkola-Vuoti, L., Oikkonen, J., Onkamo, P., Karma, K., Raijas, P., & Jarvela, I. (2011). Association of the Arginine Vasopressin Receptor 1A (AVPR1A) Haplotypes with Listening to Music. *Journal of Human Genetics, 56*(4), 324–329.

van Eijck, K., & Knulst, W. (2005). No More Need for Snobbism: Highbrow Cultural Participation in a Taste Democracy. *European Sociological Review, 21*, 5513–5528.

White, C. G. (2001). *The Effects of Class, Age, Gender and Race on Musical Preferences: An Examination of the Omnivore/Univore Framework* (Master of Science). Virginia: Virginia Polytechnic and State University (etd-09072001-101445).

Yee, A. H. (1989). *A People Misruled: Hong Kong and the Chinese Stepping Stone Syndrome.* Hong Kong UEA Press.

Zapata, G. P., & Hargreaves, D. J. (2017). The Effects of Musical Activities on the Self-Esteem of Displaced Children in Colombia. *Psychology of Music, 46*(1). https://doi.org/10.1177/0305735617716756

Zweigenhaft, R. L. (2008). A Do Re Mi Encore: A Closer Look at the Personality Correlates of Music Preferences. *Journal of Individual Differences, 29*, 45–55.

CHAPTER 4

Personality, Gender, and Education

The previous two chapters have begun to outline some of the contextual variables and processes that influence how particular music comes to take on significance in our lives. We have discussed how memory and nostalgia for past eras and lifestyles work together in forging strong emotional bonds with certain pieces of music, as well as how our family and culture and the degree to which we may have experienced discontinuity in our environment all play a role in our music preferences. In this chapter and the next two to follow, we look more closely at numerous personal variables that also play a role in shaping how we use music and the music we are attracted to.

PERSONALITY

Personality can have an important impact on the type of music people are drawn to and how they make use of it in their daily lives. Among the many functions that music can serve is its value as an 'identity badge'—a means by which people express their values and advertise these to other people (North & Hargreaves, 1999). Individuals, beginning in adolescence, tend to select music that is popular among people with whom they share values, and may even use music as the way they communicate their allegiance to a particular cultural or societal group. Thus, the type of people one chooses to associate with, the type of lifestyle one prefers, one's beliefs—in other

© The Author(s) 2019
S. Garrido, J. W. Davidson, *Music, Nostalgia and Memory*, Palgrave Macmillan Memory Studies,
https://doi.org/10.1007/978-3-030-02556-4_4

words, an individual's very temperament and personality—are reflected in that individual's music choices.

Music listeners themselves seem to believe that their choices in music reveal a lot about their personalities and values (Rentfrow & Gosling, 2003). In fact, studies have shown that music is a common topic among strangers who meet, and that information about music preferences reveals very different information about personality from that obtained through other topics of discussion and can be a surprisingly accurate way of assessing personality (Rentfrow & Gosling, 2006).

Marc Delsing and colleagues (Delsing, Ter Bogt, Engels, & Meeus, 2008) explain this association between personality and music choices by means of the 'uses and gratifications' approach, arguing that people choose particular types of music because of how it satisfies particular personality characteristics. For example, extraverts—who enjoy social interactions—will tend to prefer music that either facilitates or simulates social interactions. Their study confirmed that people with high scores in extraversion and agreeableness tended to prefer pop music and dance music, i.e. music that tends to be associated with social occasions.

Another function that music can serve is to regulate our emotions, moods and arousal levels. Individuals all have what is known as an 'optimal stimulation level'. This is the level of arousal or alertness at which we feel most comfortable and operate best. People who are introverted, for example, tend to feel more comfortable at relatively low levels of arousal, and therefore tend to avoid situations that feel over-stimulating, or to tire of stimulating situations more quickly than other people. Extraverts on the other hand tend to prefer to operate at higher levels of arousal and may look for increased stimulation at every opportunity.

The type of music that will cause arousal will also differ depending on various personal variables. For example, cognitively complex or highly intelligent individuals tend to require more complex music in order to reach their optimal level of arousal (Rentfrow & Gosling, 2003). Other people with high levels of sensation seeking, who enjoy novel and intensely exciting situations and are therefore likely have high levels of optimal stimulation, have been found to prefer music like rock or heavy metal and to avoid genres such as sound track and religious music (Litle & Zuckerman, 1986). Other studies have shown that heavy metal fans in fact tend to experience higher levels of resting arousal than lovers of more laid back genres (Gowensmith & Bloom, 1997; McNamara & Ballard, 1999).

Furthermore, since music can have such a powerful impact on emotions and moods, individuals develop different ways of using music to regulate affective states. Some may use music as a form of distraction from negative emotions, others may use it to help soothe anxiety, while others may use it for cathartic purposes or to give them energy and motivation. For example, one study about adolescents (Schwartz & Fouts, 2003) found that young people tended to prefer music that reflected their personality as well as the particular developmental issues with which they were dealing. The young people considered in that study were using music as a way to work through issues and concerns they were experiencing. Thus, an individual's habitual coping style and the mood regulation strategies they have developed involving music—which are again largely related to personality—will all play a role in the music people are attracted to at key moments in their life.[1]

The fact that music preferences are so heavily connected to personality is borne out by the number of studies that have consistently found associations between certain personality traits and genre preferences. Many such studies have looked at correlations between music preferences and the Big Five personality traits or the five factor model, which posits that personality can be categorized on five dimension: openness to experience, conscientiousness, extraversion, agreeableness, and neuroticism (Goldberg, 1993). For example, Stephen Dollinger (1993) found that highly extraverted people preferred high arousal music such as jazz, while those with high levels of excitement seeking were attracted to a different type of high arousal music—hard rock. In addition, openness to experience was associated with the enjoyment of a diverse range of genres including those outside the mainstream. Broader musical tastes and a liking for more diverse styles such as classical is also associated with high scores in intuition on the Myers Briggs Type Indicator (Pearson & Dollinger, 2004).

Other studies have made similar findings. Peter Rentfrow and Samuel Gosling (2003), for example, found that a preference for highly cheerful music was related to extraversion, while people with high levels of openness to experience preferred complex, intricate music. Similarly, studies have found that openness to experience is associated with a preference for 'Elite' music, or non-mainstream music such as classical or jazz (Delsing et al., 2008), while other studies show that extraversion is related to an attraction to music with a strong bass line such as rap and

---

[1] See Chap. 4 for more information about music, mood regulation and coping styles.

dance music (McCown, Keiser, Shea, & Williamson, 1997). Such findings have been replicated across numerous cultures and samples (Dunn, Ruyter, & Bouwhuis, 2012; Langmeyer, Gulghor-Rudan, & Tarnai, 2012; Miranda, Gaudrea, Debrosse, Morizot, & Kirmayer, 2012). In fact, such preferences may be closely related to chemical responses that occur when listening to music, with one study showing that changes in plasma norepinephrine, B-endorphin and growth hormone when listening to techno music, was associated with high scores in novelty-seeking (Gerra et al., 1998).

One study attempted to look into the association between personality traits a little more deeply, by looking at particular facets that appear to underlie each of the dimensions in the five-factor model. Richard Zweigenhaft (2008), demonstrated that both facets of extraversion—gregariousness and excitement seeking—were associated with a liking for rap and hip-hop music, while the fantasy aspect of openness to experience was associated with a liking for international music, and the aesthetics aspect (people who value and are sensitive to the arts) was associated with a liking for opera. Thus it is evident that music preferences interact with our personality in complex ways, from our social habits to our ways of taking meaning from the world around us.

Similarly, these traits can influence how people both perceive and use music. For example, Jonna Vuoskoski and Tuomas Eerola (2011) found that neuroticism was positively correlated with the perception of sadness in music, while there was a negative correlation between extraversion and the perception of sadness in music. Tomas Chamorro-Premuzic and Adrian Furnham (2007) found that neuroticism was also related to how people use music. They report that participants in their study who were high in openness to experience, had high IQs and were intellectually engaged, tended to use music in rational, cognitive ways, while people with high scores in neuroticism and introversion were more likely to use music for emotion regulation purposes. Neuroticism is closely associated with depression and negative mood states, and people with high scores in neuroticism tend to be more susceptible to environmental stressors. The fact that people with high scores in this trait tend to use music for emotion regulation purposes is therefore not surprising, given that emotional coping is considered to be one of the less adaptive ways of dealing with negative emotions (Li, DiGiuseppe, & Froh, 2006). Similarly, considerable research has indicated that tendencies to ruminate—another form of emotional coping—are also associated with a liking for sad music, and with negative mood outcomes from music listening (Garrido, 2017; Garrido, Eerola, & McFerran, 2017; Garrido & Schubert, 2015).

Our results from the MLAP study of this volume confirm the relationship between personality, coping style and how people use music in their lives. For example, as we will describe in more detail in Chap. 7, people with generally maladaptive coping styles, reported a greater non-use of music during childbirth than other participants. Our results also suggested that whether or not music would be useful to a birthing mother during labour is highly dependent on personality, with some mothers reporting that it was an important way to cope with stress and pain, and other reporting that music was too distracting. Similarly, songs that parents may select to sing to their children also differed between the coping styles of the individuals Individuals with generally adaptive coping styles were more likely to select songs with a positive valence for putting their children to sleep than other people (see Chap. 8).

Personality and coping style were also found to be related to the lyrical content of songs selected for coping with heartbreak in our MLAP data as we will report in Chap. 10. In that chapter we relate findings indicating that people with high scores in neuroticism were more likely to listen to songs with themes of death, or with a focus on the past and on the person causing the heartbreak Other people with generally unhelpful coping styles also tended to select songs with lyrics reflecting inhibition, helplessness and anger.

While these findings will be discussed in greater detail in Part II of this volume, it is evident even from this brief discussion that personality influences our music selections and preferences in several profound ways. Firstly, our temperament is directly related to our optimal level of stimulation and therefore whether we are attracted to music that will increase or decrease our arousal levels. Secondly, music selections are a reflection of values and an expression of our social and cultural allegiances, a way that we can align ourselves with like-minded others. Thirdly, our music choices are directly related to how we respond to adversity in our lives, at both a temperamental level and via learned coping strategies.

GENDER

Evidence also indicates that music preferences are related to one's gender. For example, females tend to like popular music styles more than males (Rawlings & Ciancarelli, 1997; Zweigenhaft, 2008). This has been confirmed not only by academic studies but in marketing research. Musicstats.org for example, found that pop music is the music of choice for females, while it rates among the lowest choices for men. On the other hand, men tend to prefer electronic music, rock, hip-hop/rap, or heavy metal, while heavy metal was the genre least preferred by women.

Again, these differences are likely related to differing chemical responses to music as well as social functions that music performs. One study using electrophysiological measures indicated that women displayed elevated response curves to arousing music such as heavy metal, while men did not, suggesting a hypersensitivity to aversive stimuli in women (Nater, Abbruzzese, Krebs, & Ehlert, 2006). Other studies have linked music preferences to how traditional attitudes about gender roles and relationships are expressed in the music (Schwartz & Fouts, 2003). Colley (2008) argues that mainstream popular music has lyrics that tend to focus on emotions and relationships, while heavy metal and rock music may be more concerned with themes of rebellion and aggression which are of more interest to men in general. However, Colley further argues that our self-perceptions in relation to gender are also involved. Gender schema theory proposes that the degree to which gender influences an individual's processing of information through gender norms, depends to a large extent on the degree to which the individual perceives themselves as possessing the traits stereotypical of their sex. Men, who may be more likely to be discouraged from identifying with things generally perceived as female, may therefore be more likely to avoid music genres that seem to be more feminine. Rap appears to be a style that is broadly appealing across genders, despite the fact that it often expresses misogynistic views (White, 2001).

Being female is also related to 'ominivorousness', or a liking for a broad range of musical genres (White, 2001). Similarly, research indicates that females may have higher scores on a trait called 'music empathy', or the ability to decode emotions in a musical context (Garrido & Schubert, 2011; Kreutz, Schubert, & Mitchell, 2008). However, Eckart Altenmueller and colleagues (Altenmüller, Schurmann, Lim, & Parlitz, 2002) have found that females demonstrated greater valence-related variations in brain-activation patterns to the music they listened to, indicating that their emotional response to music may be more variable than that of males.

There also appear to be differences in the way males and females use music. Adrian North and colleagues (North, Hargreaves, & O'Neill, 2000) found that female adolescents used music more for mood regulation purposes, while male adolescents used it more for identity formation and to create an impression with others. Other research has shown that women may be more likely to use music in ruminative ways or for self-reflection than males, who tend to listen to music that they find absorbing (Garrido & Schubert, 2013).

Our MLAP data also revealed some significant gender differences in song selections across the various key life moments investigated in our study. In general, men were more likely to select rock and hard rock than females, while females were more likely to select soul/jazz and traditional music choices than males. Unlike previous studies, no significant differences were found in our sample between genders on the selection of pop, electronic, RNB/hip-hop, or classical/instrumental music. Females were also more likely to rate their song selections as having a more positive valence than males, and were significantly less likely to have some experience in playing a musical instrument or singing than male participants. However, no differences were found on arousal ratings of the music selections, and no significant differences were found between genders for the reported reasons for their song selections.

Social Class and Education

Richard Peterson coined the term 'cultural omnivore' in 1992 to describe people who have expansive and widely encompassing cultural tastes, who, in other words, can appreciate both 'highbrow' (intellectual or elite) and 'lowbrow' (popular, vulgar or less sophisticated) music. These rather crude latter expressions came from the pseudo-science of phrenology or the measuring of the features of the skull, and the notion that people with larger foreheads have more brains. Thus the term 'highbrow' came to denote something associated with intelligence and high culture.

This distinction has not always existed of course. At various time periods in history, such as early in the history of the U.S. when democracy and equality were paramount, the elitism of European history was rejected and concerts would often include all sorts of music from classical to minstrel singing (Roy, 2001). However, by the twentieth century, the boundary between the upper and lower classes had been re-established. Dimaggio (1982) explains how these distinctions have been important for the maintenance of the status of the dominant status group in a culture and thus 'their' culture needed to be recognized yet be relatively inaccessible to the 'lower' social classes.

Opera is an interesting example of the processes by which popular culture can become 'highbrow'. Opera developed from the comedic entertainments of the Italian nobility. The acts of the comedies were usually interspersed with musical *intermedi* which involved both solo and choral singing, and which eventually became more elaborate than the comedic performances themselves. When the first public opera house opened in 1637, opera moved from the realms of the wealthy to that of the popular, a trend which increased with the rise of the middle class in the eighteenth century. In the nineteenth century, Italian operas translated into English were being performed in a range of culture venues across the United States. However, operas in their original Italian and without the popular songs often incorporated in them were a taste that was only held by a minority and so led to the development of a culture of opera that appealed to class divisions.

Similarly, in England, in the nineteenth century, composers were beginning to depend more on the wealthy bourgeoisie for their income. Prices of concert tickets at various venues such as the concerts of the London Royal Philharmonic Society, created audiences that excluded those unable to afford them. For the middle class, music became a means of displaying status. Piano sales and sales of sheet music also increased in this period, with the middle class again desirous of displaying their culture and aesthetic taste. Thus by the early decades of the twentieth century we find theories of 'mass culture' in abundance, with the upper classes professing to like only 'high culture' while everybody else was believed to form a mass group of listeners with undiscriminating tastes (White, 2001). These processes of change in what is considered 'highbrow' may be almost cyclical, as the middle classes become upwardly mobile and begin to adopt the tastes of the upper classes, which in turns prompts the upper classes to appropriate aspects of 'lowbrow' culture in order to distinguish themselves (Veenstra, 2015).

However, Richard Peterson and Roger Kern (1996) argued that cultural exclusivity is no longer valued as it was in the past, and that 'snobs' are becoming 'omnivores'. The acceptance of a wide range of music now provides cultural capital, or a sense of sophistication in taste, rather than listening only to genres previously considered elitist such as opera or classical. Thus, popular music no longer needs to be spurned as a demonstration of class, but rather class and sophistication are displayed through the acceptance of a wide range of genres. Many proponents of opera and classical music are striving to make them more accessible to the broader public, such as the through the movement to sing opera in the mother tongue of the country in which it is performed. (See for e.g. this recording by the Philharmonia Orchestra with La Boheme by Puccini in English).[2]

In fact, empirical research demonstrates that while one's income level is not necessarily predictive of music taste, one's educational level often is. For example, Tak Wing Chan and John Goldthorpe (2007) found that the higher an individuals' educational level, the more likely they were to be a musical omnivore. Similarly, Gerry Veenstra's (2015) study of over 1595 people from various backgrounds found that while people with the lowest education levels were eight times more likely to dislike classical music than the more educated ones, 'higher class' groups tended to like a broader range of genres, while 'lower class' groups preferred heavy metal, rap and disco. This may explain why some studies have found no specific differences in attraction to particular genres based on education level or employment (North & Davidson, 2013), since education levels seems to be associated with a liking for a wide range of genres rather than any specific type of music.

Our MLAP sample was made up of participants with a wide range of educational levels, with 34% having a high school education, 17% having a professional certificate or diploma, 28% having a bachelor's degree, and 20% having a postgraduate qualification. Some significant differences in genre preferences were found between groups in our sample. For example, people with a postgraduate qualification were more likely to select a song from the Soul/Jazz cluster than people from other educational groups. Classical music selections increased in tandem with educational level, with 17% of postgraduates nominating a classical music piece, compared to only 8% with a high school only education. People with a tertiary education were also less likely to nominate a popular music choice than people with a high school education or a professional certificate or diploma. The group with a professional certificate or diploma were the group most likely to select a song from the hard rock cluster (4%) with postgraduates scoring the lowest on this genre (<1%). However, postgraduates were more likely than any other group to nominate traditional or world music for their song selections. Significant differences were also found on valence ratings of the song selections, with people with a postgraduate qualification being likely to rate their song as of more positive valence than those with a high school education.

---

[2] Tracks 17–49: La Boheme sung in English, Philharmonia Orchestra.

Some differences also existed in the reasons people with different educational levels gave for their song selections. For example, people with a postgraduate education were more likely to select music that expressed their personal views (14%) than other groups, with people with a high school education reporting this reason for their song selections less often than other groups (11%). Similarly, people with a postgraduate education were more likely to select music that represented a historical era that they like than any other group. On the other hand, people with only a high school education were more likely to select music that allowed them to wallow in negative emotions when experiencing a case of heartbreak and were less likely to select music that would have a positive mood impact than other groups.

Thus, education levels may have a direct influence on one's music selections. This may in part be due to the fact that greater education perhaps exposes one to a greater variety of people, situations and musical experiences. However, it may also be that music again becomes an expression of values and social allegiances since people in particular educational groups were more likely to select music from similar genres as their peers. Thus more educated people demonstrated a willingness to encompass non-mainstream genres such as classical and world music, while people with relatively low levels of education were significantly more likely to select pop music, and people with professional certificates or diplomas who may work in trade or industry were more likely to select hard rock than other educational groups.

CONCLUSIONS

This chapter has revealed how a number of personal variables interact in shaping our musical preferences. Our perceptions of gender roles and of how closely we ourselves fit traditional gender stereotypes can have a deep effect on our music selections. The socio-economic and societal sub-groups with which we identify will influence both the music we are exposed to, and that which we find acceptable or preferable. Our personality in turn, affects both how we use music to regulate mood and affect, and what we choose to express about ourselves through our music choices. Our lifestyle and personal experiences also play into this intricate mix. In particular, the strategies we develop for coping with life experiences, especially adverse events, also has a profound influence on how we use and respond to music. It is to this topic that we turn our attention in the following chapter.

REFERENCES

Altenmüller, E., Schurman-, K., Lim, V. K., & Parlitz, D. (2002). Hits to the Left, Flops to the Right: Diffe-ent Emotions During Listening to Music are Reflected in Cortical La:eralisation Patterns. *Neuropsychologia, 40*, 2242–2256.

Chamorro-Premuzic, T., & Furnham, A. (2007). Personality and Music: Can Traits Explain How People Use Music in Everyday Life? *British Journal of Psychology, 98*(2), 175–185.

Chan, T. W., & Goldthorpe, J. H. (2007). Social Stratification and Cultural Consumption: Music in England. *European Sociological Review, 23*(1), 1–19.

Colley, A. (2008). Young People's Musical Taste: Relationship with Gender and Gender-Related Traits. *Journal of Applied Social Psychology, 38*(8), 2039–2055.

Delsing, M. J. M. H., Ter Bogt, T. F. M., Engels, R. C. M., & Meeus, W. H. J. (2008). Adolescents' Music Preferences and Personality Characteristics. *European Journal of Personality, 22*, 109–130.

Dimaggio, P. (1982). Cultural Entrepreneurship in Nineteenth Century Boston: The Creation of an Organizational Base for High Culture in America. *Media, Culture & Society, 4*, 33–50.

Dollinger, S. J. (1993). Research Note: Personality and Music Preference: Extraversion and Excitement Seeking or Openness to Experience? *Psychology of Music, 21*(1), 73–77.

Dunn, P. G., Ruyter, B. D., & Bouwhuis, D. G. (2012). Toward a Better Understanding of the Relation Between Music Preference, Listening Behavior, and Personality. *Psychology of Music, 40*(4), 411–428.

Garrido, S. (2017). *Why Are We Attracted to Sad Music?* Cham, Switzerland: Palgrave Macmillan.

Garrido, S., Eerola, T., & McFerran, K. (2017). Group Rumination: Social Interactions Around Music in People with Depression. *Frontiers in Psychology, 4*, 490. https://doi.org/10.3389/fpsyg.2017.00490

Garrido, S., & Schubert, E. (2011). Individual Differences in the Enjoyment of Negative Emotion in Music: A Literature Review and Experiment. *Music Perception, 28*(3), 279–295.

Garrido, S., & Schubert, E. (2013). Adaptive and Maladaptive Attraction to Negative Emotion in Music. *Musicae Scientiae, 17*(2), 145–164. https://doi.org/10.1177/1029864913478305

Garrido, S., & Schubert, E. (2015). Music and People with Tendencies to Depression. *Music Perception, 32*(4), 313–321. https://doi.org/10.1525/MP.2015.32.4.313

Gerra, G., Zaimovic, A., Franchini, D., Palladino, M., Guicastro, G., Reali, N., … Brambilla, F. (1998). Neuroendocrine Responses of Healthy Volunteers to 'Techno-Music' Relationships with Personality Traits and Emotional State. *International Journal of Psychophysiology, 28*(1), 99–111.

Goldberg, L. R. (1993). The Structure of Phenotypic Personality Traits. *American Psychologist, 48*, 26–34.

Gowensmith, W. N., & Bloom, L. J. (1997). The Effects of Heavy Metal Music on Arousal and Anger. *Journal of Music Therapy, 34*(1), 33–45.

Kreutz, G., Schubert, E., & Mitchell, L. A. (2008). Cognitive Styles of Music Listening. *Music Perception, 26*(1), 57–73.

Langmeyer, A., Gulghor-Rudan, A., & Tarnai, C. (2012). What Do Music Preferences Reveal About Personality? *Journal of Individual Differences, 33*, 119–130.

Li, C. E., DiGiuseppe, R., & Froh, J. (2006). The Roles of Sex, Gender and Coping in Adolescent Depression. *Adolescence, 41*(163), 409–415.

Litle, P., & Zuckerman, M. (1986). Sensation Seeking and Music Preferences. *Personality and Individual Differences, 7*(4), 575–578. Retrieved from http://www.sciencedirect.com/science/article/B6V9F-45Y7R7H-76/2/f75eef-9ade7fa7864ce8baf48f68f654

McCown, W., Keiser, R., Shea, M., & Williamson, D. (1997). The Role of Personality and Gender in Preference for Exaggerated Bass in Music. *Personality and Individual Differences, 23*(4), 543–547.

McNamara, L., & Ballard, M. E. (1999). Resting Arousal, Sensation Seeking, and Music Preference. *Genetic, Social and General Psychology Monographs, 125*(3), 229–250.

Miranda, D., Gaudrea, P., Debrosse, R., Morizot, J., & Kirmayer, L. (2012). Music Listening and Mental Health: Variations on Internalizing Psychopathology. In A. R. M. Raymond, G. Kreutz, & L. Mitchell (Eds.), *Music, Health and Wellbeing* (pp. 513–530). New York: Oxford University Press.

Nater, U. M., Abbruzzese, E., Krebs, M., & Ehlert, U. (2006). Sex Differences in Emotional and Psychophysiological Responses to Musical Stimuli. *International Journal of Psychophysiology, 62*(2), 300–308.

North, A. C., & Davidson, J. W. (2013). Musical Taste, Employment, Education, and Global Region. *Scandinavian Journal of Psychology, 54*, 432–441.

North, A. C., & Hargreaves, D. J. (1999). Music and Adolescent Identity. *Music Education Research, 1*(1), 75–92.

North, A. C., Hargreaves, D. J., & O'Neill, S. A. (2000). The Importance of Music to Adolescents. *British Journal of Educational Psychology, 70*, 255–272.

Pearson, J. L., & Dollinger, S. J. (2004). Music Preference Correlates of Jungian Types. *Personality and Individual Differences, 36*, 1005–1008.

Peterson, R. A., & Kern, R. M. (1996). Changing Highbrow Taste: From Snob to Omnivore. *American Sociological Review, 61*(5), 900–907.

Rawlings, D., & Ciancarelli, V. (1997). Music Preference and the Five-Factor Model of the NEO Personality Inventory. *Psychology of Music, 25*(2), 120–132.

Rentfrow, P. J., & Gosling, S. D. (2003). The Do Re Mi's of Everyday Life: The Structure and Personality Correlates of Music Preferences. *Journal of Personality and Social Psychology, 84*(6), 1236–1256.

Rentfrow, P. J., & Gosling, S. D. (2006). Message in a Ballad – The Role of Music Preferences in Interpersonal Perception. *Psychological Science, 17*(3), 236–242.

Roy, W. G. (2001). *Making Societies: The Historical Construction of Our World.* Pine Forge Press.

Schwartz, K. D., & Fouts, G. T. (2003). Music Preferences, Personality Style, and Developmental Issues of Adolescents. *Journal of Youth and Adolescence, 32*(3), 205–213.

Veenstra, G. (2015). Class Position and Musical Tastes: A Sing-Off Between the Cultural Omnivorism and Bourdieusian Homology Frameworks. *Canadian Review of Sociology, 52*(2), 134–159.

Vuoskoski, J. K., & Eerola, T. (2011). The Role of Mood and Personality in the Perception of Emotions Represented by Music. *Cortex, 47*(9), 1099–1106.

White, C. G. (2001). *The Effects of Class, Age, Gender and Race on Musical Preferences: An Examination of the Omnivore/Univore Framework* (Master of Science). Virginia: Virginia Polytechnic and State University (etd-09072001-101445).

Zweigenhaft, R. L. (2008). A Do Re Mi Encore: A Closer Look at the Personality Correlates of Music Preferences. *Journal of Individual Differences, 29*, 45–55.

CHAPTER 5

Setting the Mood: Throughout History and in the Modern Day

The power that music has to influence our emotions and moods is one of the primary reasons that people report listening to it (Saarikallio, 2011). In fact, people generally prefer to listen to music that has the most impact on their emotions (Schubert, 2007). Memories encoded in association with deep emotional responses are also often more vivid and durable (Kensinger & Schacter, 2008). The music that we respond to the most emotionally is therefore also most likely to leave an intense impression in our memory and thus to trigger the most powerful memories. Therefore how we respond to music emotionally influences both how we use it to regulate affective states and how particular pieces of music come to take on meaning in our lives.

Music psychologists Patrik Juslin and Daniel Västfjäll and their colleagues (Juslin, Harmat, & Eerola, 2013; Juslin, Liljestrom, Vastfjall, & Lundqvist, 2010; Juslin & Västfjäll, 2008) argue that there are eight mechanisms via which emotions are evoked by music:

1. *Brain stem reflexes*—an unconscious and automatic activation of physiological systems that cause an individual to signals of danger from the acoustic environment,
2. *Rhythmic entrainment*—the unconscious compulsion to adjust bodily rhythms to externally heard rhythms,
3. *Emotional contagion*—the activation of mirror neurons that cause an automatic empathic response to emotions expressed by others

S. Garrido, J. W. Davidson, *Music, Nostalgia and Memory*, Palgrave Macmillan Memory Studies, https://doi.org/10.1007/978-3-030-02556-4_5

4. *Evaluative conditioning*—the automatic emotional responses elicited by the repeated pairing of a musical stimulus with something else leading to an emotional response by association,
5. *Episodic memory*—the triggering of specific memories that themselves evoke emotions,
6. *Visual imagery*—the conjuring up of visual images that produce an emotional response,
7. *Musical expectancy*—the violation of culturally acquired knowledge of musical conventions,
8. *Aesthetic judgment*—a subjective evaluation of the aesthetic beauty of the music.

The first three mechanisms involve instinctive biological mechanisms that are likely related to the evolutionary functions of music in the development of human society (Huron, 2001). However, the remaining mechanisms likely trigger both physiological and cognitive responses that are mediated by individual experiences and context-specific knowledge. Much of the time the relationship between memory, emotion and music is a two-way street with music triggering thought processes travelling in both directions: music can trigger memories through associative processes and other mechanisms mentioned above which in turn elicits an emotional response, while emotional responses incurred in relation to music can encode vivid memories of the circumstances in which the music was heard (see Fig. 5.1).

Although the terms mood and emotion are often used interchangeably, they are in fact distinct although related constructs. Emotions tend to be of relatively short duration and high intensity, that are invoked in response to a particular stimuli and that are largely uncontrollable, while moods can be more long-term affective states which may be relatively removed from

Fig. 5.1 Bi-directional relationship between memories and emotions

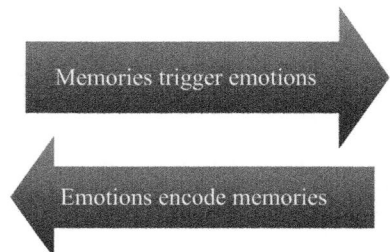

Memories trigger emotions

Emotions encode memories

any particular trigger and are experienced with less intensity (Garrido, 2014). However, the two have a "transactional relationship" (Lane & Terry, 2000, p. 18) in that an individual's current mood can influence their emotional response to a stimulus, which in turn can feed into a long-term mood state. Thus, the mood we are in when we hear a particular piece of music can influence both how we perceive the emotions being expressed in it, and the emotions we will experience in response to it. The emotions we experience in response to the music in turn have an impact on the ultimate effect the music will have upon our mood.

Just as emotions are often evoked via cognitive processes, the relationship between emotional responses and moods is mediated by thought processes as well. One study, for example, found that music which triggered unhappy memories or negative thoughts tended to result in negative mood outcomes, while the invocation of happy memories or positive thinking patterns by music resulted in positive mood effects (Garrido, Bangert, & Schubert, 2016). Thus, the emotions we experience while listening to a piece of music may differ from its effect on our overall mood, and music's ability to evoke powerful memories is closely entwined with its value as a tool for both evoking emotions and regulating mood.

Affective Regulation Using Music Throughout History

The Ancients

Music has been used for centuries as part of deliberate strategies to improve health and wellbeing, in part, for its ability to influence affective states (Garrido & Davidson, 2013). For many centuries an understanding of music was therefore believed to be a crucial part of the training of medical practitioners. In fact, it was only during the seventeenth and eighteenth centuries with the dichotomy between the arts and sciences that occurred as part of the scientific revolution, that music became of less interest in the health sciences.

Many ancient cultures believed in the power of music to influence moods, even those of unborn children. Over 4000 years ago in ancient China, for example, flute music was prescribed to calm an overexcited foetus (Brettingham-Smith, 1993). Evidence exists that the ancient Egyptians were using music for therapeutic purposes as early as 1500 BC

(Bunt, 1994). Another often-cited example is that of the biblical account of King Saul of Israel whose moods were quieted by the harp played by David.

In Western cultures belief in the power of music to regulate affective states goes back to ancient Greek philosophers such as Homer (*c.* eight-century BC) and Pythagoras (*c.* 500 BC). Homer recommended that music be used to counteract negative emotions such as anger, sorrow, fear and emotional fatigue.

Pythagoras also experimented with the use of specific notes and intervals played on a one-stringed instrument called a monochord to determine their relative effects on listeners. Using the mathematics of harmonic ratios, Pythagoras determined that the universe as a whole could be divided according to similar ratios, and that the planets all therefore corresponded to particular musical notes or intervals which could be invoked to create 'harmony' in both earthly and heavenly realms. This theory became known as the 'harmony of the spheres'. On this basis Pythagoras and his followers developed a framework of guidelines for 'prescribing' music to address particular physical and mental imbalances.

Although none of Pythagoras' own writings are known to have survived, his theories were adopted and enlarged upon by his disciples and ideas attributed to Pythagoras can be found in the writings of many philosophers in the succeeding centuries. By the time of Plato (*c.* 428–348 BC) certain tones and tone series were even believed to correspond to particular planets. The moon, for example, was believed to produce the note 'A' and the notes of the Mixolydian mode, and the sun, the note 'D' and the notes of the Dorian mode.

A second theory which stemmed from Pythagorean theory of the harmony of the spheres was the 'doctrine of ethos'—the idea that particular musical modes or scales could influence moods in particular ways. It was believed that each mode or 'harmonia'—a one-line melody on which much Greek music was based—had a specific quality that could influence a person's mood in unique ways. In fact, the word 'mode' is etymologically related to the word 'mood', a further indication of the long-standing connection between music and mood (Stevenson, 1952). On the basis of this theory, Pythagoras developed specific melodies for alleviating sadness and sang "paeans"—a song form expressing triumph—to ease rage and anger. Similarly, in Plato's *Republic* (Book III) we find an account of a dialogue between his Plato's brother Glaucon and Socrates in which Socrates apparently encouraged the use of Dorian and Phrygian modes to inspire men to bravery while calling the Ionian and Lydian modes 'relaxed' and saying that its use would encourage drunkenness, softness and indolence. Lydian mode on the other hand, was said to invoke sorrow.

While the fragmentary evidence available limits our understanding of the exact notes used in ancient Greek modes, the version of the Dorian mode that Socrates advocated for inspiring bravery was the principal mode in the old Greek musical system and was believed to draw on the powers of the Sun. It likely consisted of the tones: C D E F# G# A# B C (Hamilton, 1953). With its relatively large interval sizes this mode is closer to our modern day major scale—a scale commonly perceived as expressing positive emotions in Western music—than to a minor scale. The Lydian mode, on the other hand, which was believed to invoke the power of Mercury, involved smaller interval sizes and a flattened 16th note, and thus to the modern ear would likely seem more closely related to a minor scale—commonly associated with sadness—than some other modes. It is interesting that there appears to be some similarity between the believed mood effects of certain modes to the ancient Greeks with the emotions commonly associated with scale forms in present-day Western music. However, what is of particular interest here is the way Socrates used particular modes to neutralize or stabilize undesirable affective states.

One reported instance of the use of music to calm undesirable mood states is found in the works of Boethius (*c.* 480 AD) in his treatise *De Institutione Musica.* Here Boethius recounts a tale of a young man who had become wrought up by the sound of the Phrygian mode. The man had reportedly discovered his 'harlot' in the home of another man, and, with the added incitement of the music, was preparing to burn down the other man's house. Pythagoras reputedly calmed the man down by changing the music to the Spondaic mode, a rhythmic mode involving long, slow sustained notes. Boethius similarly reports that Timotheus of Miletus from Lacedaemonia steered the youths of Sparta astray from virtue by altering the pitches in an octave so that they were closer together, like chromatics (Leach, 2006). Thus, to the ancient Greeks, both 'tonal' modes and rhythmic patterns could invoke undesirable mood states that could be counteracted through the use of opposing modes.

Aristotle also advocated the use of certain modes to alter affective states, commenting further on the effects of specific rhythms, saying that "some fix the disposition, others occasion a change in it; some act more violently, others more liberally" (*Politics*, Book VIII, Part V). Aristotle also made some interesting comments distinguishing the immediate emotional response of the listener from the long-term effect on mood, describing the emotions that people could experience in response to music such as "excitement" and "frenzy", while suggesting that experiencing these emotions could leave people feeling "purged", thus resulting in a mood that is "lightened and delighted" (*Politics*, Book VIII, Party VII).

Another doctrine of the ancient Greeks that had an influence on understandings about the relationship between music, mood and wellbeing, was the concept of the balance of the humours which was in circulation around the time of Hippocrates (*c.* 400 BC). According to that theory four bodily fluids or humours need to be balanced within the body to achieve emotional and physical health: blood, phlegm, yellow bile, and black bile. Illnesses and disturbances of moods were understood to be caused by an imbalance between these bodily humours. However, it was believed that music was capable of restoring the balance.

Medieval Period

These ideas of the ancient Greeks were to continue to influence theory in the following centuries. During this period, Christianity and the liturgy were spreading, influencing both the development of music and musical theory. Ideas from the ancient Greeks became intertwined with Egyptian and Arabic philosophy as well as newer Christian beliefs, becoming known as Neo-Platonism (Gouk, 2004).

Two of the most notable medieval writers on music and its influence on mood were Boethius and Cassiodorus (480–573). We have already seen how Boethius recounted numerous tales of the use of music to influence mood by the ancient Greeks. His text *De Institutione Musica* was an important treatise in medicine, which in some Italian universities was part of the 'faculty of arts and medicine' (Cosman, 1978). Drawing on the works of Pythagoras, Plato and Aristotle, Boethius divided music into several spheres: *musica mundana*—the heavenly music of the motion of the spheres; *musica humana*—the rhythms and cycles of the human body; and, *musica instrumentalis*—the music made by humans using physical instruments. In much the same way that Pythagoras likened the universe to a monochord with its harmonic ratios, the Neo-Platonists described the connection between the spheres by analogy to a lyre. They argued that just as the vibrations of the string on an instrument can cause other strings tuned to the same pitch to vibrate in sympathy, so humans could vibrate in harmony with the celestial bodies if they could be brought into 'tune'.

Cassiodorus, kinsman to Boethius and his successor in the role of *magister officiorum* of Rome, followed Boethius' belief in the value of music to regulate affect. He wrote in a letter to Boethius (*c.* 538) requesting his assistance in finding a harp player, who could "tame the savage hearts of barbarians" with his "sweet sounds" for Clovis, King of the Franks (Cassiodorus, 1886). He writes of the power of music:

> Harmful melancholy he turns to pleasure; he weakens swelling rage; he makes bloodthirsty cruelty kindly, arouses sleepy sloth from its torpor, restores to the sleepless their wholesome rest, recalls lust-corrupted chastity to its moral resolve, and heals boredom of spirit which is always the enemy of good thoughts. (Cassiodorus, 1886)

Cassiodorus also reiterated the doctrine of ethos, saying:

> Phrygian arouses strife, and inflames the will to anger; the Aeolian calms the storms of the soul, and gives sleep to those who are already at peace; the Ionian sharpens the wits of the dull, and as a worker of good, gratifies the longing for heavenly things among those who are burdened by earthly desire. The Lydian was discovered as a remedy for excessive cares and weariness of spirit: it restores by relaxation, and refreshes it by pleasure. (Cassiodorus, 1886)

Cassiodorus here argues for a different effect for the Phrygian mode compared to Socrates and Aristotle, possibly because the modes in the medieval mode were likely not the same as the ancient Greek modes. Interestingly, however, in the anecdote described above where Boethius reports Pythagoras using music to calm a distressed man, the overwrought state of the man is attributed to his hearing music in the Phrygian mode, despite the fact that Socrates and Aristotle reported using the music to inspire bravery. It is possible that in fact, certain modes were recognized as being able to inspire enthusiasm in one individual while causing another to become overwrought. Similarly, a mode that might in one individual encourage lethargy, could calm down the overexcited nerves of another.

Another writer in this period whose work was to be highly influential in later centuries, was the second-century Greek physician Galen (Galenus).

In his treatise *On Temperaments*, Galen expanded on theories about humoural medicine by proposing that personalities could be characterized according to humoural balances as either phlegmatic, choleric, sanguine or melancholy. Galen also wrote extensively in *De Pulsibus* on the influence that music could have on the human pulse.

Martianus Cappella was another important writer on music in the fifth century, who reported the cure of the mentally ill by music. Cappella's work *De Nuptiis Philologiae et Mercurii* (On the Marriage of Philology and Mercury), which was influential for almost all of the medieval period, was an allegorical tale in which seven maids representing the seven arts describe the arts they personify. The final one represents music (Harmony). This was an important work in ensuring the survival of the Pythagorean ideas about the harmony of the spheres into the Renaissance period.

Further dissemination of Platonic theory occurred in the eighth and ninth centuries when Europe began to achieve a degree of unity under Charlemagne. Charlemagne's conquests involved the acquisition of manuscripts including those of Boethius and Cappella, which were then copied and dispersed throughout the empire resulting in a revival of interest in Pythagorean philosophy particularly among monastic scholars. Monastic scholars with their strong interest in the mathematics of the universe and the corresponding pitches and ratios, basically dominated thinking on music until the thirteenth century (Callahan, 2000).

One abbess and composer, Hildegard of Bingen (*c.* 1098–1179) showed an interest in the practical use of music writing two medical treatises *Physica* and *Causae et Curae*. Her theories differed somewhat from the usual doctrine of humours, although she does employ the humoural classification of personalities derived from Galen. For Hildegard, music was a psychic force that could offset melancholy which occurred as a result of mankind's banishment from paradise. According to Hildegard, music could once again unite mankind with the heavenly choirs, and Hildegard's own compositions embody this in rapturous melodies which defied the simplicity of the plainchant most often heard in her time (Holsinger, 1993). For example, *O Ecclesia*[1] celebrates St Ursula, a woman who had rejected an earthly marriage for one to God. As a leader of a company of Christian women, Ursula was a focus of Hildegard's devotion. On her works she wrote:

---

[1] Track 50: O Ecclesia, Hildegard von Bingen, performed by Sequentia.

Underneath all the texts, all the sacred psalms and canticles, these watery varieties of sounds and silences, terrifying, mysterious, whirling and sometimes gestating and gentle must somehow be felt in the pulse, ebb, and flow of the music that sings in me. My new song must float like a feather on the breath of God.

When the words come, they are merely empty shells without the music. They live as they are sung, for the words are the body and the music the spirit.

Other medieval medical practitioners who included music theory in their treatises include Peter of Abano of Italy (1257–1315), who recounted the theories of Boethius, arguing that all physicians should follow his recommendations. Gentile da Foligno (d. 1348), an Italian professor and doctor, promoted the idea that musical consonance and musical mathematical properties could be found in the human pulse. Thus, high and low pitches, according to da Foligno, corresponded to strength and weakness in the pulse, while the speed of the pulse corresponded to meter in music (da Foligno, 1510). A healthy pulse was considered to be equal and steady while irregularities of rhythm were indicators of ill health.

Jacopo da Forli (c. 1364–1414) similarly argued that the variations of a pulse, like the different voices in a group of singers could be either harmonious or dissonant, and could be influenced by emotions among other things. Six rhythmic modes—a medieval concept in which the relative duration of notes were determined by their position within a rhythmic series—were commonly used for writing *ars antiqua* motets and other music at the time. Peter d'Abano (c. 1257–1316) directly applied these rhythmic modes in a medical context to regulating the pulse, advising use of specific modes for activating a sluggish pulse and other ones for calming a rapid or erratic one (d'Abano, 1303).

Other medieval scholars and physicians also mentioned the therapeutic powers of music. William of Auvergne, a French priest who served as Bishop of Paris from 1228 to 1249, dedicated a chapter to music in his treatise *De Universo*, describing how music could be used to treat insanity, melancholia and other mental disturbances. Similarly, Franciscan monk Bartholeus Anglicus (c. 1203–1272) describes a condition akin to depression in his encyclopedia, *De Proprietatibis Rerum*, suggesting that music would be of assistance in treating it. Twelfth-century Welsh chronicler Geraldus Cambrensis also says "The sweet harmony of music … greatly cheers the drooping spirit, smooths the wrinkled brow, promotes hilarity ... There are no sufferings which music will not mitigate, and there are some which it cures" (Cambrensis & Forester, 1894).

The Renaissance and Elizabethan Era

Renaissance scholars, especially in Italy, also demonstrate the influence of the ancient Greeks. A direct line can be traced from the works of Boethius to some of the major writers on music in the Renaissance period, including Gentile da Foligno, Marsilio Ficino and H. Cornelius Agrippa. This period would also see a synthesizing of theoretical strands of thought that had developed in earlier centuries, with concepts from Pythagorean cosmology becoming fused with Galenic medicine and monastic writings on church modes.

Evidence of the fusion of these theories can be seen in the writings of Ramis de Pareja such as *Musica Practica* (1482). Here de Pareja lists the Pythagorean beliefs about the influence of the modes on the humours, drawing upon Islamic Neo-Platonist writings to attribute the power of the modes to particular planets to which they correspond. Like philosophers in earlier centuries, he gives specific musical prescriptions for altering affective states. For example, he recommends the Dorian mode for drying 'watery phlegm' by drawing on the power of the sun resulting in equanimity and calm. Hypophrygian mode was advised for mitigating the effect of yellow bile and soothing the soul through the power of the planet Mercury. Lydian mode was said to reinforce happiness by imparting the power of Jupiter, while Hypolydian and Mixolydian modes were said to cause sadness and melancholia. In contrast, Hypomixolydian could draw on the power of the stars to suppress black bile and increase happiness and bliss.

Similar ideas come from the Italian priest, theologian, astrologer and physician Marsilio Ficino (1433–1499). His work *De Vita Libri Tres (Three Books on Life)* (1489) merging ideas from both Platonic theory and Christianity, outlined the specific musical characteristics of each planet and offering a complex set of techniques for creating songs to attract beneficial powers from the planets. Ficino's understanding of the mechanisms involved here show evidence of the influence of the Neo-Platonist interpretation of the harmony of the spheres. He believed that sound, by causing air to vibrate, could connect directly with the ear and thus convey those vibrations to the soul and spirit. Therefore, carefully chosen music, according to Ficino, was the most effective tool for restoring physical and mental health and balance. Ficino's astrological model was highly influential for many centuries until around the end of the eighteenth century when neurological and mechanical theories came to the fore (Wigram, Pedersen, & Bonde, 2002).

Emerging theories of aesthetics also began to intermingle with the Platonic theory in this period. Johannes Tinctoris, for example, was a composer and music theorist born in Flanders around 1440s. In his work *Complexus Effectuum Musices* (1475) he describes 20 different emotive effects that music can have. Rob Wegman (1995) writes that in the works of Tinctoris, "sweetness" in the music was the key to having a positive effect on the emotions of the listener. The concept of "sweetness" seems to have been mostly akin to consonance but could also relate to instrumental or vocal timbre as well. Thus, theories about music deriving from astrology and medicine were shaping the ideas of composers themselves, a trend which was to see the arts and sciences become further separated in subsequent centuries.

Baroque Period, Classicism and the Enlightenment

Music composition during this period was marked by a focus on the "passions" or "affections" and the development of compositional techniques for expressing them. The "doctrine of affections" drew on Neo-Platonic theory in speculating that specific tonalities, rhythms or melodic phrases could directly represent particular affective states. The interest in the passions that emerged in this period was stimulated at least partially by a revival in interest in the works of Aristotle and Cicero, in particular of Aristotle's *Poetics* (Palisca, 2001), and coincided with a corresponding interest in the application of dramatic and narrative techniques to music composition. It was also a product of an age of rationalism in which there was a desire to impose order on emotions (Nagley & Bujic, 2001). These changing interests among composers led to the eventual founding of opera in Italy in the early seventeenth century and the development of standard musical devices and performance gestures that were used to express particular emotions.

An interesting example of the development of a set of musical techniques for communicating emotion is found in the eighth book of madrigals by Claudio Monteverdi.[2] In his foreword to the volume, Monteverdi

---

[2] See Chap. 9 for more information.

(1929) states that the human mind has three principal passions or affections including anger, temperance, and humility or supplication. These three affections, Monteverdi argues, correspond to the pitch ranges of the human voice. He was likely influenced in this by the work of Italian humanist Girolamo Mei (1519–1594) who wrote a detailed study of Greek music theory. Monteverdi also quotes directly from Plato's *Republic*, (although he attributes his source to Plato's *On Rhetoric*), that is discussed earlier in this chapter where Plato mentions specific modes that can inspire bravery in men going out to battle. Monteverdi then uses specific musical devices that closely model Platonic philosophy to represent bravery and the contrasting emotion of love throughout the course of his book of madrigals.

However, in parallel to the increasing interest by composers in the power of music to depict and evoke emotions, the seventeenth and eighteenth centuries were witnessing the scientific revolution. In medical and scientific realms much of the Platonic theory of previous centuries began to be regarded as superstition, and music began to be firmly relegated to the domain of the arts without the status of a science that equaled the rigour of medicine or mathematics (Gouk, 2004). Thus interest in the capacity for music to be harnessed as a tool for influencing affective states and mental health waned in the world of science at the very time of its rising importance to the creators of music itself.

Nevertheless, some physicians adopted the scientific methods that were becoming important in this period, drawing on the 'doctrine of affections' to empirically investigate the effect of music on emotions and moods. Dr. Robert Burton, English clergyman and scholar, for example, wrote extensively about music based largely upon his own experiences with depression in *Anatomy of Melancholy* (1621). He describes music as "a sovereign remedy against despair and melancholy" (Memb VI, Subs III). Similarly, Richard Browne, an English apothecary recommends music as a cure for spleen, vapours, melancholy and madness in his *Medicina Musica, or a Mechanical Essay on the Effects of Singing, Musick and Dancing* (1729).

Accounts also emerge from this period of the use of music to treat cases of melancholy among prominent individuals. King Philip V of Spain, for example, suffered from bouts of depression and the famed male soprano Farinelli was reputedly engaged to perform for him to treat his low moods. Similarly, Princess Izabella Czartoryska of Poland claimed that her recovery from melancholia began with hearing the music of Benjamin Franklin's glass harmonica (Lipowski, 1984). Other royals including King George II of England and King Ludwig of Bavaria were also treated for depression using music (Cook, 1981).

A consciousness of the importance of targeting musical selections to the symptoms of the patient was also evident in the words of eighteenth-century physician William Pargeter (1792) who wrote:

> a considerable share of knowledge in music, then, will be requisite to select those compositions and instruments and that arrangement of the instru-mental parts as may, with an exact correspondence with the *pathos animi*, attract and fascinate the attention, and influence the temper of the animal spirits … Whether it should be executed in the *allegro, andante or dolce-largo* or *presto* time; and whether the tone should be *forte* or *fortissimo*—or *piano* or *pianissimo*. This must be regulated by the feelings of the patient. (pp. 107–108)

This concept that music can have a distinctly different effect on the individual depending on their temperament and affective state has been an important thread throughout the history of music in the regulation of affective states. Scholars and theorists throughout the ages have also rec-ognized the power music has to influence affective states in non-desirable directions as well as in positive ways. As the next section of this chapter will review, this is a view that has been borne out by empirical research in the last few years, despite the predominantly popular view that music is a uni-versal cure-all.

Mood Altering and Self-Medicating with Music in Modern Times

Modern understandings about the way music works and its impact on the brain, mind and body have come a long way since the time of Plato. However, the latter half of the twentieth century saw a tendency to focus on the benefits of musical engagement without regard for the potential for music to be used negatively. A trend can also be observed towards bulk administration of musical interventions without accounting for individual differences. Research in the last few years, however, is beginning to re-emphasize the need for music to be considered as a force that can have both negative and positive effects and that needs to be tailored to the individual in order to have positive outcomes on affective state and wellbeing.

Theories that are useful for understanding how music works as a regulator of affective state have emerged particularly from the field of media and communications. For example, Dolf Zillmann (1988) proposed that media choices (including music) are motivated by a desire to either diminish a negative mood or perpetuate a good mood. For example, women in a negative mood are more likely to select positive news items to read (Biswas, Riffe, & Zillmann, 1994) or to choose comedy programs on television—both designed to improve their negative mood. Music consumption patterns appear to be similar. William Thompson and colleagues (Thompson, Schellenberg, & Husain, 2001), for example, found that after listening to classical music enjoyment ratings are higher for an up-tempo piece in a major key than they are for a slow piece in a minor key. In a subsequent study (Husain, Thompson, & Schellenberg, 2002) the authors found that when listeners are played different versions of the same piece of music in which the tempo and mode have been altered, they generally prefer the happiest-sounding versions in fast tempos and major keys. Thus, it appears that in general, people 'self-medicate' by choosing to listen to music that will shift moods in positive directions.

However, there are times at which people do choose to listen to music that will not immediately improve their affective state. When people are in a sad mood, for example, they may select music that is mood-congruent rather than mood altering. Patrick Hunter and colleagues (Hunter, Schellenberg, & Griffith, 2011) found that after sad mood induction the typical preference for happy music disappeared in their participants. Other studies indicate that when feeling depressed, people are less attracted to energetic and mood-improving music (Dillman Carpentier et al., 2008; Punkanen, Eerola, & Erkkila, 2011).

While the immediate effects of listening to mood-congruent music may be a prolongation of the negative mood, Randy Larsen (2000) has argued that the ultimate goal may still be to achieve a positive mood state, but that gratification of this desire is delayed in order to obtain other psychological benefits. For example, Suvi Saarikallio and Jaakko Erkkila (2007) reported that adolescents often use music to engage in mental work such as contemplating and reappraising events that have triggered negative emotions. They also use music to help them discharge or release negative emotions, or to obtain solace through emotional validation. Other studies have similarly found that people typically use mood-congruent music as catharsis for negative emotions or to reflect on and make sense of life events (Garrido & Schubert, 2011a, b, 2013; Van den Tol & Edwards, 2015; Van den Tol, Edwards, & Heflick, 2016).

However, the evidence also suggests that the use of mood-congruent music is generally a temporary strategy designed to help people work through emotions, and that eventually the preference for happy music re-emerges. For example, where the situation which evoked the negative emotions is perceived to be unresolvable and therefore sadness is of no value in motivating change, study participants tend to prefer to listen to happy music (Tahlier, Miron, & Rauscher, 2013). Furthermore, when some resolution of the sad emotions has been achieved, listeners will also return to listening to music evoking positive emotions (Dillman Carpentier et al., 2008).

Nevertheless, these healthy processes in which music is used to manage negative emotions or to induce positive mood states, seem to malfunction in some individuals. Depression is, by definition, a disorder of affect dys-regulation in which people tend to have less access to effective strategies by which to regulate affective states. They often engage in behavior that prolongs negative affective states and show reduced motivation to engage in behavior that could alleviate those negative states (Forbes & Dahl, 2005). Thus whether or not music listening choices will have the desired effect on mood has much to do with the habitual coping style of the individual.

Research has consistently shown that rumination—an involuntary focus on negative and pessimistic thoughts about one's self, the world and the future which is distinct from healthier processes of self-reflection (Joorman, 2005)—is associated with negative mood outcomes from listening to mood-congruent music (Garrido et al., 2016; Garrido & Schubert, 2013, 2015a, b). Our MLAP research also demonstrated the link between coping styles and music choices. Chapter 7 will reveal in more detail, for example, that people with high scores in rumination and behavioural disengage-ment—another maladaptive coping style—are less likely to have access to music as an effective means for coping with the stress of childbirth. In Chap. 8, we will show how parents with positive coping styles tend to sing songs to their children with a more positive valence or that are humorous and ironical. Similarly, the data presented in Chap. 10 will demonstrate that people with less effective coping styles are more likely to deal with heartbreak using songs that reflect past-oriented themes and anger. People with adaptive coping styles, on the other hand, tend to select songs with lyrics revealing a degree of cognitive insight that suggested their use of music for positive psychological processes. Thus, as will become evident throughout the rest of this volume, when associated with maladaptive coping styles, music does not always have a positive effect on affective states.

The potentiality for music to influence affective states is not only utilized on an individual level, but can be recruited for numerous political and economic purposes as well (Brown, 2006). Steven Brown argues that music is used to foster internal group harmony and to consolidate solidarity against other groups, in part by stimulating conformity to behavioural norms and codes, and by reinforcing group ideologies. Thus, he argues, music is ultimately a form of behavioural control. Music can also be used to mobilize group emotions which will reinforce loyalty to the group or antipathy towards those outside the group. Thus Brown argues that music is not only a mood-altering drug, but an "associative enhancer of communication" (p. 20) which makes use of affective stimulation to amplify the messages being communicated. The persuasive potential of music is utilized in religious rituals, to influence consumer behavior, and to manipulate affect in film and television.

In many cases music also serves important ritual purposes. Chapter 11, for example, will reveal how many people select traditional music choices for weddings such as Wagner's Bridal Chorus or the overture from Mendelssohn's *A Midsummer Night's Dream*, despite the fact that the meaning of marriage has changed greatly since the time this music was first used in a wedding. However, this music has come to form part of the overall picture of what a wedding should look like for people from many diverse cultural backgrounds. In fact, the example of weddings, nicely illustrates Brown's argument about how music is used to manipulate behavior. Commercial motivations along with social and cultural movements have shaped popular beliefs about the importance of romance in marriage in the twenty-first century, and along with this, have created a picture of the fairy-tale wedding complete with music, to which many modern-day couples aspire. While many couples choose to put a more individual stamp on wedding rituals, for many the traditional concept of a wedding is still the ultimate symbol of romance. Music enhances this cultural concept, playing on the emotions of the participants via mechanisms of association and symbolism.

The previous chapters of this volume have discussed how situational variables such as family upbringing and culture, as well as personal variables such as gender, personality and habitual mood regulation strategies influence the emotions we experience in response to music, how we use it, and how personal meaning is formed around music. Do these emotional responses and functions of music stay stable throughout our lifespan? The following chapter will examine how music preferences and use develop throughout different stages of the lifecycle.

References

Biswas, R., Riffe, D., & Zillmann, D. (1994). Mood Influence on the Appeal of Bad News. *Journalism & Mass Communication Quarterly, 71*(3), 689–696.

Brettingham-Smith, J. (1993). The Sick Child and Music. *Child's Nervous System, 9*(4), 193–196.

Brown, S. (2006). Introduction: "How Does Music Work?" Toward a Pragmatics of Musical Communication. In S. Brown & U. Volgsten (Eds.), *Music and Manipulation: On the Social Uses and Social Control of Music* (pp. 1–30). New York: Berghahn Books.

Browne, R. (1729). *Medicina Musica: Or, a Mechanical Essay on the Effects of Singing, Musick, and Dancing, on Human Bodies*. Uppingham: John Cooke.

Bunt, L. (1994). *Music Therapy: An Art Beyond Words*. Psychology Press.

Burton, R. (1621). *Anatomy of Melancholy*. Oxford University Press.

Callahan, C. (2000). Music in Medieval Medical Practice: Speculations and Certainties. *College Music Symposium, 40*, 151–164.

Cambrensis, G., & Forester, T. (1894). *The Historical Works of Giraldus Cambrensis: The Topography of Ireland*. London and New York: George Bell & Sons.

Cassiodorus, M. A. (1886). *The Letters of Cassiodorus: Being a Condensed Translation of the Variae Epistolae of Magnus Aurelius Cassiodorus Senator* (T. Hodgkin, Trans. Vol. II). London: Frowde.

Cook, J. D. (1981). The Therapeutic Use of Music: A Literature Review. *Nursing Forum, 20*(3), 252–266.

Cosman, M. P. (1978). Machaut's Medical Musical World. *Annals of the New York Academy of Sciences, 314*(1), 1–36.

d'Abano, P. (1303). *Conciliator differentiarum quae inter philosophos et medicos versantur.*

da Foligno, G. (1510). *Primus Avicenne Canonis Cum Argutissima Gentilis Expositione*. Pavia: Jacob de Burgofranco.

Dillman Carpentier, F. R., Brown, J. D., Bertocci, M., Silk, J. S., Forbes, E. E., & Dahl, R. C. (2008). Sad Kids, Sad Media? Applying Mood Management Theory to Depressed Adolescents' Use of Media. *Media Psychology, 11*, 143–166.

Forbes, E. E., & Dahl, R. C. (2005). Neural Systems of Positive Affect: Relevance to Understanding Child and Adolescent Depression? *Development and Psychopathology, 17*, 827–850.

Garrido, S. (2014). A Systematic Review of the Measurement of Mood and Emotion in Music Studies. *Psychomusicology, 24*(4), 316–327.

Garrido, S., Bangert, D., & Schubert, E. (2016). Musical Prescriptions for Mood Improvements: A Mixed Methods Study. *The Arts in Psychotherapy, 51*, 46–53.

Garrido, S., & Davidson, J. (2013). Music and Mood Regulation: A Historical Enquiry into Individual Differences and Musical Prescriptions Through the Ages. *Australian Journal of Music Therapy, 24*, 89–109.

Garrido, S., & Schubert, E. (2011a). Individual Differences in the Enjoyment of Negative Emotion in Music: A Literature Review and Experiment. *Music Perception, 28*(3), 279–295.

Garrido, S., & Schubert, E. (2011b). Negative Emotion in Music: What Is the Attraction? A Qualitative Study. *Empirical Musicology Review, 6*(4), 214–230.

Garrido, S., & Schubert, E. (2013). Adaptive and Maladaptive Attraction to Negative Emotion in Music. *Musicae Scientiae, 17*(2), 145–164. https://doi.org/10.1177/1029864913478305

Garrido, S., & Schubert, E. (2015a). Moody Melodies: Do They Cheer Us up? A Study of the Effect of Sad Music on Mood. *Psychology of Music, 43*(2), 244–261. https://doi.org/10.1177/0305735613501938

Garrido, S., & Schubert, E. (2015b). Music and People with Tendencies to Depression. *Music Perception, 32*(4), 313–321. https://doi.org/10.1525/MP.2015.32.4.313

Gouk, P. (2004). Raising Spirits and Restoring Souls: Early Modern Medical Explanations for Music's Effects. In V. Erlmann (Ed.), *Hearing Cultures: Essays on Sound, Listening and Modernity* (pp. 87–105). Oxford and New York: Berg.

Hamilton, E. (1953, 27th January, 2016). *The Modes of Ancient Greece*. Retrieved from http://www.nakedlight.co.uk/pdf/articles/a-002.pdf

Holsinger, B. W. (1993). The Flesh of the Voice: Embodiment and the Homoerotics of Devotion in the Music of Hildegard of Bingen. *Signs, 19*(1), 92–125.

Hunter, P. G., Schellenberg, E. G., & Griffith, A. T. (2011). Misery Loves Company: Mood-Congruent Emotional Responding to Music. *Emotion, 11*(5), 1068–1072.

Huron, D. (2001). Is Music an Evolutionary Adaptation? *Annals of the New York Academy of Sciences, 930*, 43–61.

Husain, G., Thompson, W. F., & Schellenberg, E. G. (2002). Effects of Musical Tempo and Mode on Arousal, Mood, and Spatial Abilities. *Music Perception, 20*(2), 151–171.

Joorman, J. (2005). Inhibition, Rumination and Mood Regulation in Depression. In R. W. Engle, G. Sedek, U. V. Hecker, & D. N. McIntosh (Eds.), *Cognitive Limitations in Aging and Psychopathology: Attention, Working Memory, and Executive Functions* (pp. 275–312). New York: Cambridge University Press.

Juslin, P. N., Harmat, L., & Eerola, T. (2013). What Makes Music Emotionally Significant? Exploring the Underlying Mechanisms. *Psychology of Music*. https://doi.org/10.1177/0305735613484548

Juslin, P. N., Liljestrom, S., Vastfjall, D., & Lundqvist, L.-O. (2010). How Does Music Evoke Emotions? Exploring the Underlying Mechanisms. In P. N. Juslin & J. A. Sloboda (Eds.), *Handbook of Music and Emotion: Theory, Research, Applications*. Oxford: Oxford University Press.

Juslin, P. N., & Västfjäll, D. (2008). Emotional Response to Music: The Need to Consider Underlying Mechanisms. *Behavioral and Brain Sciences, 31*, 559–621.

Kensinger, E. A., & Schacter, D. L. (2008). Memory and Emotion. In M. Lewis, J. M. Haviland-Jones, & L. F. Barrett (Eds.), *Handbook of Emotions*. New York: The Guilford Press.

Lane, A. M., & Terry, P. C. (2000). The Nature of Mood: Development of a Conceptual Model. *Journal of Applied Sport Psychology, 12*, 16–33.

Larsen, R. J. (2000). Toward a Science of Mood Regulation. *Psychological Inquiry, 11*, 129–141. https://doi.org/10.1207/S15327965PLI1103_01

Leach, E. E. (2006). Gendering the Semitone, Sexing the Leading Tone: Fourteenth Century Music Theory and the Directed Progression. *Music Theory Spectrum, 28*(1), 1–21.

Lipowski, Z. J. (1984). Benjamin Franklin as a Psychotherapist: A Forerunner of Brief Psychotherapy. *Perspectives in Biology and Medicine, 27*(3), 361–366.

Monteverdi, C. (1929). *Madrigas, Book VIII: Madrigali guerrieri et amorosi* (S. Appelbaum, Trans.). New York: Dover.

Nagley, J., & Bujic, B. (2001). Doctrine of Affections. *Grove Music Online. Oxford Music Online*. Retrieved from http://www.oxfordmusiconline.com/subscriber/article/opr/t114/e94

Palisca, C. V. (2001). Baroque. *Grove Music Online. Oxford Music Online*. Retrieved from http://www.oxfordmusiconline.com/subscriber/article/grove/music/02097

Pargeter, W. (1792). *Observations of Maniacal Disorders*. London; Reading: Printed for the Author.

Punkanen, M., Eerola, T., & Erkkila, J. (2011). Biased Emotional Preferences in Depression: Decreased Liking of Angry and Energetic Music by Depressed Patients. *Music and Medicine, 3*(2), 114–120.

Saarikallio, S. (2011). Music as Emotional Self-Regulation Throughout Adulthood. *Psychology of Music, 39*, 307–332.

Saarikallio, S., & Erkkila, J. (2007). The Role of Music in Adolescents' Mood Regulation. *Psychology of Music, 35*(1), 88–109.

Schubert, E. (2007). The Influence of Emotion, Locus of Emotion and Familiarity Upon Preferences in Music. *Psychology of Music, 35*, 499–515.

Stevenson, R. (1952). Thomas Morley's "Plaine and Easie" Introduction to the Modes. *Musica Disciplina, 6*(4), 177–184. Retrieved from http://www.jstor.org/stable/20531854

Tahlier, M., Miron, A. M., & Rauscher, F. H. (2013). Music Choice as a Sadness Regulation Strategy for Resolved Versus Unresolved Sad Events. *Psychology of Music, 41*(6), 729–748.

Thompson, W. F., Schellenberg, E. G., & Husain, G. (2001). Arousal, Mood and the Mozart Effect. *Psychological Science, 12*, 248–251.

Van den Tol, A., & Edwards, J. (2015). Listening to Sad Music in Adverse Situations: How Music Selection Strategies Relate to Self-Regulatory Goals, Listening Effects, and Mood Enhancement. *Psychology of Music, 43*(4), 473–494.

Van den Tol, A., Edwards, J., & Heflick, N. A. (2016). Sad Music as a Means for Acceptance-Based Coping. *Musicae Scientiae, 20*(1), 68–83.

Wegman, R. C. (1995). Sense and Sensibility in Late-Medieval Music: Thoughts on Aesthetics and 'Authenticity'. *Early Music, 23*(2), 298–312.

Wigram, T., Pedersen, I. N., & Bonde, L. O. (2002). *A Comprehensive Guide to Music Therapy: Theory, Clinical Practice, Research and Training* (Vol. 1). Jessica Kingsley Publishers.

Zillmann, D. (1988). Mood Management Through Communication Choices. *American Behavioral Scientist, 31*(3), 327–340.

CHAPTER 6

Music Throughout the Life Span

Most people recall certain times of their lives with particular vividness. For many, those most poignant of autobiographical memories come from the period when they were aged between 10 and 30 years (Rubin, 2002). Researchers report what is often termed a 'reminiscence bump'—or a peak in recall—for memories from that phase of an individual's life (Rubin, Wetzler, & Nebes, 1986). For example, author Ian Inglis, who writes about popular music performances in his book "Performance and Popular Music: History, Place and Time" (2006), cites two powerful quotes from Brian Kendall's study of the Beatles performances in Canada (1997). Two Canadian adults reflected on their attendance at a Beatles concert in 1964 when they were teenagers. Eric Twimane, for example, noted:

> Never in all the years since have I been as emotionally high as I was during that concert. The music and the charisma…simply can't be matched. You couldn't take your eyes off them. I still compare every concert to that one. None have measured up

Similarly Edith Manea stated:

> It's difficult to even describe my feelings. I was exactly where I had dreamed of being for months. I went to see them. And, my god, there they were. (Kendall, 1997, pp. 128–129)

© The Author(s) 2019
S. Garrido, J. W. Davidson, *Music, Nostalgia and Memory*, Palgrave Macmillan Memory Studies,
https://doi.org/10.1007/978-3-030-02556-4_6

The period from adolescence to early adulthood is a key period in development of personal identity—a process known as individuation—during which an individual's sense of self begins to emerge as distinct from their family. It is also a period during which many key life events tend to take place. Barring unexpected disruptions to one's life in later years, individuals tend to go through more changes and novel events during adolescence and early adulthood than in subsequent decades, a fact which likely heightens the emotional resonance of memories from this period. Emotions can be particularly intense in adolescence and so the memories we form around music tend to be especially potent during that period. Music can thus seem to take on a deep level of symbolism of the self and one's own identity during this period.

Not only are memories from the reminiscence bump more easily retrieved and clearly recalled, but items from this period of one's life are generally preferred. For example, Jerome Sehulster (1996) found that most people's favourite films were films they had viewed in their twenties. Similarly, several researchers have reported that people most often express a strong liking for music that was popular when they were in their early twenties (Holbrook & Schindler, 1989). This remains true even when cross-cultural differences are examined. While the content of music preferences may differ between people from different cultural backgrounds, what is apparent is that musical taste mostly derives from what individuals were exposed to in their youth (Cohen, 2002). These preferences appear to remain relatively stable over the lifespan, especially in the case of music, although with some exceptions as discussed below.

Carol Krumhansl and Justin Zupnick (2013) reported that memories encoded in adolescence and early adulthood in their participants interacted with the music they were exposed to by family in what they call 'cascading reminiscence bumps'. They report that, in addition to the reminiscence bump of adolescence and early adulthood, individuals may also show a preference for music that was popular before their birth as a result of exposure to the music of their parents in the home environment during childhood.

However, some studies suggest that there are age-related differences in how we process and perceive music. For example, some research has suggested that older people have a reduced ability to recognize a set of newly learned melodies (Halpern, Bartlett, & Dowling, 1995). In one detailed study involving more than a quarter of a million participants, Arielle Bonneville-Roussy and colleagues (Bonneville-Roussy, Rentfrow, Xu, &

Potter, 2013) found that preferences for intense music decreased with age while preferences for mellow and sophisticated music increased with age in ways that were closely associated with personality changes that tend to occur with maturity. Thus, the authors suggested that rather than music preferences being relatively stable from adulthood onwards, changes in personality that occur along with aging in turn influence changing musical preferences. They point to the fact that social roles change throughout the life stages, with adolescence characterised as a 'storm and stress' period of identity formation, while middle adulthood is more about stabilizing intimate relationships and careers.

A further suggestion made by Bonneville-Roussy and colleagues is that changes in music taste may be related to changes in auditory perception that occur with aging. As people age, hearing impairments may be more prevalent, individuals show a decreased capacity to perceive high-pitched sounds, and tend to be more sensitive to volume and intensity (Buus & Florentine, 2002). Thus, there appear to be a number of developmental variables that can influence music preferences throughout the lifespan. Music preferences may not be as stable as one might assume.

Our MLAP data did reveal some age-related differences. Older participants were more likely to select spiritual music, instrumental or traditional choices for their key life moments than younger people, while younger people were more likely to listen to RNB or electronic music than older people. While these findings could primarily reflect the types of genres that participants are most familiar with, there were also differences in their reasons for song choices. Older participants reported selecting music that expressed their views or that was personally significant or because they liked elements of the music, while the most strongly nominated reason for song choices by younger people was because they were a fan of the artist.

In this chapter, we shall continue to explore the memories and emotional experiences people have with music from their childhood through to very old age. In so doing, we shall consider cultural and historical context and personal situational variables. Indeed, personal history and life experiences play a large role in emotional response and personal taste in relation to music. Also, as outlined in Chap. 2, personal memories become entangled with particular pieces of music. This can be to such a strong degree that it becomes impossible to hear a particular piece of music without thinking of a specific person, place or event. Indeed, evidence shows that music is one of the strongest triggers of nostalgic remembrance (Barrett et al., 2010; Zentner, Grandjean, & Scherer, 2008).

As mentioned in the previous chapter, the twentieth century brought many changes to culture and society at large. Perhaps one of the most significant developments was the concept of the teenager and youth culture (see also Chap. 9). Its roots have several different accounts, one being that universalistic norms began to emerge in the twentieth century as a consequence of modernism, where interaction in a modern culture made everyone learn the same set of norms (Haferkamp & Smelser, 1992). Furthermore, compulsory schooling separated children from adults and, as a consequence of peer group interactions, adolescent or youth culture emerged (Inglis, 2006). It has also been posited that the concept of the teenager emerged in response to hormonal and growth developmental stages, with the time between childhood and adulthood being filled with questions about self-identity.

But, teenagers are not the only age group that has been impacted by the modern world. For instance, a quicker pace of life and technology means that a fifty-year old in 2018 has access to many more life experiences and opportunities than their counterpart of 1918. More than this, with improvements in hygiene, medicine, diet and welfare, people are living much longer and so lead much more diverse lives than their forebears. These technological developments also mean that lifespan access to music has also changed. Historically, an individual would have been constrained by the locality in which they lived and the culture into which they were born (Inglis, 2006). Today, place, space, experience, and belief are ever changing, and as a consequence, individuals develop along with their environment and the times in which they live. This means that someone in their fifties now would have experienced particular forms of school music and youth music, and as they face older age they may anticipate a relationship with music which may be much more personalised than ever before, owing to the rapid rate of technological advancement and the accessibility of many kinds of music digitally and in live contexts. As a consequence of these ever-emergent experiences, the use of music as both guiding and responding to personal and environment variables may vary in ways never previously imagined. However, for the sake of discussion, this chapter explores a rather generalised sense of a lifespan, looking at individuals and time periods.

First Memories

There have been numerous studies of children's musical tastes and experiences, specifically in relation to how they acquire musical skills. For many there is a very strong tie between the motivations required to engage in learning, their self-identity and memories of positive earliest experiences with music (McPherson, Davidson, & Faulkner, 2012). For example, in a study of adolescent musicians in the 1990s, many recalled how a specific musical work or event stimulated them towards initial participation in music, often when they were very young (Howe & Sloboda, 1991). They also remembered being drawn to the sounds of specific instruments. For some, this first hearing could be described in vivid detail. One boy talked about the incredible impact hearing the oboe had on him, how he could still remember that sound and how it was a strong incentive to being learning. Another spoke about falling in love with the sounds of one specific song and playing it over and over again, as if it were impossible to sate her desire to hear it. In fact, both continued to love these aspects of their musical lives, showing how that initial impact grew and developed over time.

Raymond MacDonald, David Hargreaves and Dorothy Miell edited a volume on musical identities in which they highlighted a distinction between 'identities in music' and 'music in identities' (MacDonald, Hargreaves, & Miell, 2002). The former relates to how one sees oneself as a musician. In a study of 42 young musicians aged between 8–18 years of age in receipt of a specialist musical education, it was discovered that the majority could not imagine a future without music in their lives (Howe & Sloboda, 1991). Their specialist music school days began and ended with a music practice session, and while a full school curriculum was delivered, students took fewer public examinations in other subjects, devoting themselves principally to music study. In one case, the child had grown up in a family of musicians, each playing a range of string and woodwind instruments. So, when the doctor came to visit the home during a bout of sickness, the child immediately assumed the doctor was another musician, carrying a musical instrument in the black medical bag. Meaning and emotional association with music was dominant in the child's life experience and his perception. Historical cases from Western culture would certainly reveal similar accounts of deep absorption in musical activities in early childhood being key to establishing a lifelong interest and commitment to music.

Consider, for example, the famous jazz musician Louis Armstrong, who was born in the first years of the twentieth century. His early life was literally a musical playlist (Collier, 1983). Born into extreme poverty in New Orleans, Mississippi, the three-year-old Armstrong used to tramp the streets playing a toy tin-horn to call out for rags, bones or bottles, to help his brother with his junk round. At the same time, he and other children begged on street corners, literally singing for their supper. This was going on outside of the greatest jazz halls of the era. He was absorbing the music of the New Orleans music scene—Joe "King" Oliver and Bunk Johnson. Developing in that musical culture and focussed on music, it is not surprising that Armstrong not only developed a musician identity, but that music became his main medium of communication, employment and connection.

The role of the environment in shaping musical experience and the memory of it cannot be underplayed. Reminiscing on his achievements, Armstrong acknowledged that the musical knowledge and related memories he acquired during those early years were formative. In fact, in his childhood he frequently found himself in the New Orleans Colored Waifs' Home for Boys. These potentially traumatic periods were recalled with fondness as times when crucial social and musical alignments were formed. In that home, Armstrong made a strong bond with the musical instructor, Peter Davies, who supported music making, even making Armstrong child bandmaster (Bergreen, 1997).

Of course, in most Western cultural contexts, the numbers of the population playing an instrument or having frequent performance engagement with music are in the minority, and many have traumatic associations with the experience often owing to bad teaching or peer bullying (McPherson et al., 2012). Contrary to the child whose experience led him to believe all black bags could be musical instrument cases, the vast majority of children do not see themselves as possessing a musician's identity. For those who do persist and learn, that minority position often makes them determined to take up this role. For example, the work by Davidson, Howe, and Sloboda (1997) revealed that some budding young musicians had been teased about the sounds their musical instruments made or had been bullied about the appearance their faces took when playing the instrument. While the memories of these challenging social encounters were strong, the potentially negative feedback was turned into a positive, motivating the children to strive harder, to stand out from the crowd. One girl said it was the affirmation she achieved from being 'different' that kept her going with her musical studies and so helped her to develop an identity as a musician. So, her love of music shaped her identity and made her resilient to the comments of others. She remembered these experiences as formative and positive.

Looking at how music and emotional effects typically coexist, it is possible to see that recollections of strong positive early memories help to shape young musicians' emerging identities. It seems that a 'first trigger' for music captures short-term attention and engages an emotional reaction. For some, this earliest experience can afford a very strong, epiphany-like impact which may be sufficient to motivate them for some time. But, it is well-established that music-focused 'situational interest' only persists if it is maintained (Hidi & Renninger, 2006). For those who go on to develop competency as adult musicians, external support in the form of key individuals is often necessary to stimulate and support a routine of practice and lessons—Armstrong's music instructor at the children's home, for example. Indeed, in the study of young musicians in specialist music education, they understood that their personal interest was complemented by factors such as performing their daily music exercises to a carer figure, where the praise and support they felt endorsed their sense of engagement and musician identity. Although some of the interviewees were close to the events they were describing (e.g. a 14 year old talking about experiences as a 9 year old), it was clear that their memories of these experiences were very strong and influential (Davidson et al., 1997).

A more recent study tracing the emergence of musicians in 160 students as they transitioned from childhood to early adulthood revealed a highly complex set of autobiographical memories of their learning (McPherson et al., 2012). The researchers framed these memories within Edward Deci and Richard Ryan's self-determination theory (Deci & Ryan, 1985; Ryan & Deci, 2000) and Arnold Sameroff's theory of transactional relations (Sameroff, 2010). These theories, focused on motivation, are important when considering identity as a musician and the role of memory in establishing it.

Deci and Ryan explain the motivation to engage in terms of senses of competency, autonomy and relatedness (Deci & Ryan, 1985; Ryan & Deci, 2000). What this implies is that when one feels endorsed in one's actions, a sense of control over what one does and is yet connected to others, motivation flourishes. Of the 160 student musicians in Gary McPherson, Jane Davidson and Robert Faulkner's 2012 study (McPherson et al., 2012), this was certainly the case for those who became successful self-determined musicians. With memories of being supported for small achievements and feeling good about making music, accounts of learning were self-endorsing: their memories of music and music learning were positive and powerful.

Sameroff's theory (2010) explores the transactional relations between self-regulation and environment or other regulation. In this theoretical framework, agents in the home, school, community and wider society operate critically to transform biological, social and psychological experiences. Again, how these experiences are processed, stored and retrieved by the music learner clearly influences the cycle of future investment in a musician identity. The overarching outcome of the study of the young learners was that when there was a present sense of competency, autonomy and relatedness and a realistic model for future achievement, the experience and memory of the learning was positive, self-endorsing musician identity. Useful examples of this complex relationship between musical development, experience and memories of those experiences are found in the cases of two of the study participants, Andrew and Simonne, below (see Davidson & Faulkner, 2013 for more details).

CASE STUDIES: ANDREW AND SIMONNE

Andrew was a young professional trombone player, twenty-one years old at the point at which he was re-interviewed, having first been studied as an eight-year old. Andrew's mother was a piano teacher and accompanist, and so Andrew had been introduced to a musician identity from birth.

When Andrew was in primary school and first heard his school's wind band, he was transported out of himself by the quality of the sound and the look and feel of the brass instruments. Not only that, once he began lessons, he developed a close and long-lasting relationship with his teacher that included Andrew visiting the teacher in the pit of the Sydney Opera House, during a professional performance. The visit, and the feelings and associations it left with Andrew—strong and powerful memories—continued to sustain him beyond the initial love of the trombone, through to a desire to play trombone as a career. In terms of emotional impact and depth of feeling and commitment to music learning, Andrew also loved his "own" instrument and regularly performed at local and state band championships, where a sense of relatedness and positive memories and feelings were promoted, generating further desire to develop as a musician.

For Simonne, memories of early childhood experience and subsequent exposure revealed a complex musician identity. Firstly, there were no strong memories associated with starting her instrument, the French horn. She had been flattered that a teacher had asked her to learn the instrument, but there was nothing special or emotionally associated with the horn—no sound or epiphanic memory of hearing or seeing the instrument. She continued with lessons making slow progress until, not surprisingly, she decided to give up learning. However, an interview with Simonne and her mother within the first year of studying the horn revealed that Simonne had always been fascinating by vocal performance, and by 16 years of age, she took up singing where she discovered the profound emotional and aesthetic pleasure this musical identity provided:

> I don't know … with a certain sound of, aesthetic sound I guess, very technical and I guess technique was the most important thing. Then I started listening to music, it was just that there is, there are different kinds of aesthetics with the voice, not just one. (Davidson & Faulkner, 2013, p. 382)

At her interview in her 20s, Simonne had begun to explore new performance and song-writing opportunities. Simonne's sense of pleasure at song-writing and performance came from memories and emotions related to her voice and sharing her musical creativity with close friends. But what of music in the construction of other identities or 'music in identities' as MacDonald, Hargreaves and Miell referred to them (MacDonald et al., 2002)?

MUSIC IN IDENTITIES

As Chaps. 3 and 4 revealed, music aids people to express strong associations such as nationality, gender, and preferred social groups across the lifespan. For the young child, this can be membership of a school or cultural group. As an example, in non-specialist schools music might underpin a celebration of cultural diversity, with song, dance and costume parades forming part of a rich and stimulating participatory experience that goes on to influence the child in the longer term. In fact, such a commonly practised example reveals the extent to which music helps people to show their cultural distinctiveness, yet offers access to it to others through the music and associated feelings of celebration that often surround performance (Baily & Collyer, 2006).

The case of popular culture is even stronger. The second author of this volume—Jane Davidson—recalls being given a recording of an extremely popular singer for her tenth birthday. At her party, she played this recording time and again, revelling in not only possessing this cherished sonic item, but also loving the sound, the pop star whose voice was being brought close to her, and the overall clothing fashion and associated cultural accoutrements of the time. The music brought together a whole series of cultural values with which she associated as part of the tween culture of her generation. Interestingly, she recalls her friends being irritated at the number of times she played the specific recording at her party. It seems that her absorption and emotional reaction to the music itself was not shared by her friends, though in terms of the tween culture, all were as enthusiastic about the artist.

However, this love of the music and the artist did not continue across Jane's lifespan. The attraction to all elements of the experience were time- and context-specific. As Jane has aged, so too has her musical taste. As indicated by the examples in the opening of this chapter, she has become increasingly interested by more complex music. Even music she enjoyed in her formative student and young adult phases, while still listened to for its reminiscence value—remembering the people, places and events—is no longer loved and played for more aesthetic purposes. As Russell (1997) has highlighted, there is a very strong association between musical taste, social group and lifestyle. So, as these factors interact, it would be rather unusual if Jane's tastes in listening to musical genres did not change, or perhaps one could say, 'mature' over the lifespan.

Stepping away from Western cultural contexts to those of Africa, we can see how social practices influence children as they grow up, particularly as their lives more obviously combine traditional historical cultural practices with modern global pop ones. Research of this type has been undertaken by a range of researchers from Western anthropologists to indigenous African scholars themselves. An example can be found in a project exploring children's musical lives in Limpopo Province in South Africa (Davidson & Emberly, 2012).

In state schools in Limpopo, children are taught traditional song and dance by experts. Such practices often result in out-of-school competitions between a range of school and community groups, where the goal is both for fun but also the continuation of traditional cultural practice.[1] These educational schemes are highly successful and popular. In addition, many families still practice traditional culture at home. For example, after the working day, groups of women often congregate to share stories, as well as to perform traditional songs and dances such as Malende and

---

[1] See such a dance at Tshirunzananana Primary School, https://www.youtube.com/watch?v=ECZAyVPuttU, Smithsonian Folkways collection.

Tshigombela. As the women participate their children are present, often in the background, but assimilating the meaning of the songs, their complex rhythms and the dance steps. When ready, the child will begin to participate in a safe and informal manner.

During a recent visit to Thohoyandou—the state capital of Limpopo—and its surrounding villages, the second author (Jane Davidson) spent some time with a VhaVenda family and found the children freely improvising on the traditional drums, making up variations on their latest favourite pop song, in a hybrid manner. They danced around the drum in a circle, as their families would do in the traditional dance, but their movements and words were contemporary, interfacing hip-hop and VhaVenda traditional dance. This engagement revealed how vital and affirming both genres of music were to the social worlds of these children and illustrated how their cultural identity was practised in and through music. Memories of these events will no doubt leave strong traces for these children, perhaps offering the nostalgia bumps of the cascading proportions mentioned at the start of the chapter.

Looking to the broader engagements of adulthood, the interplay of culture and identity are found in the next set of examples, as we consider the musical engagements of adults from early adulthood to old age. We begin with an example from Icelandic culture, which has a strong association with traditional culture and much intergenerational interaction.

Case Study: Hreimur Choir, Iceland

The data explored here comes from a male choir which draws together singers from a population who live in geographically isolated conditions, spread across an area of scarcely populated north-east Iceland. It brings together a group of same sex participants for weekly social exchange. Despite factors that might seem to be grounds for creating a singing group to reduce the marginalized experience of remote living, all of these men are from the same unifying musical ecology, which constitutes an incredibly socially inclusive broader ecology as music features as a part of the Icelandic society's DNA. Thus, the Hreimur Choir is a positive example of how a collective cultural memory trace of community music can continue to foster social cohesion and inclusion, even though the perceived function of the group is vocal excellence (the choir having been regular competitors in international competitions). In this brief example, Hreimur choir is considered in terms of cultural memory as part of musical/social ecology and the theory of self. The researcher, Robert Faulkner both lead and reflected on his experiences of the choir in his monograph, *Icelandic Men and Me* (Faulkner, 2013).

The cultural ecology of this choir stems back to Iceland's rich musical past with the epic sung narrative which enjoyed an attentive participatory audience. There is a deep cultural memory trace going back to the significance of social singing for all Icelanders. How the choristers approached songs and reflected on the stories they contain, revealed much about their personal and cultural identity. Indeed, in this regard, this choir shows how we can use historical knowledge and music to sustain and develop as a cultural group. Icelanders typically sing in many different daily contexts both in family and the broader community in a diverse range of social activities. For the choristers, all of this fed back into their choir singing and their motivation to participate in it. Indeed, this specific singing group offered the choristers strong agency within Icelandic society—shaping and expressing their social identities, or persona (Weber, 2000). A collective and positive memory of endorsing social experiences were built through membership in it.

Beyond the choir and its musical demands, it provided a platform to enact intergenerational relationships as well as lineage—singing with children and grandchildren. Faulkner explored this, showing the vocal behaviour of the individuals in this choir as becoming the representation of kinship, an important Icelandic social construct, and a vital aspect of nostalgia and reminiscence (Faulkner, 2013). But this kinship was such that the choir itself became a representation of family, with the bonds of commitment to the group being like a family. In fact, the kinship bonds of Icelandic community were represented through five father and son pairs, four brothers from one family, and two pairs of brothers from other families. The music making became a site where family memories were generated and passed on.

In addition to the familial social identities, the concept of the social collective revealed itself to be central to choir ecology and ethics of Hreimur choir. As well as supportive leadership from Robert, the men always offered one another a positive and caring support. For instance, one man knew he did not have solo potential, but within the group his high register and light timbre was credited as helping the overall sound. The other singers often referred to the value of the collective sound. In studying these vocal interactions and the participants' lived experiences of them, a layered account of the complex interactions between self and social identity can be unravelled between individuals, the group sound and songs. All of these inputs were strengthening the bonds between choristers, and lead to long term deep relationships that were bound together with personal and collective memories of the experiences in the choir. All of this lead to both 'peak' epiphanic memories and connections to a historical nostalgia: imagining that their forebears had sung across the same valleys, or been in these comforting social spaces with others, making music together.

It is possible to see that being in this choir generated an environment in which the chorister's self was both safe yet expanding into the group and into an imagined future history, building from the past and present. Indeed, looking at the 'Spiritual' aspects of Self, the singing these men undertook seem to incorporate the idea of the voice travelling outwards beyond the physical realm, also to a future of collaboration and more music-making.

Case Study: Choirs to Celebrate and Embrace Old Age

While the Hreimur choir has deep historical and cultural foundations, in this section we discuss a collective of people making music together explicitly for social companionship and physical health benefits. In a longitudinal applied research project, the second author (Jane Davidson) founded six singing groups, aiming to address the social isolation frail, aged people face. Jane worked with a team of others including expert facilitators to create the musical content and social presentation, and designed intermittent survey-style questionnaires, face-to-face interviews and group discussions to sample on-going experience (Davidson, 2011; Davidson & Faulkner, 2010; Davidson et al., 2014; Lee, Davidson, & Krause, 2016).

Although six choirs were created, three are discussed here. One was in a residential care unit for people living with dementia. The other two were recruited by engaging aged health care service providers to promote participation to people in receipt of their care services such as home help or gardening. The participants were challenging to recruit, many living in isolated conditions such as being alone or in rundown homes with no infrastructure for frail individuals. Others were in state government units, but often with no passers-by and few material comforts. Poor physical health, e.g., multiple and interrelated physical health issues severely limited capacity to travel independently and indeed many were not in proximity to bus or train routes.

The choirs for these older participants became highly meaningful in the lives of all members. It is know that social isolation, depression and other chronic health problems can be countered by meaningful social engagement (Bunker, Colquhoun, & Murrary, 2003; Sorkin, Rook, & Lu, 2002), and this was certainly the case with the two singing groups targeting those living in community settings. For some participants, it became the only social outing of the week, and while the singing activities were initiated for group cohesion there were significant aspects of the shared musical encounters that aided participants far beyond social bonding. For example, people, some in their mid-80s at the formation of the groups, reported new feelings of excitement, energy, clarity and focus they had not experienced before. Some pinpointed the experience of having to learn new music, remembering melodies and words as being invigorating; for others, it was simply the experience of being the focus of attention when they went on stage to perform. The music was an active ingredient in expanding life experience.

In fact, recent work has been focused attention away from growing old as an inevitable process of decline to one where 'successful ageing' includes unleashing creative potential (Cohen, 2006). This work has refuted Erik Erickson's lifespan stages which portrayed older age as a time of isolation and despair. The driving force behind the theorisation of older age as an expansive, liberation phase that people enter in later life, typically from mid-fifties to mid-seventies, was psychiatrist Gene Cohen. His own research programs in the innovative Center on Ageing at the National Institute of Mental Health in Maryland, U.S., revealed that older people who participated in creative activities such as arts and music in particular, enjoyed feelings associated with flourishing, such as happiness, and had fewer trips to their GP than those in control groups (Cohen et al., 2006). He also found that between their sixties and eighties, people focus on giving back to others, completing unfinished business, and leaving a legacy for future generations such that major life themes are re-stated, offering a great sense of pleasure in their re-affirmation (Cohen, 2005, 2006).

Cohen advocated that optimal interventions to assist with 'successful ageing' focus on the distinct potential of the individual, rather than on the clinical problems that individual faces, and furthermore argued that creative expression promotes health via several interrelated facets (Cohen, 2006). Opportunities to experience a sense of autonomy and competency are provided by creative engagement, which in turn have a positive influence on health outcomes. Furthermore, various forms of creative activity (such as singing in a choir) provide opportunities for social engagement, which have a positive influence on general health and reduced mortality (Avlund, Damsgaard, & Holstein. 1998; Glass, de Leon, Marottoli, & Berkman, 1999) These choirs certainly had these goals, but also were seen to more than fulfil their remit. Indeed, when research funding ceased, the older participants had embraced their new musical identities and new social groups to such an extent, that they themselves went out to find sponsorship and support for the continuation of the choirs.

While these choirs offered new and expansive horizons, they were also moments for reflection and reminiscence. Many participants related these peaks with strong musical contexts and as the choirs developed, specific songs were used to get people focused on and thinking about specific times in their lives. As one member suggested, this was beautiful, to look back, but it could be a bittersweet experience:

> I wouldn't say I got teary, but when you haven't heard those songs for so many years and your memory goes back … to when you sort of … family, company and that.

So, as the years of choir membership have passed by, the participants' and their families have formed new friendships from within the choirs which have led to new networks permitting the groups to be self-sustaining. Many members have passed from their seventies to their late eighties and nineties, and despite challenges of mobility and chronic health conditions such as arthritis, this musical experience has become the most significant event in their weekly calendar. Indeed, reflecting on membership between 2008 and 2016, participants discussed themes that emerged that shaped on-going long-term motivation for participation: Importance of singing in my life (even when singing had never been a part of their previous childhood or adult experience); the enormous pleasure of singing; the experience of spiritual and uplifting emotions; feelings of challenge and achievement; strength in overcoming age, disease, and hardship; fellowship with others and finding purpose and meaning in group singing (Lee et al., 2016). All of these aspects are related to meaning and emotion. And, all of these aspects are known to deliver some degree of neuro-protection to the cognitive function of older people. Indeed, being in the musical activity often was described as helping the participants with short-term memory problems (Davidson & Almeida, 2014).

For those with dementia, the choir offered lucidity and focus (Davidson & Almeida, 2014) and for their family carers who also joined the group, it gave respite and the opportunity to enjoy normalizing and equalizing participation with their loved one. The group had a positive effect on the self-esteem of the person living with dementia and provided the carer with a view of their loved that is positive, showing a capable and strong participatory role. In fact, music is one of the most powerful resources in dementia treatment given that people with dementia retain the capacity to process and participate in music until late in the disease trajectory (Garrido et al., 2017).

A summary of the many studied benefits of music for people living with dementia include: cognitive stimulation which permits the acquisition of new knowledge, a phenomenon which until recently was not considered possible; a sense of contributing which in turn increases confidence, motivation and self-esteem; also, increased energy and motivation for physical exercise; as well as a sense of personal transcendence which feeds into positive mood and overall sense of wellbeing (Clift, Hancox, Staricoff, & Whitmore, 2008). This indicates that for those living with dementia, music offers much more than a memory prompt, it enables them to endorse their sense of self through both autobiographical and musical memories (Baird & Thompson, 2018). Sadly though, people with dementia do report that as their disease progresses, participation in their regular community music group or choir can be threatened (Clark, Tamplin, & Baker, 2018). This can be due in part to cognitive decline preventing them from processing music notation or instructions. So, music-based dementia programs delivered by a professional, particularly a qualified music therapist who is trained in a clinical model of diagnosis and treatment, can offer additional benefits, as a trained therapist has a sense of which music might be more appropriate to the needs of the individuals and are attuned to the ways in which dementia can progress (Clark et al., 2018).

Of course in the community, care for persons living with dementia comes typically from a family carer, such as a spouse or a child (Brooks, Ross, & Beattie, 2015). These people often have a heavy burden and as symptoms of dementia increase, they have to manage their own psychological stress of seeing the person they love in decline, and having to cope with these symptoms can be extremely challenging (Davidson & Almeida, 2014). Family carers often have to make hard decisions about treatment and finances. They often face significant grief as they reflect on the loss of their pre-dementia relationship. Thus, support for the carer is also vital. It has been shown that music with carers can give them a window of time to regain their own self-esteem and respite from the tensions of caring; they can also release emotionally through the music. In fact, carers who engaged in music therapy along with their loved one indicated a delay in admission to residential care for the person living with dementia (Boltz, Chippendale, Resnick, & Galvin, 2015). It seems that the interrelationship between music, emotion and memory in all its forms feeds into these outcomes: the carers develop positive associations with the person living with dementia, they also remember them with a positive nostalgia as they regain something of the former lucidity through the music.

The long-term experiences in these choirs for older people are consonant with the broader literature on the value of singing for wellbeing at any point in life e.g., challenges that are both physical (e.g., controlling breathing, remaining alert and focused) and intellectual (e.g., learning new songs, memorizing song lyrics) is supported by previous research reporting improved cognitive performance and psychological benefits after participating in a short-term music training program (Davidson & Garrido, 2015) and replicates findings of work with older people with mood disorders and people who were able to work on illness and trauma through singing (Bailey & Davidson, 2005; Bonde, 2014; Hays & Minichiello, 2005; von Lob, Carmic, & Clift, 2010).

The work on singing for older people reveals that music making can provide a socially acceptable way for vulnerable older people to seek out new social life and their experiences can channel old memories and create new ones. Using the singing voice also provides a strong connection between the person, their sense of self and their past identity. This is particularly poignant with older people because the singing voice persists even when the speaking voice has deteriorated (Austin, 2009). Research shows that group singing music therapy interventions in residential dementia care result in improved confidence, motivation, communication and social interaction (Dassa & Amir, 2014; Ridder & Aldridge, 2005; Ridder, Stige, Qvale, & Gold, 2013; Robertson-Gillam, 2008). Thus, for the person with dementia, their singing voice displays a more coherent and expressive access to their core self than spoken conversation. The use of voice seemingly aided the carer hear the 'former' voice of their loved one and provided a valuable access that person's former self (Davidson & Almeida, 2014).

On Performance and Performers Across the Lifespan

As established at the start of this chapter, reminiscence bumps are often associated with having either attended, heard or participated in a musical performance, most likely an artist from your own youth. The MLAP project asked about people's memories, preferences and the contexts in which they experienced music. People referred to key pieces and artists, but above all they also mentioned the alchemy of the situation—its performativity—as having a powerful effect on them. For most, this was through their experiences of pop performance.

Frith (1996) has argued that what makes pop performance compelling to the audience is the multi-layered performance task in which they have to 'become' the character in the song. To do this their 'performance involves gestures that are both false (they are only put on for the occasion) and true (they are appropriate to the emotions being described, expressed, or invoked)' (p. 208). Frith adds that the solo pop singer always creates 'a tension between an implied story (content: the singer in the song) and the real one (form: the singer on the stage)' (p. 209). This means that 'Pop stars must keep both their star personality and a song personality in play at once' (p. 212). This, in effect, offers much for the audience to experience.

Some performers, especially in the popular idiom, generate incredibly memorable performances that mobilise the different layers of the performance through extra musical effect such as expressive use of codes of social etiquette in the behaviours between co-performers, and co-performer and audience. An analysis of singer Annie Lennox (see Davidson, 2001) showed how she skilfully prolonged silences between phrases of a well-known song to elicit audience participation through the sense of anticipation the silence created.[2] This application of technique along with a good deal of stage persona certainly influence experience of the performance. Indeed, some have noted that the performance persona offers the audience a different access to the musician. A close long-term friend of Elvis Presley said of his performances:

> It was like a different Elvis. It was like a light coming on that stage—the electricity from the audience and the electricity from him, it was unbelievable. (Patti Perry, cited in Guralnick, 1999, p. 351)

[2] See https://www.youtube.com/watch?v=lv4SGL06qTU for an example.

It is possible to see that once this transaction between performer and audience has taken place, both parties may wish to replicate the experience. It is perhaps not surprising, therefore, that as rock stars age, their fans age with them, following them from gig to gig, eagerly aiming to recapture the strong emotions of their previous experiences of live performances.

Having explored different life phases and some of the different types of musical engagements that may stimulate powerful memories and even protect our memories as we age, it is perhaps fitting to end this chapter looking at how music has been used as a framework for people to assert not only their identities, but also their life choices and political beliefs. We end as we began, looking at youth culture. Just as pop music was created by youth for youth in the middle of the twentieth century, it is perhaps not that surprising that this same youth precipitated huge social change just a decade later. In the United States of America, young people, typically university students, often played key roles in civil uprisings. The Civil Rights Movement and protests against the Vietnam War are two such historic examples. In both cases, music was entwined with the demonstration and the building of solidarity between supporters. This final case study looks at contemporary Australian life and looks at political and social activism using choral music.

CASE STUDY: MUSIC, ACTIVISM, MEMORY AND EMOTION

Large choruses such as The San Francisco Gay Men's Chorus[3] have been trailblazers in their commitment to perform in conservative regions of the United States to challenge the prejudices felt historically (Schattenkirk, 2014). Activism and identity building work has been undertaken by Same Sex Attracted and Gender Questioning (SSAGQ) choirs, though this has been more recent. One main strategy for activism has been the development of youth choruses (Leske & Wilson, 2013). The Melbourne Gay and Lesbian Youth Chorus is an off shoot of Australia's oldest SSAGQ choir, The Melbourne Gay and Lesbian Chorus. The Youth Chorus was started in 2005 with the explicit aim of offering a safe and supportive musical and social place for young people of diverse gender and sexuality. Its mission statement actively promotes positive self-identification and rehearsals pro-

[3] To see a performance of this choir go to https://www.youtube.com/watch?v=9SRLKbrkNoo

vide mentoring and aim towards increasing autonomy and competency for all. In its twelve-year history, stories of pride and self-emergence are well-recorded (Leske, 2017). An indicative comment from a chorister's attendance at their first rehearsal encapsulates this positive experience:

> I remember finding them to be very good looking and very comfortable with each other. [yep] [giggles]. Um … and they're all like hugging everyone and like screaming when their friend arrived, because it was the first day of the year they'd just had a bit of a break. And so everyone who was … not new … was very excited … to be there, and knew each other really well. (Leske, 2017, p. 192)

Tracing the chorus and its function, Ben Leske found it was treated as a 'safe bubble' for choristers to feel able to express one's self in a supported manner (Leske, 2017). The key experience of solidarity the participants are able to express fits with Lee Higgins's concept of musical hospitality (Higgins, 2012), where choristers can choose how much hospitality they wish to receive: rehearsals and not performances, solos or not, publicise their personal involvement in the group or keep their participation anonymous. The term 'gentle activism' was coined by Leske to capture the chorus' function to support each individual and to more broadly represent gender diversity and equality. Examples of this work include the choristers' decisions to change gender pronouns and imagery in the music, also to give women low bass parts and men soprano parts, in a subversion of the traditional choral setup (Leske, 2017).

CONCLUSION

The role of music as an agent for social and political change has a persuasive history, supporting, challenging, and above all being cognitively processed as music, not speech. The experience of rehearsing, performing and listening to music can lead to hugely important and transformative personal experiences, that can develop across the life course. These merge in later life to offer important emotional experiences to be remembered and enjoyed, and in turn, feed back into everyday living. This chapter has illustrated the powerful impact of music across the lifespan for a range of groups. The life stages and experiences are diverse: the experience of music and its impact on mature persons as they grapple with the challenges of later life; music's power on youth; and how social prejudice and oppression can be addressed, as in the case of SSAGQ people.

References

Austin, D. (2009). *The Theory and Practice of Vocal Psychotherapy: Songs of the Self.* Jessica Kingsley Publishers.

Avlund, K., Damsgaard, M. T., & Holstein, B. E. (1998). Social Relations and Mortality. An Eleven Year Follow-up Study of 70-Year-Old Men and Women in Denmark. *Social Science & Medicine, 47*(5), 635–643.

Bailey, B. A., & Davidson, J. W. (2005). Effects of Group Singing and Performance for Marginalized and Middle-Class Singers. *Psychology of Music, 33*(3), 269–303. https://doi.org/10.1177/0305735605053734

Baily, J., & Collyer, M. (2006). Introduction: Music and Migration. *Journal of Ethnic and Migration Studies, 32*(2), 167–182. https://doi.org/10.1080/13691830500487266

Baird, A., & Thompson, W. F. (2018). The Impact of Music on the Self in Dementia. *Journal of Alzheimer's Disease, 61*(3), 827–841.

Barrett, F. S., Grimm, K. J., Robins, R. W., Wildschut, T., Sedikides, C., & Janata, P. (2010). Music-Evoked Nostalgia: Affect, Memory, and Personality. *Emotion, 10*(3), 390–403.

Bergreen, L. (1997). *Louis Armstrong: An Extravagant Life.* Broadway Books.

Boltz, M., Chippendale, T., Resnick, B., & Galvin, J. E. (2015). Testing Family-Centered, Function-Focused Care in Hospitalized Persons with Dementia. *Neurodegenerative Disease Management, 5*(3), 203–215. https://doi.org/10.2217/nmt.15.10

Bonde, L. O. (2014). Music and Health Promotion – In the Life of Music Therapy and Music Psychology Researchers: A Pilot Study. *Voices: A World Forum for Music Therapy, 14*(1).

Bonneville-Roussy, A., Rentfrow, P. J., Xu, M. K., & Potter, J. (2013). Music Through the Ages: Trends in Musical Engagement and Preferences from Adolescence Through Middle Adulthood. *Journal of Personal and Social Psychology, 105*(4), 703–717.

Brooks, D., Ross, C., & Beattie, E. (2015). *Caring for Someone with Dementia: The Economic, Social and Health Impacts of Caring and Evidence Based Supports for Carers – Paper 42.* Brisbane: Alzheimer's Australia.

Bunker, S., Colquhoun, D., & Murrary, D. (2003). Stress and Coronary Heart Disease: Psychosocial Risk Factors, National Heart Foundation Position Statement Update. *Medical Journal of Australia, 178*, 272–276.

Buus, S., & Florentine, M. (2002). Growth of Loudness in Listeners with Cochlear Hearing Losses: Recruitment Considered. *Journal of the Association for Research in Otolaryngology, 3*, 120–139.

Clark, I. N., Tamplin, J., & Baker, F. A. (2018). Community-Dwelling People Living with Dementia and Their Family Caregivers' Experiences of Therapeutic Group Singing: A Qualitative Thematic Analysis. *Frontiers in Psychology, 9*, 1332.

Clift, S., Hancox, G., Staricoff, R., & Whitmore, C. (2008). *Singing and Health: Summary of a Systematic Mapping and Review of Non-Clinical Research.* Canterbury, UK: Sidney De Haan Research Centre for Arts and Health.

Cohen, A. (2002). Introduction to the Special Volume on Psychogeromusicology: Psychology of Music and Aging Comes of Age. *Psychomusicology, 18*(1–2), 3.

Cohen, G. (2006). Research on Creativity and Aging: The Positive Impact of the Arts on Health and Illness. *Generations, 30*(1), 7–15. Retrieved from https://www.ingentaconnect.com/content/asag/gen/2006/00000030/00000001/art00003

Cohen, G. D. (2005). *The Mature Mind: The Positive Power of the Aging Brain.* Basic Books.

Cohen, G. D., Perlstein, S., Chapline, J., Kelly, J., Firth, K. M., & Simmens, S. (2006). The Impact of Professionally Conducted Cultural Programs on the Physical Health, Mental Health, and Social Functioning of Older Adults. *The Gerontologist, 46*(6), 726–734. https://doi.org/10.1093/geront/46.6.726

Collier, J. L. (1983). *Louis Armstrong: An American Genius.* Oxford: Oxford University Press.

Dassa, A., & Amir, D. (2014). The Role of Singing Familiar Songs in Encouraging Conversation Among People with Middle to Late Stage Alzheimer's Disease. *Journal of Music Therapy, 51*(2), 131–153.

Davidson, J., & Emberly, A. (2012). Embodied Musical Communication Across Cultures: Singing and Dancing for Quality of Life and Wellbeing Benefit. In *Music, Health and Wellbeing* (pp. 136–149). Oxford, UK: Oxford University Press.

Davidson, J., & Faulkner, R. (2013). Music in Our Lives. In S. B. Kaufman (Ed.), *The Complexity of Greatness: Beyond Talent or Practice* (pp. 367–389). New York: Oxford University Press.

Davidson, J., & Garrido, S. (2015). Singing and Psychological Needs. In G. Welsh, D. Howard, & J. Nix (Eds.), *The Oxford Handbook of Singing.* Oxford: Oxford University Press.

Davidson, J. W., McNamara, B., Rosenwax, L., Lange, A., Jenkins, S., & Lewin, G. (2014). Evaluating the Potential of Group Singing to Enhance the Well-Being of Older People. *Australasian Journal on Ageing, 33*(2), 99–104. https://doi.org/10.1111/j.1741-6612.2012.00645.x

Davidson, J. W. (2001). The Role of the Body in the Production and Perception of Solo Vocal Performance: A Case Study of Annie Lennox. *Musicae Scientiae, 5*(2), 235–256. https://doi.org/10.1177/102986490100500206

Davidson, J. W. (2011). Musical Participation: Expectations, Experiences, and Outcomes. In *Music and the Mind.* Oxford: Oxford University Press.

Davidson, J. W., & Almeida, R. A. (2014). An Exploratory Study of the Impact of Group Singing Activities on Lucidity, Energy, Focus, Mood and Relaxation for Persons with Dementia and Their Caregivers. *Psychology of Well-Being, 4*(1), 24. https://doi.org/10.1186/s13612-014-0024-5

Davidson, J. W., & Faulkner, R. (2010). Meeting in Music: The Role of Singing to Harmonise Carer and Cared for. *Arts & Health: An International Journal of Research, Policy and Practice, 2*(2), 164–170. Retrieved from http://sfx. unimelb.hosted.exlibrisgroup.com/sfxlcl41?sid=sage&iuid=234858&aulast= &date=2010&atitle=Meeting in music%3A The role of singing to harmonise carer and cared for&title=Arts %26 Health%3A An International Journal of Research%2C Policy and Practice&volume=2&issue=2&spage=164

Davidson, J. W., Howe, M. & Sloboda, J. (1997). Environmental Factors in the Development of Musical Performance Skill in the First Twenty Years of Life. In D. Hargreaves & A. C. North (Eds.), *The Social Psychology of Music* (pp. 188–203). Oxford: Oxford University Press.

Deci, E. L., & Ryan, R. M. (1985). *Intrinsic Motivation and Self-Determination in Human Behavior*. New York: Plenum.

Faulkner, R. (2013). *Icelandic Men and Me: Sagas of Singing, Self, and Everyday Life*. Ashgate.

Frith, S. (1996). *Performing Rites: On the Value of Popular Music*. Cambridge, MA: Harvard University Press.

Garrido, S., Dunne, L., Chang, E., Perz, J., Stevens, C., & Haertsch, M. (2017). The Use of Music Playlists for People with Dementia: A Critical Synthesis. *Journal of Alzheimer's Disease, 60*, 1129–1142. https://doi.org/10.3233/ JAD-170612

Glass, T. A., de Leon, C. M., Marottoli, R. A., & Berkman, L. F. (1999). Population Based Study of Social and Productive Activities as Predictors of Survival Among Elderly Americans. *BMJ: British Medical Journal, 319*(7208), 478–483. Retrieved from http://www.ncbi.nlm.nih.gov/pmc/articles/ PMC28199/

Guralnick, P. (1999). *Careless Love: The Unmaking of Elvis Presley*. Little Brown.

Haferkamp, H., & Smelser, N. J. (1992). *Social Change and Modernity*. University of California Press.

Halpern, A. R., Bartlett, J. C., & Dowling, W. J. (1995). Aging and Experience in the Recognition of Musical Transpositions. *Psychology and Aging, 10*(3), 325–342.

Hays, T., & Minichiello, V. (2005). The Meaning of Music in the Lives of Older People: A Qualitative Study. *Psychology of Music, 33*(4), 437–450. https://doi. org/10.1177/0305735605056160

Hidi, S., & Renninger, K. A. (2006). The Four-Phase Model of Interest Development. *Educational Psychologist, 41*(2), 111–127. https://doi. org/10.1207/s15326985ep4102_4

Higgins, L. (2012). *Community Music: In Theory and in Practice*. New York: Oxford University Press.

Holbrook, M. B., & Schindler, R. M. (1989). Some Exploratory Findings on the Development of Musical Tastes. *Journal of Consumer Research, 16*(1), 119–124.

Howe, M., & Sloboda, J. (1991). Young Musicians' Accounts of Significant Influences in Their Early Lives. 2. Teachers, Practising and Performing. *British Journal of Music Education, 8*(1), 53–63. https://doi.org/10.1017/S0265051700008068

Inglis, I. (2006). History, Place and Time: The Possibility of the Unexpected. In *Performance and Popular Music: History, Place and Time*. Aldershot: Ashgate.

Kendall, B. (1997). *Our Hearts Went Boom: The Beatles' Invasion of Canada*. Toronto: Viking.

Krumhansl, C. L., & Zupnick, J. A. (2013). Cascading Reminiscence Bumps in Popular Music. *Psychological Science, 24*(10), 2057–2068.

Lee, J., Davidson, J., & Krause, A. E. (2016). Older People's Motivations for Participating in Community Singing in Australia. *International Journal of Community Music, 9*(2), 191–206.

Leske, B. (2017). *Performing Difference: Exploring the Social World of the Melbourne Gay and Lesbian Youth Chorus* (PhD). The University of Melbourne. Retrieved from http://hdl.handle.net/11343/194521

Leske, B., & Wilson, J. (2013). Community Through Song: Australia's First Gay and Lesbian Youth Chorus. *Sing Out: Journal of the Australian National Choral Association, 30*(2), 26–27.

MacDonald, R. A. R., Hargreaves, D. J., & Miell, D. (2002). *Handbook of Musical Identities*. Oxford: Oxford University Press.

McPherson, G. E., Davidson, J. W., & Faulkner, R. (2012). *Music in Our Lives: Rethinking Musical Ability, Development and Identity*. Oxford: Oxford University Press.

Ridder, H. M. O., & Aldridge, D. (2005). Individual Music Therapy with Persons with Frontotemporal Dementia: Singing Dialogue. *Nordic Journal of Music Therapy, 14*(2), 91–106.

Ridder, H. M. O., Stige, B., Qvale, L. G., & Gold, C. (2013). Individual Music Therapy for Agitation in Dementia: An Exploratory Randomized Controlled Trial. *Aging Mental Health, 17*(6), 667–678.

Robertson-Gillam, K. (2008). *The Effects of Singing in a Choir Compared with Participating in a Reminiscence Group on Reducing Depression in People with Dementia* (PhD). Western Sydney University.

Rubin, D. C. (2002). Autobiographical Memory Across the Lifespan. In P. Gtaf & N. Ohta (Eds.), *Lifespan Development of Human Memory* (pp. 159–184). Cambridge, MA: MIT Press.

Rubin, D. C., Wetzler, S. E., & Nebes, R. D. (1986). Autobiographical Memory Across the Adult Lifespan. In D. C. Rubin (Ed.), *Autobiographical Memory*. Cambridge: Cambridge University Press.

Russell, P. (1997). Musical Tastes and Society. In D. Hargreaves & A. C. North (Eds.), *The Social Psychology of Music* (pp. 141–160). Oxford: Oxford University Press.

Ryan, R. M., & Deci, E. L. (2000). Self-Determination Theory and the Facilitation of Intrinsic Motivation, Social Development, and Well-Being. *American Psychologist, 55*(1), 68–78. Retrieved from https://ezp.lib.unimelb.edu.au/login?url=https://search.ebscohost.com/login.aspx?direct=true&db=edsbl&AN=RN074551075&site=eds-live&scope=site

Sameroff, A. (2010). A Unified Theory of Development: A Dialectic Integration of Nature and Nurture. *Child Development, 81*(1), 6–22. https://doi.org/10.1111/j.1467-8624.2009.01378.x

Schattenkirk, K. (2014). Matthew Shepard, Music and Social Justice: Discourse on the Relationship Between Homophobic Violence and Anti-Gay Sentiment in Two Performative Contexts. *ERAS Journal, 16*(1), 83–96.

Sehulster, J. R. (1996). In My Era: Evidence for the Perception of a Special Period of the Past. *Memory, 4*(2), 145–158.

Sorkin, D., Rook, K. S., & Lu, J. L. (2002). Loneliness, Lack of Emotional Support, Lack of Companionship, and the Likelihood of Having a Heart Condition in an Elderly Sample. *Annals of Behavioural Medicine, 24*, 290–298.

von Lob, G., Carmic, P., & Clift, S. (2010). The Use of Singing in a Group as a Response to Adverse Life Events. *International Journal of Mental Health Promotion, 12*(3), 45–53. https://doi.org/10.1080/14623730.2010.9721818

Weber, R. J. (2000). *The Created Self: Reinventing Body, Persona, and Spirit.* W.W. Norton.

Zentner, M., Grandjean, D., & Scherer, K. R. (2008). Emotions Evoked by the Sound of Music: Characterization, Classification and Measurement. *Emotion, 8*, 494–521.

Historical and Psychological Variables Reflected in Music Choices for Key Life Events

CHAPTER 7

Birth

In the previous section of this volume we considered some of the factors that influence how particular songs come to take on personal significance in the lives of an individual. We considered how our family, our culture—both historically and in the present day, our personality and our life experiences merge in shaping our music listening choices and musical behaviours. In Part II we illustrate how these processes occur, by considering many of the most significant rituals that take place across the lifespan and the way music is and has been used within these rituals in a variety of temporal and geographical contexts. Each chapter considers a number of historical and cross-cultural examples. In addition, we present data from hundreds of people from the MLAP website in relation to the music that holds personal value for them because of its connection to key moments such as falling in love, getting married, the birth of their children and the death of a loved one.

Historical and Cross-Cultural Practices

As a rite of passage, becoming a parent is one of the most unforgettable. Few events are quite as life-altering, especially for the mother, who bears the physical task of bringing the child into the world and may forever carry the bodily scars of doing so. While in Western lands more and more people are choosing not to have children or are deferring parenthood until later in life, in some cultures becoming a mother is regarded as the ultimate rite into womanhood (Okereke, 1994). Birth can be both an ordeal and a source of exquisite joy for the parents. Hormonally, the presence of neuro-chemicals such as oxytocin and serotonin, essential to the post-birth bonding of mother and child and the success of breast-feeding, also serve as natural pain relievers and can cause euphoric highs in the birthing mother (Browning, 2001; Wagner, 2009). The simultaneous presence of these two extremes of emotion in childbirth situations makes birth a uniquely emotional and poignant experience.

Historically the domain of women, in many cultures the birth of a child is an occasion for strengthening the bonds between female members of a community (Drinker, 1995). It is also an occasion in which music and dance feature strongly, echoing the primitive cries of pain and joy of the birthing mother. In fact, some scholars argue that the role that music has played in rituals associated with childbirth throughout history underpins the whole relationship of women to music in the modern world (Drinker, 1995; Stein Hunt, 1993).

Our systematic review of the literature revealed that in historical and cross-cultural contexts music has played a role in three key events surrounding the birth of a child: the birth itself, announcing the birth to the wider community immediately after the birth (or in modern times, the coming home of the mother and child from hospital), and formal celebrations of the child's arrival some time after the birth such as in a name-giving ceremony or in the re-integration of the mother to the community. This closely resembles the three phases of rites of passage identified by Van Gennep (1960): preliminal, liminal and postliminal. The preliminal stage often involves a separation of the individual from the surrounding community, as when an expectant mother withdraws from communal life in order to prepare for her 'lying in' (Hill, 1985). A short time after the birth, in many cultures there is a formal announcement of the birth of the child to the community. In this, the liminal phase, a transition is taking place during which the parents are adjusting to their new status within the community and the changes to their family. This stage may also include a degree of seclusion and separation. The postliminal phase is a period of incorporation in which the parents are re-entering the community around them and may formally introduce the child to the community by means of a christening or name-giving ceremony. As we shall see, music plays an important role in all three phases in cultures from around the world.

Music for Labour and Childbirth

Childbirth is often an event from which men are excluded (Drinker, 1995). Historically, in many cultures across the world, birth is a time when the female members of a community come together to express their support of the birthing mother, both by providing practical assistance with the birth, and by providing emotional support and encouragement. Thus numerous cultures around the world have developed 'birth songs' which are sung by the waiting women in an expression of solidarity for the woman in labour.

In medieval Europe there was little available to women to relieve the pain and anxiety of childbirth, and mortality rates for both infants and mothers were high (Schofield, 1986). In a society where marriage took place at a young age, many of those who died in childbirth would have been teenagers. Numerous folk remedies were utilized to hasten a slow birth or to deal with pain. Herbal poultices sometimes even of dung would be applied (Marchant, 2009), and other remedies such as the opening of all doors and cupboards or placing stones in the opening of the vagina were employed (Niebrzydowski, 2009; Wrigley, 2005). Hildegard of Bingen also suggested rubbing the thighs of a woman with a stone called 'sard' when the delivery is taking a long time (von Bingen, 1998).

Births generally took place at home with the assistance of female relatives and maybe a midwife (Kitzinger, 1997). While doctors needed a knowledge of obstetrics, the need to maintain respectability meant that they were seldom involved in women's health issues (Wrigley, 2005). In the case of wealthy or titled women a doctor may have been on standby in an antechamber, but it was the midwife who actually attended the patient. It wasn't until the end of the eighteenth century that male doctors began to be involved in childbirth. It was around this time that drugs like morphine and chloroform were developed. The rate of hospital births began to increase. By the twentieth century with the development of powerful drugs for counteracting infection, medical intervention in childbirth saw the reduction of deaths in childbirth and specialized maternity hospitals were established. Birth inductions and cesarean sections are now commonplace, with births frequently being under the charge of male doctors rather than in the hands of traditional midwives.

When a medieval woman went into labour she was surrounded by women—her "god-sibs" (sisters in God)—women from the surrounding village and female relatives who stayed with the mother-to-be and cared for her during her labour and after the birth of the child (Kitzinger, 1997). Singing and praying was often a part of the proceedings in what Kitzinger calls "an exclusively female process of bonding in love and power" (p. 211).

This female bonding may have been even more important in the eighteenth and nineteenth centuries when people were settling in new lands such as North America, and would often have been isolated from their own female relatives (Kitzinger, 1997). In these situations women would travel long distances to support a fellow female during her birth with the understanding that she would be similarly supported when giving birth herself.

Cross-cultural examples of childbirth rituals display a similar pattern of female connection often involving song and dance. In modern times, music in labour is used by such geographically diverse groups as the Laotians in Indochina, the Navaho in North America, and the Cuna in Panama (Newton & Newton, 1972). In Sierra Leone, traditional women's songs for pregnancy and childbirth are taught to all female initiates during their coming of age rites (Stein Hunt, 1993). Similarly, in Fiji, the women sing to help women giving birth using a sighing wailing sound, evolved from the cry of childbirth (Drinker, 1995). African pygmy women who are giving birth may typically sing along with their midwives whilst walking along the riverbanks (io Elima, n.d.). This is similar to the custom of the people of Nubia in Africa. In India music and singing forms known as "sohar" are sung in anticipation of birth as well as during labour when female relatives and neighbours come to support the mother-to-be (Tewari, 1988).

Dancing also plays a role in some cultures. In Kenya, the women of the village surround the home of the woman who is in labour, and perform a strongly rhythmic dance accompanied by hand clapping which continues until the child is born (Moreno, 1995). Unlike much African music which is polyrhythmic, these birth songs are performed with a single strong rhythm for both dancing and clapping designed to match the rhythm of the birth. In other African tribes each child has a unique birth song which is believed to have been given to the mother from the spirit world before the child is even conceived (Some, 1999). The song is then sung to the mother while she is giving birth. It is thus the first sound that the child will hear and will be used on many occasions throughout the child's life into adulthood.

Some cultures make particular use of song when the birth is difficult. In Southern Albania, for example, the midwife will summon a male relative who sings a song to induce the child to come out (Bezo & Albanologjike, 2013). The Cuna Indians of Panama likewise invoke music when the labour is progressing with difficulty (Dundes, 2004). In that culture, a shaman is called by the midwife who then sits beneath the birthing hammock of the mother and sings a repetitive song calling upon the spirits to help the baby be released from the womb. Similarly, in Scandinavia, in medieval times, songs were sung to invoke the assistance of goddesses when the birth was not progressing well (Jacobson, 1984).

Music is also used to divert bad luck from the mother and child in some circumstances. Some African people such as the Tsonga of Mozambique and the Northern Transvaal, for instance, consider the birth of twins to be a curse and have a song and dance to counteract the bad luck it is believed to bring (Johnston, 1982). In this particular culture, one woman lies down while the other dancers circle around her, mimicking the movements of a midwife during a birth. It may be that the aim is to try to fool the gods into believing that the two children are born of different mothers.

Announcing the Birth

In most cultures, the mother and child and sometimes the father will enjoy a period of postpartum seclusion from their community or tribe for some period after the birth, as reflected in the English term "confinement" (Eberhard-Gran, Garthus-Niegel, Garthus-Niegel, & Eskild, 2010). Periods of seclusion can range from 4–5 days to a much longer period of 40 days or so. This forms the liminal stage or a period of transition and adjustment to the birth, according to Van Gennep's model. During this period of transition it is often customary for some kind of formal announcement of the birth of the child to take place, usually by the close relatives of the parents or the women who attended the birth. Despite the seclusion of the mother, the celebrations may be a highly social event for the rest of the village. In medieval Europe this time period would include the christening of the child, which the mother often did not herself attend. The child would be presented for baptism at the church by the 'god-sibs' who had attended the birth.

At times the announcements themselves are performed in song-form. The Igbo people of Africa, for example, announce the birth of a child with a special musical genre called "oro'nu" (Onyeji, 2004). Once again, this music is the exclusive domain of the women of the village and takes the form of a call-and-answer accompanied by spontaneous dance. Among the Ututu of Nigeria, the first announcement of a new birth is made by the woman's mother-in-law to the father of the child. The mother-in-law then uses song to call the other women of the village (Okereke, 1994). The women sing "omumu nwa" songs accompanied by a wooden musical instrument known as an "aja" while dancing around the home several times. If she has the baby in a hospital the ceremony may be postponed until the child and mother arrive home. Similarly, in the Baltic states, a call and response style song is used to welcome a new infant into the world (Drinker, 1995).

Other songs used during this period may be to celebrate the infant's safe arrival or protect him or her from danger. Igbo women perform songs of thanksgiving and prayers for the child's continued health during a ceremony to officially welcome the new child into the community, known as "omugwo" (Onyeji, 2004). Amongst the Macha Galla of Ethiopia, women kneel in a room near the mother and baby shortly after the birth, singing and moving their upper bodies in a birth song of celebration (Bartels, 1969). The group of singers grows in size as the days progress until the fifth day on which name-giving ceremony is held. The singers improvise, creating stories around the bravery of the mother and gratefulness for the successful birth. The Wakuénai of Venezuela have specialist performers who sing sacred vocal music on many formal ritual occasions, including a chanting ritual of protection for the child about one week after its birth (Hill, 1985). After the birth of their child pygmy women perform a dance of celebration imitating the motions of the birth. The performance is a dance of life which not only celebrates the birth of her child, but is a symbolical rejuvenation of the whole tribe (Drinker, 1995). In various parts of Albania too, it is customary for the women of the mother's home village to dance a 'confinement dance' in which the old women of the village dance around the baby and mother. Among other functions, this serves to introduce the newborn to the cultural system of the village (Bezo & Albanologjike, 2013).

In some cultures, birth songs of celebration are limited to the arrival of a male child, such as in the Judeo-Spanish songs of the Mediterranean (Cohen, 2010). In India similarly, if the newborn is a boy, friends and relatives are formally invited to the singing of "sohar" which takes place over a period of around 6–12 days after the birth (Tewari, 1988). The songs are sung exclusively by women with or without the accompaniment of musical instruments such as drums or cymbals. If the newborn is a girl the celebrations will be small or not held at all.

These traditions of post-partum seclusion or collective female bonding in the postpartum period discussed above are less often seen in modern times in Western countries than they are in agrarian societies of the present or the past. The increase in the number of women who work means that female relatives are often unavailable to support women with new babies. In addition, the modern nuclear family means it is less common for extended family to be closely involved with care of the child and mother after birth (Eberhard-Gran et al., 2010). There is also less emphasis on rest for recovering mothers. Even after hospital births became common, mothers often enjoyed a relatively long lying-in period of up to 14 days in hospital (Eberhard-Gran et al., 2010). Today the period of hospital rest may be a lot less, perhaps only a day or two. Thus for some, the liminal stage of childbirth rituals today may be limited to small gatherings of close family and friends at the location of the birth or after the mother and child arrive home from hospital. In modern Western countries, music may be nearly non-existent from transitional stage rituals.

Re-integration into the Community and Celebrations of the Birth

Amongst people for whom a period of seclusion is customary after birth, a special ceremony of reintegration for the mother or parents may be held. In some cultures the naming of the child also takes place at this time. These postliminal celebrations signal the return of the mother to her duties in the community, as well as the child's acceptance into the society. They may also hold symbolic importance to the community, signaling the health and prosperity of the group as a whole, or reinforcing locally held world-views. It is at this time too, that often the mother attains a new status in the community if it is her first child, as she is now viewed in some traditions as having the right to a 'voice' in the family or in the society of women. In other cultures, this status is only attained if the child is a boy.

In many cultures, the custom of isolating a mother after birth has its origins in the concept of childbirth being an 'unclean' process. In Western cultures, this stems from the Biblical command to the Jews that "A woman who becomes pregnant and gives birth to a son will be ceremonially unclean for seven days, just as she is unclean during her monthly period" (Leviticus 12:2, New American Standard). In the Jewish tradition, this period of uncleanness ended with a ceremonial offering at the temple. Various versions of this were carried into the Christian tradition.

For example, in Medieval England, a month or so after the birth of the child women often attended a 'Churching'. This was a ceremony held at the local church in which women who were considered 'unclean' from having recently given birth, were able to be 'purified' so as to be readmitted to the church community (Niebrzydowski, 2011). The woman was veiled and brought to the church accompanied by her god-sibs. The ceremony was often conducted outside the church or in the entrance-way to the church and involved the singing of psalms by male clerics and a sprinkling with holy water. Despite the implications of uncleanness and exclusion implicit in this ritual and in the song-texts used, evidence suggests that women did not view this as a shameful event, but rather as a celebration of fertility and feminine power (Niebrzydowski, 2011). The Churching of Elizabeth Woodville, the Queen consort of King Edward IV of England, for example, was reported to be an extravagant affair with 60 female attendants, 42 chapel singers and priests carrying holy relics (Niebrzydowski, 2011).

Hindu people similarly believe that the birthing mother is unclean after childbirth. She is not allowed to touch food that others will eat or cook for the family during that period. However, in other cultures in which seclusion takes place for the purpose of rest and recovery, the reintegration ceremony has a different significance. In Kenya, 41 days after the birth of the child, the mother reassembles the women of the village who danced for her during the birth to re-create the birth dance. This time, she joins in with the dancers, symbolizing her initiation into motherhood and her new status within the society of women (Moreno, 1995). Among the Wakuénai of Venezuela the specialist chanter performs a musical ritual of spirit naming over food that the mother has cooked. This signals the mother's return to the general activities of the village and is a ritual also designed to protect the child.

Naming ceremonies variously take place during the mother's seclusionary period, afterward or at the point of her reintegration. In Christian cultures, the official naming of the child and celebration of his birth may take place in a baptism ceremony or christening. Baptisms in Christian ceremonies tend to involve less music than other religious services like weddings or funerals since they are often incorporated into the general church services. Few hymns were written specifically for baptisms, but hymns for general worship might be included in a service. In Victorian

England a christening might have been held at the family home. Friends and relations of the family would form a quartet of singers to sing popular lullabies and hymns.

Royal christenings in England follow an established tradition, often performed by the Archbishop of Canterbury as the spiritual head of the Church of England and held in the Music Room at Buckingham Palace. They usually include the singing of hymns and anthems, including at times specially composed songs such as "Jubilate"[1] composed by Prince Albert for the christening of his daughter Princess Helena in 1846. Composers of the royal courts of England traditionally composed special pieces of music to mark the birth of members of the royal family. Edward Elgar's *Nursery Suite*,[2] for example was composed to celebrate the birth of Princess Margaret and her sister (now Queen Elizabeth II) (Davidson & Garrido, 2014).

In other cultures, music is an integral part of the naming ceremony. For Hindus, naming ceremonies known as "namakarana" typically take place 11 days after the child's birth when the mother and child are considered to be 'clean' once again (Gatrad, Ray, & Sheikh, 2004). This often involves music in the form of the chanting of sacred hymns by priests.

When the Edo people of Nigeria hold a naming ceremony, family and friends gather together to give the child gifts and eat special foods. The ceremony holds the function of separating the child from the spirit world and uniting them with the community (Ogie, 2002). In ceremonial song, the eldest female of the family asks the mother several times what the child is to be named. The mother replies each time with a name that is not considered suitable and the women then reject the name in song. The purpose of these false names is to fool evil spirits and distract them from the child's true name (Ogie, 2002). When the question is asked for the seventh time, the real name of the child is then publicly announced.

Similarly, the Nigerian Yoruba hold a naming ceremony on the seventh day after the birth of a girl and on the ninth day after the birth of a boy. The ceremony is led by the oldest member of the family and includes the playing of drums and reciting of traditional poetry. Its purpose among other things is to initiate the child into both the joys and hazards of daily life (Akinnaso, 1980). Native American naming ceremonies conducted by the tribal elders also include singing and dancing. These ceremonies situate

[1] Track 51: Jubilate, Chapel Royal Choir.
[2] See Tracks 3–7: Nursery Suite. Edward Elgar.

the child within the kinship structure of their community and incorporate them into their spiritual life (Red Horse, 1997).

Modern Day Playlists

Music for Labour and Childbirth

Studies on the benefits of music therapy have reported decreased levels of anxiety and pain perception in women who used music during labour as opposed to those who did not (Browning, 2001; Labrague, Rosales, Rosales, & Fiel, 2013; Phumdoung & Good, 2003). In these studies, often the music therapist prepares a recording that the study participant listens to during labour. However, the efficacy of the music therapy program is often influenced by the soothing presence of the therapist who may have a previously established relationship with the participant. It is also common for expecting mothers to practice relaxing with the same music at home prior to the birth, thus setting up a conditioned response to the music that can enhance its effectiveness in relaxing the listener during the actual birth.

Researchers suggest that music therapists and doulas select anxiolytic music (calming music) (Browning, 2000) with relatively slow rhythms, smooth melodies and little dynamic change (Spintge, 1989) such as music by Irish singer-songwriter Enya which is often listed on birthing CDs.[3] Browning (2000) reports that the 11 women in her study responded well to music which was primarily instrumental, classical or New Age. The music helped them to pace their breathing, to distract them or focus them on the task at hand, or to facilitate visual imagery which helped them relax.

However, few studies have examined the use of music during childbirth by people who do not have the benefit of a trained therapist. In a survey of websites and blogs for expectant mothers, Davidson and Garrido (2014) report recommendations from mothers similar to those suggested by music therapists. They found that New Age music, nature sounds and soothing instrumental versions of well-known classical tunes were popular choices, although some humorous choices were reported too. However, no studies to date that we are aware of, have systematically examined the extent to which mothers and parents follow these suggestions and

[3] Track 52: Caribbean Blue, Enya.

voluntarily choose to listen to music during childbirth without the assistance of a music therapist. Therefore, the question arises, to what extent do individual mothers (and parents) include music in their birth plans? How effectively do they use music? What kind of music do they choose and why?

We explored these questions on the MLAP website by asking 262 parents whether they had used music during the birth of their children. The majority had not used music (n = 195) and several said they could not remember (n = 27). Of the parents surveyed, only 40 reported having deliberately used music during the birth of their children, the majority of these being women (n = 32), and the majority being people who were themselves musicians of varying levels of experience (n = 33). Statistical analysis revealed that there were significant differences in age between people who reported having used music during birth and those who had not, with younger participants being more likely to have used music than older participants.

The most frequent type of music selected was instrumental music such as classical or ambient music (n = 14, 35%). Non-instrumental selections included rock, jazz, pop, and singer-songwriter, with the majority having male singers (n = 15, 37.5%). Participants were also asked to rate the music they had selected on two dimensions of valence (pleasantness or unpleasantness) and arousal (sleepy or alert). These dimensions are commonly used in the psychology literature to categorise emotions. Calming music for example, would usually be rated as of positive valence (pleasant) but low arousal (sleepy), while exciting music would similarly be positive valence but would be high arousal (alert). On average, participant selections were of positive valence (m = 4.3),[4] and of relatively high arousal (m = 3.3). Despite this, the majority of people said they had selected music that was calming or soothing (n = 13, 32.5%) or that reminded them of cherished times in their lives (n = 9, 22.5%). Other reasons given for the selection were that the music had personal significance or that they were big fans of the artists.

We also wanted to see whether the use of music during childbirth was related to differences in the ways people cope with difficulties. Coping styles refers to the strategies people use to deal with stress and conflict (Snyder, 1999) which can be either adaptive (helps to reduce stress), or maladaptive (is ineffective in reducing stress or results in increased stress).

---

[4] A score of 3 would indicate a neutral midpoint on both valence and arousal dimensions.

To measure these we included the Coping Orientations to Problems Experienced scale and the Rumination-Reflection Questionnaire (see Chap. 1 for more details).

Results revealed that people who did not use music during childbirth scored significantly higher than those who did use music on Rumination and Behavioural Disengagement, both of which are generally considered to be maladaptive coping styles. Rumination is a largely involuntary tendency to dwell on negative thoughts and feelings, which is closely associated with depression (Lyubomirsky & Nolen-Hoeksema, 1995; Nolen-Hoeksema, 1991). Behavioural disengagement can also be associated with depression, since it involves feelings of helplessness and a reduction of efforts to deal effectively with a stressor (Carver, Scheier, & Weintraub, 1989). It is often observed when the individual expects a negative outcome and has little belief that there is anything that can be done to avert or mitigate that outcome. While we did not find any significant relationship between the use of music during birth and any particular adaptive coping style, these results suggest that people who did not use music are less adept at finding effective means for coping with stress and perhaps felt a sense of helplessness in the face of the birth.

In order to investigate the topic more closely, we invited parents from an online parenting site to comment further on how they felt about using music in childbirth. Numerous women responded to our post by saying that they had not used music. However, eight women agreed to be interviewed or provided us with written comments about the role music had played in the birth of their children.

Several of the participants described having used soothing music (or sounds) during birth. For example, one woman whose child was born in a birth centre[5] listened to a CD of whale songs for about 8 hours. She described it as being "soothing, a perfect backdrop to natural birth", and particularly liked the fact "that there was no set rhythm, just the natural flow of the whale songs". Rhythm was also mentioned by another participant who said that during the birth she only liked listening to "chilled out songs—anything upbeat or fast really irritated me". Similarly, one participant had planned to listen to an Indian raga during the birth because "they start so soothing and spacious". However, she reported that "as the

---

[5] A centre run by midwives that promotes natural birth and may or may not be attached to a hospital.

raga sped up and the labour intensified, I couldn't stand it. I nearly fell on my face trying to run over and turn it off".

Other music selections were chosen because of the spiritual connotations they had for the mother. For example, one participant chose to listen to Julie Fowlis, a Gaelic folk singer, describing the music as "haunting and uplifting by turns" and stating that it "speaks to some spiritual side of me". She mostly had this music on softly in the background so that it was "not intrusive". The fact that the lyrics were not in English also meant that her mind did not get "too caught up" in their meaning. Another participant listened to Dead Can Dance, a group that construct spacious sound-scapes that are influenced by Gaelic folk music and Gregorian chant and use African polyrhythms and Middle Eastern mantras (see Chap. 1 for more details). Another listened to the chanting of Krishna Das who is known for his inspiring Hindu kirtan yoga chanting.

One participant found recorded music less helpful, but described that singing internally during the birth was a particularly powerful experience. Helen Reddy's song "I Am Woman" was a song she had habitually listened to over the years while at the gym or "when I needed a pick me up". This song came into her head during the labour and she developed a routine of "listening" to the song in her head during each contraction and singing the chorus internally "I am strong. I am invincible. I am woman" as she breathed deeply through the contractions. "I think it helped me to stay calm and really focused".

On the other hand, one participant who is a musician herself described in detail her reasons for choosing not to use music during the birth. Music had played an important role in her life from a very young age. However, she described herself as very emotional and felt that her response to the music might have been distracting or even annoying during the labour. She explained that although she loves music, she also enjoys silence. She also had some fear that if the birth was a "scary or painful experience" she would be reminded of it every time she heard that music in the future.

Thus, it appears that there are several benefits that the women who were interviewed were able to gain from their use of music. Participants appear to have particularly benefited from music that helped them to focus and be calm, that added a sense of spirituality to their situation or that enhanced their perceptions of personal strength. This was useful even in the case of the participant who merely sang the music to herself internally. Music that was too "intrusive" or that had rhythms that did not match the arousal needs of the birthing mother at the time, tended to cause tension and irritation. For some people, particularly those who perhaps tend to be more sensitive to the emotional arousal of music, silence may in fact work better.

Taken together, the results from our survey and qualitative data tend to suggest that while for some people music might be too distracting, for others it can serve as an important way of coping with the stress and pain of childbirth, helping them to feel stronger and calmer in the face of the intensely demanding situation. The age differences between participants who reported using music and those who did not, also suggests that the use of music in labour is something that is becoming increasingly popular and acceptable in modern times. Therefore the fact that many mothers do not use music could be more to do with cultural and situational factors, or with a lack of awareness of the usefulness of music as a coping strategy in childbirth situations.

The results further indicate that despite the fact that soothing music is what is most regularly suggested in the literature, some women benefited from music that was more rousing. In fact, even though the soothing properties of the music was the most frequently chosen reason for the music selection, the average arousal rating of the self-selected music was much higher than what would generally be regarded as 'calm'. Whether the music needed is calm or rousing likely has much to do with individual arousal levels and how sensitive the individual is to external stimulation.

Celebrations of the Birth

For many people in the modern day who choose to have their child born outside of the home, the day the baby comes home from the hospital or place of birth is a special event. However, there are few rituals that surround this occasion in Western countries. The child's clothing may be carefully selected and some close family members may be present to greet the new member of the family, however these tend to be informal events, unlike some of the more formal rituals that mark the event in other cultures as discussed above.

In the past, a christening or baptism may have been the most important post-birth event to mark the arrival of the new child. This is still the tradition among practicing Christians today. Prince William of England had an anthem composed especially for his christening in 1982, entitled "Blessed Jesu! Here we Stand". This anthem was also sung by the Choir of Her Majesty's Chapel Royal at the christening of Prince George, son of Prince

William. Prince George's christening was a much less formal affair than his father's had been. Other music used in Prince George's christening included processional music of Bach's "Fantasia in G" on the organ, the anthem "The Lord Bless You and Keep You" by John Rutter, along with the hymns "Breathe on Me, Breathe on God" and "Be Thou My Vision" and recessional organ music of Widor's Toccata from Symphony No. 5.

However, the number of people who formally christen or baptize their children is on the decline. Today, many non-religious people perform a naming ceremony as an alternative to a christening or baptism. A formal ceremony may be led by a celebrant, in which the infant is formally named and 'mentors' (rather than godparents) nominated. Music may often be played or poetry read to mark the occasion. Davidson and Garrido (2014) report that a survey of online sites reveals some popular music choices to be "Beautiful Boy" by John Lennon or "Wonderchild" by Mary Black. Well-known classical tunes like Vivaldi's Spring concerto from "The Four Seasons" or Handel's "Water Music" are also popular.

Thus, while for many traditional beliefs and ceremonies play an important role in celebrating the arrival of a new child into the community, others are finding new ways to commemorate the event that involve more personal expressions of joy including through music.

The Trajectory from the Past to the Modern Day

While music is not always an integral part of birth, one aspect of childbirth that seems to be common in many traditional cultures and across many time periods is the surrounding of the birthing mother by the other women of their family and sometimes even of the entire village during the birth. The presence of other women provided not only practical assistance with the birth, but was or is a source of strength and comfort to the birthing mother. Where music is involved in birth in traditional cultures, the music appears the serve the primary function of enhancing female solidarity and imbuing the mother with the collective strength of the female community.

In Western societies, as modern medicine has advanced, women have often found themselves without these traditional supports while going through the ordeal of giving birth. In past decades even the father of the child being born was often not allowed in the hospital birthing room (Heggenhougen, 1980). A woman may have found herself in a sterile, clinical, hospital environment without any familiar faces, in many cases, treated as a passive participant in an event being staged by the medical practitioners.

More recently, although grateful for the added life expectancy for both mother and child that modern medicine provides, parents have striven to wrest back at least some control over birth. Often times this is by choosing home-births or births in clinics with midwives who take a more holistic approach to childbirth. For others who still want to enjoy the relative safety of the hospital environment, this may be about having the freedom to choose birthing methods, or about creating a personal space within the hospital setting in which the birth can take place. Hospitals are responding to this in many parts of the world by allowing parents greater latitude to make choices about the conditions within their birthing units. Music has oftentimes provided an effective means for parents to create a more personal and individual atmosphere as well as a feeling of control within their birth experience (Browning, 2001).

As the modern MLAP data demonstrates, some women appear to use music in ways that perhaps displays a desire to compensate for the absence of her female tribe in many modern birthing environments. The desire for powerful female voices, tribal rhythms or chanting, and nature sounds perhaps reflects a subconscious yearning to return to something more primal or at the very least to take the experience from a clinical to a spiritual level. Many theorists argue that it is the power of music to promote social cohesion and bonding that is behind its evolutionary development, that music in fact formed a kind of 'vocal grooming' that enabled groups of primates to connect themselves together in cohesive units (Dunbar, 1998). Women in primitive societies required the support of other women in order to successfully birth their children. Thus in some cultures, specialized musical forms have evolved as an expression of female solidarity during the physically vulnerable time of giving birth. In modern times music can continue to serve this function even in the absence of the tribe themselves, by making the woman feel that she has the collective strength of hundreds of generations of women behind her in her ordeal.

In tribal societies, traditional singing and dancing associated with birth also serves the function of situating the experience of the individual within the universal principles of the culture (Dundes, 2004). The mother is reminded of the purpose of the birth and its role in the regeneration of the community as a whole. Her role as a woman and destiny as a mother is reaffirmed through song and dance (Okereke, 1994). In Wakuénai myth, for example, music is believed to be the force which shaped the world.

Thus, the musical rituals surrounding birth, re-enact the birth of the world (Hill, 1985). In modern times, music can again serve the role of empowering the mother in her role as a giver of life, giving her a sense of connection with the women who have taken on this role throughout history.

As well as these more spiritual functions, there is also extensive evidence of physiological and psychological benefits from the use of music during childbirth. The gateway theory of pain relief holds that listening to music can diminish the perception of pain by loading the neural pathways that handle sensory input so that less information about pain gets through to the limbic system (Cousins & Bridenbaugh, 1998).

Music may modulate pain perception via psychological mechanisms as well. High levels of anxiety or fear can increase tension in the mother, which in turn can increase the difficulty of the labour and the pain associated with it, a cycle known as 'fear-tension-pain syndrome' (Dick-Read, 1949). Taz Tagore (2009), an experienced midwife, reports that the creation of a playlist for use during labour enabled one woman to begin to view the approaching birth with joyful anticipation rather than fear. She also reports that it can help some women to visualize a successful birth, and to tune into their bodies and babies rather than focusing on their fears. It can also help to drown out the sounds of a busy, impersonal hospital environment. Similarly, Browning (2001) argues: "When a woman feels she can actively manage her surroundings, and when she feels in control of her body and can actively manage her pain, she is much less likely to succumb to fear-tension-pain syndrome" (p. 74). Thus the sense of control and focus that music can bring can do much to alleviate fear and reduce tension and pain.

As noted above, in many cross-cultural settings the use of the voice is a crucial part of music in childbirth with women of the village vocalizing along with the mother throughout the birth or re-enacting this after the birth. In modern birth settings, midwives often recommend maternal vocalisations as a way to cope with pain, advocating the view that a woman should freely express herself in this way (Borrelli, Locatelli, & Nespoli, 2013). However, women of some cultures may feel more able to express pain in this way than others (Cassisi et al., 2004; Weber, 1996). For women who may feel less able to freely vocalize during childbirth, Tagore (2009) argues that music can serve the additional function of helping them to find their voices. The use of the voice such as in singing, can be of broad psychological benefit in many situations (Davidson & Garrido, 2015), providing benefits that include increasing mastery and empowerment (Ruud, 2012), or enhancing capacity for self-expression and a sense of group reciprocity (Bailey & Davidson, 2005). It is not hard to imagine how vocally liberating it would be to give birth surrounded by a tribe of chanting women. In the absence of the 'village', music may again serve the purpose of invigorating a sense of vocal freedom, adding to a feeling of empowerment and connection in the birthing mother.

Some women in our study indicated a preference for music without intrusive rhythms, or even music that tends to be atemporal such as ambient music. In traditional tribal cultures, on the other hand, rhythm sometimes forms an integral part of childbirth rituals, such as in the strongly rhythmic hand-clapping of Kenya. It is possible that the rhythm in music of this tradition makes use of the process of entrainment in order to encourage the birth to progress. Entrainment refers to the way external rhythms can interact with internal rhythms in order to bring our physiological processes into synchrony with the external rhythms. Highly arousing music, for example, can cause our physiological systems such as breathing and heart rate to begin to match the music causing increased feelings of excitement or alertness. It is interesting that despite the fact that many therapists recommend calming music, the participants in our study rated their self-selected music as mostly of relatively high arousal levels. This suggests that the use of anxiolytic music is perhaps suitable only for some women, or perhaps only for certain stages of the labour. Tagore (2009) suggests that repetitiveness may be the key aspect, with music that has a strong regular rhythm helping women to develop their own rhythm of breathing for coping with contractions, and to enter a state of flow.

When seen within the context of the historical and cross-cultural evidence outlined in this chapter, it is clear that the settings in which many women give birth in Western countries in the modern day is very different from the experiences of most women throughout history. The dangers of childbirth and the vulnerable state of a birthing mother have meant that from an evolutionary perspective, the support of the female community has been imperative to the survival of both mother and child. In some contexts this bonding has been enhanced through musical communication, as it likely has in other evolutionary contexts as well. Indeed, rates of postnatal depression are significantly lower in cultures that still offer these high levels of communal support for mothers (Stern & Kruckman, 1983).

The advent of modern medicine has greatly increased the life expectancy of both mother and child. However, with this rise in medical involvement came a shift in childbirth practices from what was primarily a female sphere into a clinical context in which the tribe of female supporters has been seen as somewhat obsolete. However, many women and parents are demonstrating a craving for more natural, even 'primitive' settings in which to bring their children into the world. Many are choosing settings that return birth to the realm of women, surrounding themselves with midwives or doulas to support them in the birth. Our studies of music selections reveal that some women express this need for nature, the primal and the feminine in their choice of music as well. However, our results also suggest that perhaps the power of music to enhance the experience of childbirth has not been fully exploited by women in the modern day. A one-size-fits-all approach is common in which therapists or medical practitioners tend to recommend the use of one type of music for all kinds of patients and at all stages of the birth. Perhaps music could be used more effectively than it is now. Individual levels of anxiety, as well as individual arousal levels and sensitivity to external stimuli could enable more personalized music selection. A further improvement on popular usage of music in childbirth may be the following of ancient tribal practices by using the female voice and steady rhythms to match the pace of the birth. While silence may indeed be preferable for some women, more individualized selection of music could enable more women even in clinical contexts to experience a sense of cohesion and focus on her task, as well as to find her own personal voice and rhythm.

As modern medicine has increased its involvement in childbirth in Western countries, liminal stage rituals are less frequently seen in this context. Women less often experience a long period of confinement and recovery after work, again in part due to the decreased levels of support available to them from female members of the community. The increasing secularization of Western cultures has also seen an erosion of post-liminal type rituals such as Christenings and baptisms, with less people choosing to celebrate the arrival of a new family member in this way. However, the need for ritual to mark such an important life event has not diminished. The rise of non-religious naming day ceremonies illustrates how people are recreating modes for commemorating such key life moment that can exist outside of traditional religious settings. Music again plays a key role, as it can provide an outlet for personal expression of the feelings of the parents surrounding the momentous occasion as well as future wishes for their child.

The topic of birth has thus provided an interesting beginning to our exploration of how historical and psychological variables come together to shape our music choices for particular key life moments. It has demonstrated that bringing together diverse historical and cross-cultural perspectives along with modern knowledge from multiple psychological disciplines, can inform us both about how modern day uses of music have developed and about what has been lost along the way, suggesting areas for future research and ways in which music can be better utilized to improve wellbeing in contemporary societies.

References

Akinnaso, F. N. (1980). The Sociolinguistic Basis of Yoruba Personal Names. *Anthropological Linguistics, 22*(7), 275–304.

Bailey, B. A., & Davidson, J. W. (2005). Effects of Group Singing and Performance for Marginalized and Middle-Class Singers. *Psychology of Music, 33*(3), 269–303.

Bartels, L. (1969). Birth Customs and Birth Songs of the Macha Galla. *Ethnology, 8*(4), 406–422.

Bezo, B. H., & Albanologjike, Q. E. S. (2013). *Ritual of Childbirth in Southeastern Coast of Albania*. Paper presented at the 1st International Conference on Research and Education, Shkodra, Albania.

Borrelli, S. E., Locatelli, A., & Nespoli, A. (2013). Early Pushing Urge in Labour and Midwifery Practice: A Prospective Observational Study at an Italian Maternity Hospital. *Midwifery, 29*(8), 871–875.

Browning, C. A. (2000). Using Music During Childbirth. *Birth, 27*(4), 272–276.

Browning, C. A. (2001). Music Therapy in Childbirth: Research in Practice. *Music Therapy Perspectives, 19*(2), 74–81.

Carver, C. S., Scheier, M. F., & Weintraub, J. K. (1989). Assessing Coping Strategies: A Theoretically Based Approach. *Journal of Personality and Social Psychology, 56*, 267–283.

Cassisi, J. E., Umeda, M., Deisinger, J. A., Sheffer, C., Lofland, K. R., & Jackson, C. (2004). Patterns of Pain Descriptor Usage in African Americans and European Americans with Chronic Pain. *Cultural Diversity & Ethnic Minority Psychology, 10*(1), 81–89.

Cohen, J. R. (2010). Judeo-Spanish Song: A Mediterranean-Wide Interactive Tradition. *Trans: Revista Transcultural de Musica, 14.*

Cousins, M. J., & Bridenbaugh, P. O. (1998). *Neural Blockade in Clinical Anesthesia and Management of Pain*. Lippincott Williams & Wilkins.

Davidson, J., & Garrido, S. (2014). *My Life as a Playlist*. Perth: University of Western Australia Publishing.

Davidson, J., & Garrido, S. (2015). Singing and Psychological Needs. In G. Welsh, D. Howard, & J. Nix (Eds.), *The Oxford Handbook of Singing*. Oxford: Oxford University Press.

Dick-Read, G. (1949). Observations on a Series of Labours with Special Reference to Physiological Delivery. *Lancet, 30*, 721–726.

Drinker, S. (1995). *Music and Women: The Story of Women in Their Relation to Music.* Feminist Press at CUNY.

Dunbar, R. (1998). *Grooming, Gossip, and the Evolution of Language.* Harvard University Press.

Dundes, L. (2004). *The Manner Born: Birth Rites in Cross-Cultural Perspective.* AltaMira Press.

Eberhard-Gran, M., Garthus-Niegel, S., Garthus-Niegel, K., & Eskild, A. (2010). Postnatal Care: A Cross-Cultural and Historical Perspective. *Archives of Women's Mental Health, 13*, 459–466.

Gatrad, A., Ray, M., & Sheikh, A. (2004). Hindu Birth Customs. *Archives of Disease in Childhood, 89*, 1094–1097.

Heggenhougen, H. K. (1980). Father and Childbirth: An Anthropological Perspective. *Journal of Midwifery & Women's Health, 25*(6), 21–27.

Hill, J. D. (1985). Myth, Spirit Naming, and the Art of Microtonal Rising: Childbirth Rituals of the Arawakan Wakuenai. *Latin American Music Review, 6*(1), 1–30.

io Elima, U. (n.d.). A Pygmy Model for Partnership Relations. *Primal Psychotherapy.* Retrieved from http://www.primal-page.com/pygmy.htm

Jacobson, G. (1984). Pregnancy and Childbirth in the Medieval North: A Topology of Sources and a Preliminary Study. *Scandinavian Journal of History, 9*(2–3), 91–111.

Johnston, T. F. (1982). The Secret Music of Nhanga Rites. *Anthropos, 77*(5–6), 755–774.

Kitzinger, S. (1997). Authoritative Touch in Childbirth: A Cross-Cultural Approach. In R. Davis-Floyd & C. Fishel Sargent (Eds.), *Childbirth and Authoritative Knowledge.* California: University of California Press.

Labrague, L. J., Rosales, R. A., Rosales, G. L., & Fiel, G. B. (2013). Effects of Soothing Music on Labor Pain Among Filipino Mothers. *Clinical Nursing Studies, 1*(1), 35–42.

Lyubomirsky, S., & Nolen-Hoeksema, S. (1995). Effects of Self-Focused Rumination on Negative Thinking and Interpersonal Problem Solving. *Journal of Personality and Social Psychology, 69*(1), 176–190.

Marchant, S. (2009). The History of Postnatal Care, National and International Perspectives. In S. Byrom, G. Edwards, & D. Bick (Eds.), *Essential Midwifery Practice: Postnatal Care.* John Wiley & Sons.

Moreno, J. J. (1995). Ethnomusic Therapy: An Interdisciplinary Approach to Music and Healing. *The Arts in Psychotherapy, 22*(4), 329–338.

Newton, N., & Newton, M. (1972). Childbirth in Crosscultural Perspectives. In J. G. Howells (Ed.), *Modern Perspectives in Psycho-Obstetrics.* Edinburgh: Oliver & Boyd.

Niebrzydowski, S. (2009). From Bedroom to Courtroom: Home and the Memory of Childbirth in a Fourteenth-Century Marriage Dispute. *Home Cultures, 6*(2), 123–134.

Niebrzydowski, S. (2011). Asperges Me, Domine, Hyssopo: Male Voices, Female Interpretation and the Medieval English Purification of Women After Childbirth Ceremony. *Early Music, 39*(3), 327–333.

Nolen-Hoeksema, S. (1991). Responses to Depression and Their Effects on the Duration of Depressive Episodes. *Journal of Abnormal Psychology, 100*(4), 569–582.

Ogie, O. (2002). Edo Personal Names and World View. In O. I. Pogosan & F. O. Egbokhare (Eds.), *New Perspectives in Edoid Studies: Essays in Honour of Ronald Peter Schaefer*. The Center for Advanced Studies of African Society.

Okereke, G. E. (1994). The Birth Song as a Medium for Communicating Woman's Maternal Destiny in the Traditional Community. *Research in African Literatures, 25*(3), 19–32.

Onyeji, C. (2004). Igbo Rural Women in Africa as Creative Personalities: Musical Processing of Socio-Economic Solidarity. *Journal of the Musical Arts of Africa, 1*, 84–101.

Phumdoung, S., & Good, M. (2003). Music Reduces Sensation and Distress of Labor Pain. *Pain Management Nursing, 4*(2), 54–61.

Red Horse, J. (1997). Traditional American Indian Family Systems. *Families, Systems, & Health, 15*(3), 243–250.

Ruud, E. (2012). The New Health Musicians. In R. MacDonald, G. Kreutz, & L. Mitchell (Eds.), *Music, Health, & Wellbeing*. Oxford: Oxford University Press.

Schofield, R. (1986). Did the Mothers Really Die? Three Centuries of Maternal Mortality in "The World We Have Lost". In L. Bonfield, R. M. Smith, & K. Wrightson (Eds.), *The World We Have Gained: Histories of Population and Social Structure*. Oxford: Basil Blackwell.

Snyder, C. R. (Ed.). (1999). *Coping: The Psychology of What Works*. New York: Oxford University Press.

Some, S. (1999). *Welcoming Spirit Home: Ancient African Teachings to Celebrate Children and Community*. New World Library.

Spintge, R. (1989). The Anxiolytic Effects of Music. In L. Matthew (Ed.), *Rehabilitation, Music and Well-Being*. St. Louis: MMB Music.

Stein Hunt, D. L. (1993). The Changing Role of Women in African Music. *Ufahamu: A Journal of African Studies, 21*(1–2), 41–49.

Stern, G., & Kruckman, L. (1983). Multi-Disciplinary Perspectives on Post-Partum Depression: An Anthropological Critique. *Social Science & Medicine, 17*(5), 1027–1041.

Tagore, T. (2009). Why Music Matters in Childbirth. *Midwifery Today* (Spring), 33–68.

Tewari, L. G. (1988). "Sohar": Childbirth Songs of Joy. *Asian Folklore Studies,* *47*(2), 257–276.

Van Gennep, A. (1960). *The Rites of Passage* (Vol. 3). Routledge.

von Bingen, H. (1998). *Hildegard von Bingen's Physica: The Complete English Translation of Her Classic Work on Health and Healing* (P. Throop, Trans.). Inner Traditions/Bear & Co.

Wagner, H. N. J. (2009). The Hormone of Love. *Brain Imaging: The Chemistry of Mental Activity* (189–190). London: Springer.

Weber, S. E. (1996). Cultural Aspects of Pain in Childbearing Women. *Journal of Obstetric, Gynecologic, and Neonatal Nursing, 25*(1), 67–72.

Wrigley, H. L. (2005). *Wise Women and Medical Men: Obstetrics and Gynecology in the Middle Ages.* Paper presented at the 14th Annual History of Medicine Days.

CHAPTER 8

Childhood

INTRODUCTION

Even from the earliest months of life, children are able to perceive and respond to music, being biologically programmed to perceive certain musical cues irrespective of cultural context. The extreme dependence of newborn humans on their parents, has made it an evolutionary imperative for infants to be able to decode prosodic speech content in adult voices in order to promote communication of emotional messages and enhance bonding between parent and child. This ability enables infants to detect musical features as well. In fact, some scholars argue that infant-carer bonding underpins the evolutionary origins of music (Dissanayake, 2008). This function of music is apparent in modern-day music for children and in historical examples and those from diverse cultures, as this chapter will demonstrate.

The biological basis of response to music is further borne out by modern-day research in music cognition in infants, which has revealed that even small babies have the capacity to perceive many of the features of music. Much of this seems related to features that are also relevant to other forms of communication from caregivers. For example, pitch is a primary means by which voices communicate emotional messages. Thus small babies can detect pitch changes of a semitone or less (Trehub, Schellenberg, & Kamenetsky, 1999), and can distinguish between consonance and dissonance (Trainor & Heinmiller, 1998). They are also able to recognize a melody even when it has been transposed to a different pitch, and display a preference for higher pitches, which often signal positive emotions.

Rhythm and movement are also important in the world of an infant, since rocking and bouncing seem to be an instinctive part of caregiving behavior across cultures. It is thought that the rocking is soothing in that it mimics the constant movement experienced in the womb. Thus perception of rhythm is fairly developed in small infants, and appears to be closely related to movement, possibly because of its relationship with biological rhythms such as walking and the heartbeat experienced in uterine (Phillips-Silver & Trainor, 2005). Indeed, children as young as 2 months can perceive rhythmic patterns, and tempo changes, and by the age of 7 months they can distinguish between duple and triple meter (Hannon & Johnson, 2005).

During these early years of life—the sensorimotor stage of development—children are focusing on absorbing and decoding the auditory cues of the world around them (Garrido, 2014). They also begin to experiment with their own vocalizations, investigating timbre, rhythm and melodic contour using their own voices. With age, however, children become increasingly sensitive to cultural norms and begin to internalize information about culturally specific musical conventions. About 2 years of age—known as the pre-operational stage—children may begin to produce formed songs that they have heard rather than merely experimenting with random sounds. A sense of key begins to stabilize around age 6 enabling children to replicate songs with some degree of tonal accuracy and to understand the cultural associations between certain musical features and emotional expression, such as the typical Western association between minor keys and sadness (Schubert & McPherson, 2006).

This acquisition of musical knowledge is thought by some researchers to have a critical period, in much the same way that language does. While children are born with certain innate processing skills that apply to music, many of these skills become lost to neural pruning if unused, with synaptic connections that are unemployed being eliminated to improve the efficiency of brain function. Similar processes occur with language learning in that children eventually focus their attention on the perception and production of sounds that are used within their own culture and lose their ability to distinguish and reproduce phonemes not commonly used in their own language (Trainor, 2005). Thus, children who grow up in musically impoverished environments may be limited in the musical skills they can acquire later in life.

Given the close association between parent-child bonding and the early development of musical perception, it is no surprise that singing to infants is a part of child care practices in cultures all over the world (Trehub & Trainor, 1998). Specific genres of songs for children are common, and include songs sung *to* children such as lullabies and 'play songs', and songs sung *by* children as part of play. All of these song-types typically feature simple, repetitive forms that enable even untrained singers to use them. We will now consider historical evidence of children's song genres and musical customs surrounding children from various cultures across the world.

HISTORICAL AND CROSS-CULTURAL PRACTICES

Singing to children appears to have its roots in ancient traditions that have survived industrialization and urbanization. The renowned scholars of children's rhymes, Iona and Peter Opie (1997) state that there are references to children's songs in the Biblical gospels, and in the Roman poets Horace (b. 65 BC) and Persius (b. 34 AD). Records of early nursery rhymes—both sung and spoken—first appear in texts from the Middle Ages, and many that are still well-known today date from as early as the sixteenth century (Opie & Opie, 1997). In fact, some argue that many may be even older, since some nursery rhymes such as 'Humpty Dumpty' are found in both England and Scandinavia in slightly varied forms suggesting that they may have been of ancient Teutonic origins (Halliwell, 1849).

Early nursery rhymes were printed in 'chapbooks', which were small, inexpensive books sold by peddlers or 'chapmen' (Neuberg, 1969). However, most were not written down until the publishing of children's books became more prevalent in the eighteenth century. They come from a variety of sources including riddles, proverbs, ballads, drinking songs, mummers plays,[1] and records of historical events. In fact the majority, except for rhymes invented to aid in learning the alphabet, were not originally intended for childish ears at all (Opie & Opie, 1997). They perhaps became common in the nursery when carers drew on other commonly heard songs when singing to children, adapting them to their juvenile

---

[1] Mummers were travelling folk performers who put on plays and other performances on the streets, in public houses or in house-to-house visits from the Middle Ages until the early twentieth century throughout Great Britain.

audience over time. It is often only the first verse of a ballad or poem from another source that has been transformed into a child's song over the centuries. The song "Lavender's Blue" for example, was once a light-hearted love song, and derives from the first verse of the ballad "Diddle, Diddle, or the Kind Country Lovers" printed in a blackletter broadside dating between 1672–1685. Some were edited to suit nineteenth century sensibilities, such as 'Little Robin Redbreast', an earlier version of which read 'Little Robin red breast, Sitting on a pole, Niddle Noddle, Went his head, And Poop went his Hole' (Cooper, 1744).

The melodies that accompany many well-known children's songs today were often derived from other sources too. Some were originally spoken and acquired a melody later, which was either adopted from other sources or composed specifically for a well-known rhyme (Opie & Opie, 1997). 'Twinkle, twinkle little star' for example has been associated with many tunes, but these days is commonly sung to the French tune 'Ah! Vous diaijie, Maman' (1761), a melody that is older than the poem (1806) and on which Mozart composed a set of variations in 1778. The melody and poem first seem to be found together in a book called *The Singing Master* from 1838 (Cryer, 2010).

Lullabies

The word "lullaby" appears to derive from the Roman word "lalla" used to describe a song to put a child to sleep. Similar words are found in Middle English by the fourteenth century (Orme, 2003). The earliest and most primitive forms may have been simple wordless hums, or soothing rhythms (de Vries, 2004). As with many song forms, in ancient traditions the words of lullabies were often believed to have a magical power. The earliest known record of a lullaby is found on a Babylonian tablet in the British museum and dates from 4000 BC, warning the crying child that it has disturbed the gods of the house. The lullaby served as an incantation to soothe the gods and avert their wrath (Farber, 1990). One of the earliest references to lullabies in European cultures comes from Bartholomew Anglicus, a 13th Century English scholar, who noted that nurses commonly soothed their charges with songs to make them sleep (Anglicus, 13th Century, II).

While songs generally vary greatly across cultures and time periods, lullabies appear to have some universal features, likely because of their primary function in putting children to sleep. However, actually enumerating the defining features of a lullaby is somewhat complicated, since songs for other purposes and texts that have little to do with putting a baby to sleep, have sometimes been appropriated as lullabies. A study of Turkish lullabies, for example, found that melodies and lyrics from both traditional laments and lullabies were fairly interchangeable (Trehub & Prince, 2010).

In general, however, lullabies tend to have simple rhythms, with a swaying, rocking style, often accompanied by rocking movements by the singer. Highly repetitive sounds like humming, nonsense syllables and onomatopoeia are prominent in lullabies across cultures, as are elongated and repetitive vowel sounds. A Swahili lullaby for example begins: "Lululu, mwana (wa) lilanji/ Luluhi, mwana (wa) kanda" (Finnegan, 1970, p. 292). Lullabies in fact, appear to share many features with the distinctive infant-directed speech that parents instinctively use with prelinguistic children worldwide (Trehub & Trainor, 1998). Babies display a clear preference for this kind of speech in which adults typically use a higher pitch, wider pitch range, simple and highly modulated intonation contours, shorter phrases, and repetition (Unyk, Trehub, Trainor, & Schellenberg, 1992). Klymasz (1968) describes lullabies sung among the Ukrainian community in Canada as making "optimum use of alliteration and assonance with a high number of liquid L's, iotized vowels and sibilants" (p. 177). In India, lullabies are sung using Neelambari raga, believed to induce peace and relaxation (Gitanjai, 1998).

Play Songs

Play songs can include both songs sung to an infant and songs sung by older children. They are often introduced a little later in the child's development than lullabies, which tend to be sung to children from birth (Garrido, 2014). Play songs include tunes such as "Mary had a little lamb", the words of which were the first words ever recorded by Thomas Edison in 1877, and "Pop goes the weasel" which was originally a dance performed at royal balls in England in the nineteenth century (Opie & Opie, 1988). They differ from lullabies in that their purpose is usually to entertain or teach a child, rather than to put them to sleep.

Often play songs accompany some kind of game or action, such as tickling the infant or the use of hand-movements (as in Incy Wincy Spider). For older children, dancing may be involved, such as in 'Here We Go Round the Mulberry Bush'. 'London Bridge' is another example of a song that involves play with similar features found all over Europe. In the game that accompanies that song, two singers form a bridge with their arms while the other players file through under the bridge. The singers playing the bridge will bring their arms down suddenly to catch one of the players going underneath. The exact meaning of the words is unknown, but several theories exist relating to the destruction of the bridge during Viking invasions or during the Great Fire of London (Gibson, 1972). 'Oranges and Lemons say the Bells of St. Clements' involves a similar game, in which the tempo of the singing speeds up until the singers forming the arch say 'chop, chop, chop, chop, chop' and bring their arms down on the child passing underneath. This one has been variously argued to derive from the days in which people about to be beheaded were paraded through the streets to the accompaniment of bells, or to the beheadings of Henry VIII's wives (Opie & Opie, 1997).

Similar song-games exist in other cultures too. Tucker (1933) for example, describes a game among the Southern Sudanese in which a group of boys sit in a circle with their legs outstretched. A singer sits in the centre chanting a song and tapping the feet of the other boys as he goes, like the counting out songs common in Western countries such as 'Eeni meeni miini moh'. The person whose foot is touched as the last syllable is spoken has to sit on his foot. When every body is sitting on both feet, the singer bows down in front of each boy with his head almost touching the boy's knees. The sitting boy has to try to get up without touching the singer's head and without his knees creaking. The boys whose knees creak are chased by the 'non-creakers' at the end of the game.

Social and Psychological Functions

The singing of songs to children serves several functions. As noted above, parent-child bonding is an important purpose of singing to infants. Spontaneous song-like interactions between parents and children have immense socio-emotional significance to the developing infant. Where it does not occur, infants may be less engaged and more fearful in social contexts (Malloch & Trevarthen, 2009). One of the other primary functions of singing to children is to regulate the child's arousal levels. There is evidence that it is effective in doing so at a biological level. Shenfield, Trehub, and Nakata (2003), for example, report that babies with low baseline levels of cortisol in their study, exhibited mild increases in response to maternal singing, while those with high baseline levels of cortisol experienced decreases. Thus singing by a mother appears to regulate the arousal levels of the child according to their needs at a given time. There is also evidence that lullabies tend to cause babies to focus their attention inwardly while play songs encourages them to become more engaged with the world around them (Rock, Trainor, & Addison, 1999).

Singing to a child, particularly a prelinguistic infant, may also serve the function of allowing the carer to express his or her own feelings. Thus lullabies may express both feelings of love and tenderness towards the child and some of the aggravations that can accompany caring for a child. 'Threat lullabies', which contain veiled messages of frustration towards children who are taking too long to go to sleep, have been found in several cultures around the world. One Iranian lullaby, for example, threatens the child with a wolf that will come if the child doesn't go to sleep (Vahman & Asatrian, 1995). Warner (2011) also argues that they may be designed to immure the child from the exact danger named, like a spell to keep a particular evil away.

Other frustrations may also be expressed by the singer. Klymasz (1968) describes a typical lullaby-singing situation in which a mother's initial purpose may be to put the child to sleep, but soon her mind wanders and the solitude and quietness of the situation may encourage the mother to express feelings that she may not otherwise express such as her conflicting feelings about motherhood. One example of such a 'protest song', is found in a Swahili lullaby. The mother sings: "What ails this child? He makes my soul suffer, he cries all night long, it cuts into my heart" (de Vries, 2004, p. 165). Thus lullabies often express more than just the desire for the child to go to sleep.

Some lullabies also express the frustrations of non-parental carers. Among the Itsuki people of Japan, lullabies were created by teenage girls who left their poverty-stricken families to work as nannies in wealthy families in parts of Japan prior to WWII. The words of the lullabies often expressed anger for their employers, or a yearning for home (Masuyama, 1989). Among the Nyoro of Uganda too, the hired nurses would sing songs that expressed frustration about their position (Finnegan, 1970). While many of these above-noted examples may have been created as genuine expressions of dissatisfaction on the part of the singer, they may often have been intended as humorous.

A further function of children's songs is to impart cultural information and values. Songs intended for older children—those beyond the sensorimotor stage of development—may particularly serve this function. Some children's songs are specifically designed to teach children basic things such as the alphabet, counting, or body parts, with their repetitive nature making them easily remembered. Rhymes and songs for remembering the alphabet date from at least as early as 1671, when John Eachard quoted a portion of one in preparing a sermon (Opie & Opie), and even today, most children learn the alphabet in song form. Songs containing lyrics that rhyme or use alliteration also teach children important pre-reading skills (Yopp & Yopp, 2000). Songs from other cultures are similarly used to teach children about their language. A Zulu song, for example, uses an amusing series of clicking sounds which is commonly used in their language in order to teach children pronunciation (Finnegan, 1970). However, the information imparted by children's songs can also include details about the social environment, such as messages about family vendettas or local prejudices (Del Giudice, 1988). Or, they may enculturate the child with regards to historical events or religious beliefs, such as the lullabies performed by adult men and women of the Yanyuwa of North Australia which provide children with an understanding of the 'Dreamtime' beliefs of the tribe (Mackinlay, 1999).

MODERN DAY PLAYLISTS

As discussed above, singing to children is a tradition of long historical origins, and in fact may even be an innate way of communicating with children, much like the song-like speech known as 'parentese' that carers all over the world instinctively adopt. Many of the songs still commonly used today have been in use for centuries. However, the concept of childhood itself is a social construction, in that it is understood differently in different cultural and historical contexts (James & Prout, 1997). Changing social conditions mean that childhood is a very different experience in Western countries in the twenty-first century to what it was in England in the sixteenth century, for example. In the modern day, children are increasingly exposed to media designed especially for them such as television shows and movies, and are exposed to a wider variety of songs than ever before.

Therefore of interest to our discussion of the role of context in musical choices in this volume, is the question of the extent to which parents today still use traditional songs that they learned from their parents when singing to their children. Do we see thematic differences, or evidence of changing cultural values when comparing traditional and contemporary children's songs? What range of parental attitudes towards children or childhood are expressed in children's songs across the centuries? How important are the functions discussed above in selecting songs to sing to children in modern times?

We explored these questions on the MLAP website by asking 532 parents or people who regularly care for other people's children to nominate a song that they would sing to a child to put it to sleep and a song they would sing to a child during play. The study participants included 378 females and 154 males with a mean age of 34.8 years, the majority of whom were not musicians themselves.

Surprisingly, the most frequently nominated genre for sleep songs was popular music (23.2%). Traditional children's lullabies such as 'Twinkle, Twinkle' and 'Rock-a-bye Baby' were the second most frequently nominated type of song (22.9%), with classical music (14.4%), rock and similar genres (10.2%), and contemporary children's songs (8%) also being selected. The most prevalent reasons given for the sleep song choice was that the song would be soothing to the child (28.3%) or to the carer singing it (27.4%), or that it was a song that had been sung to them as a child (11.9%). Participants rated the songs as being of fairly neutral valence (m = 3.1) and low arousal (m = 2.5),[2] as would be expected of songs meant to soothe or lull a child to sleep. Six parents reported making up their own songs, all of whom were people who had musical experience themselves. We also found correlations between valence and positive coping methods such as positive reinterpretation and acceptance, suggesting that people with healthy coping methods were more likely to choose songs with a positive valence to sing to their children.

In the case of play songs, traditional children's songs such as 'Old McDonald' or 'One, Two, Buckle My Shoe'[3] were the most frequently selected genre (42.2%), with contemporary children's songs including themes from television shows such as 'Bob the Builder' or from Disney movies receiving the second highest rating (34%). Popular music was selected by 10.8% of participants. The most prevalent reason given for the play song choice was that it is fun for the child (43%). Less frequently nominated reasons included that it is fun for the carer singing it (15.2%), that it is easy for children to learn (11.5%) or that the participant's own parents sang it to them as a child (9.1%). Ratings of both valence (m = 4.4) and arousal (m = 3.9) were significantly higher for play songs than for

---

[2] A score of 3 would indicate a neutral midpoint on both valence and arousal dimensions.
[3] Track 53: One, two, buckle me shoe, The Kiboomers.

sleep songs.[4] The differing reasons given for both lullaby and play song choices as well as the differing ratings given to the songs for valence and arousal tend to confirm the function of lullabies as songs to soothe and lower arousal, while play songs are intended to be entertaining and to increase arousal and social engagement.

We also conducted some analysis of lyrics[5] in order to see whether linguistic or thematic differences could be discerned between sleep songs and play songs. The analysis revealed that sleep songs contained significantly more words of over 6 letters than play songs whether traditional or contemporary, tending to confirm the idea that sleep songs may often convey more adult concepts while play songs are usually intended for the entertainment and education of the child and thus uses simpler language. Sleep songs also tended to contain more frequent use of singular personal pronouns (I and You) than play songs, while play songs contained more third person pronouns (He, She and They) than sleep songs. This suggests that sleep songs have a greater focus on the infant-carer bond than play songs, which may be more likely to foster broader social engagement, in keeping with the changing social interests of children of the age to which these songs are likely to appeal. Sleep songs also contained significantly more emotion words, both positive and negative, than play songs, while play songs tended to contain more words relating to motion than sleep songs.

Of further interest was the question of the degree to which children's songs have changed over time. We thus conducted some more in-depth thematic analysis on a randomly selected sample of sleep songs and play songs from both the traditional and contemporary categories nominated by our participants (Table 8.1). Preliminary word counts in the selected song samples revealed that the words most frequently used in sleep songs related to sleep or babies in both traditional and contemporary sleep songs, while the most frequently used words in play songs related to animals or animal sounds (e.g. 'oink' or 'moo'). All categories of songs, including play songs and sleep songs, both contemporary and traditional, contained nonsense words, humming sounds, and frequent alliteration, rhyme and repetition. Each category also contained repeated use of irony and humorous imagery. The song 'Stay Awake' sung by Julie Andrews in the film *Mary Poppins* for example, encourages the child *not* to lie down or close its eyes. However, the references to soft pillows and drifting moons

---

[4] At the level $p < 0.001$.

[5] Analyses were conducted using LIWC and NVivo software.

Table 8.1   Sleep songs and play songs selected for lyrical analysis

Traditional		*Contemporary*	
Sleep songs			
Silent Night	1818	Hushabye Mountain	1968
The Owl & The Pussy Cat	1871	Edelweiss (from *The Sound of Music*)	1959
Cradle Song (J. Brahms)	1868	Stay Awake (from *Mary Poppins*)	1964
Lavender's Blue	17th C	Baby Mine (from *Dumbo*)	1941
Rockabye Baby	17th C	Lullaby for Tom (Peter Combe)	1987
All the Pretty Horses	15th C	Counting Sheep (from *Disney Babies*)	1992
Twinkle, Twinkle, Little Star	1806 (poem)	Lullaby (Billy Joel)	1993
Play songs			
Pop Goes the Weasel	18th C	The Ning, Nang, Nong	1968
Baa Baa Black Sheep	c. 1731	Dingle, Dangle Scarecrow	1964
Oranges and Lemons	c. 1734	Newspaper Mama (Peter Combe)[a]	1988
A Tisket, A Tasket	c. 1879	Fireman Sam (theme song)	1987
Hot Cross Buns	c. 1798	Fish & Mice (Holly Throsby)	2010
One, Two, Buckle My Shoe	1805	Hakuna Matata (from *The Lion King*)	1994
Three Blind Mice	c. 1609	Juicy, Juicy Green Grass (Peter Combe)	1988
Little Miss Muffet	c. 1805	Bananas in Pyjamas	1967
Old McDonald	18th C	I Like To Sing (Justine Clarke)	2013
Mary Had A Little Lamb	1830	Big Fish, Little Fish (from *Bob the Builder*)	2008
There's A Hole In The Bucket	c. 1700	Big Red Car (The Wiggles)	1995
		Mr. Clicketty Cane (Peter Combe)	1988

[a]Track 54: Newspaper Mama, Peter Combe

demonstrate the clear intention to make the child feel sleepy. Similarly, the traditional play song 'There's a Hole In The Bucket' which derives from a song family that is at least 300 years old, plays upon the humorous image of a man (Henry) who asks the woman (Liza) how to fix the hole in his bucket. Liza's replies are full of irony as she explains step-by-step as if to a dullard, how to fix it. The last laugh is on her however, when it turns out that her instructions will require Henry to have use of the very bucket he is seeking to fix. We also found that the use of language displaying anger was correlated with a coping style that tends to use humour to deal with difficulties, suggesting that some song choices that might seem inappropriate for childish consumption were selected with irony and humour in mind too.

Sleep songs across all time periods contained similar themes relating to the beauty of the baby, wishes for their future, protection of the child (by a parent, angels or stars etc.), boats, water, rocking, and nighttime images such as the stars and moon. However, traditional sleep songs contained more references to agricultural themes such as ploughing or threshing and to flowers than contemporary sleep songs, which contained more frequent references to mechanical items such as engines. The modern day songs also contained themes of childish innocence, cleanness and happiness, which did not appear in the traditional examples.

Several themes were found in common across time periods in play songs as well. Both the traditional and contemporary play songs that we analysed had frequent references to animals, and to food, and frequently contained some kind of list (e.g. of days of the week, numbers, colours etc.) that were clearly intended to be of educational value and to help children to learn and memorize things. However, traditional play songs again contained frequent references to agricultural scenarios or to things like bells, which are seldom heard in modern society, while contemporary play songs often involved mechanical objects such as cars and bicycles, or contained themes revolving around having fun or around heroic characters. The traditional play songs also used language reflecting social conditions that are less common in Western societies in the modern day, referring to 'masters' or 'maids', or containing references to themes of debt, poverty and beheadings ('Oranges and Lemons') that would likely be considered unsuitable topics for children in modern times.

A CASE STUDY: EMMA[6]

In order to illuminate the way one's own childhood influences an individual's musical experiences and how this in turn is transmitted to one's own children, we here describe a case study of one particular participant, who grew up in a musical family and now has children of her own. Emma described many happy memories of her childhood associated with music. Her parents were both amateur musicians and so singing and playing music was a regular part of family life. Emma's mother had been an opera singer and her father played several instruments and wrote music as well. She has fond memories of sitting on her father's lap at the piano when very small, with her hands on the back of his hands and laughing at the way

---

[6] The participant's name has been changed to protect her identity.

their arms were moving about together as her father was playing the piano. When Emma later began formal music lessons at the age of 4, her parents were often deeply involved, singing or playing other musical instruments along with her as she practiced at home.

Two particular songs from Emma's childhood held special significance for her. One was a song written by Emma's father when she was born, which he used to sing to her as a baby. It told the story of a father whose little daughter was already asleep when he came home from work and how he longed to wake her up so he could play with her. The song held great meaning for her throughout her life, as it came to symbolize her close relationship with her father. Another song that was significant for similar reasons was called 'Laugh It Off Upsy Daisy' and was sung by comedian Danny Kaye and his daughter Dena. Emma described how the song was frequently sung during car-trips with her dad, particularly when they would go for a drive on their own without the rest of the family. The fact that the recording was of a father-daughter singing team and that the words are about how you can laugh off troubles when you have each other made this song another particularly poignant symbol of the musical bond between Emma and her father. As Emma described it: "The songs were like a special language that only dad and I spoke…Singing them always made us feel instantly closer"

Emma is now the mother of two pre-school aged children and music is a large part of her children's lives too:

> We probably sing at some stage every day. Maybe its just to pass the time while we are doing other things that the kids might not otherwise enjoy, like getting dressed or driving in the car. Sometimes we deliberately put some of the kids' favourite music on and sing out loud to it. Sometimes the kids might particularly ask me to sing a favourite song that they'd like to hear, or sometimes I just make something up on the spot depending on what I'm feeling at the time or what direction I would like to swing their mood in, either to calm them down or distract them from something that might be upsetting them. Sometimes the boys will even request a made-up song about a particular topic, whatever the craze of the moment is, like dinosaurs, pirates or cars or something. In fact both the kids have their own special little silly nonsense songs that I have made up for them at some stage and that we have gotten into the habit of singing together. Their song is just for them. Each boy has their own.

Emma described how her partner also sang songs to their children, and if she tries to sing the songs that their father sings to them the children get upset and say 'no, that's daddy's song'. So to the children, the songs each parent introduced were unique to that parent and somehow seemed to form part of the identity of their relationship with each parent. When asked whether she sang the same songs that her father had sung to her to her own boys, Emma replied that she didn't:

> Somehow its like those songs are sacred. They were just for me and my dad. And I'm not sure I could even sing them without breaking up anyway, because my father has passed away now and its just brings him back too vividly and painfully for me. Plus I guess, although I didn't really plan this consciously, I just wanted to create a song for each of my children spontaneously that was just about them and my bond with them, rather than just passing on what I had with my dad … you know, to celebrate what we have between us that is unique.

Emma's story illustrates the power that music has to enhance parental bonding, providing interesting insights into the influence singing has on both relationships through which it is shared, and one's relationship with music itself. It further demonstrates how, although the specific songs themselves may change, the sense that music is an important part of communicating with children is transmitted from one generation to the next. Parents seem to teach their children how to use music to create a particular mood or atmosphere, and this is likely something that children carry into adulthood, continuing to use music to modulate their moods throughout their lives.

THE TRAJECTORY FROM THE PAST TO THE MODERN DAY

Changing Cultural Values

Knowledge of what childhood was like during the medieval and early modern periods is limited. Children themselves leave few records, and in those periods fewer people in general could write. Those who could were largely adult males, often clerics, who were not interested in writing about children or childhood. Although a popular belief is that people in the medieval period treated children like 'miniature adults' and that there was no real concept of childhood at that time, research in recent decades has proven that people in medieval times had clear concepts of childhood as a distinct developmental stage of life (Orme, 2003). However, there were aspects in which children were treated more like adults than is common today. For example, the age of majority was usually much lower than it is today (as low as 12 at times), and children were often considered adults with the onset of puberty. At even earlier ages, it was possible for children to marry or enter a monastery. Given that the life expectancy was only about 30 years and that infant mortality rates were high (about 45%), parents were often eager to marry their children off young (Heins, 2001). Thus, in medieval and modern Europe children were less protected from sexual knowledge, with many families all sleeping together in a single room (Heins, 2001). In *Romeo & Juliet* for example, Juliet herself is only 13 years old, and yet the love and lust between the protagonists is taken somewhat for granted by Shakespeare. The impediment to their being together is not their age, but the feud between their respective families. Thus, Archard (2004) argues that what actually differed in the medieval period was not so much the conception of childhood as a separate stage, but in their idea of what childhood was. The ideal of childhood as representing purity, asexuality and innocence was something that developed much later.

In the twelfth century there appears to have been some level of sympathy towards childhood as evident from an increasing devotion to images of the baby Jesus in this period (Heywood, 2013). However, puritanism in the sixteenth century advocated the view that children were born tainted by original sin, needing to be controlled so as to conquer their evil impulses (Heins, 2001). Then in the seventeenth century, John Locke published his work entitled "Some Thoughts Concerning Education" (1693), which promoted the idea of children as being a 'tabula rasa', a clean slate, to be shaped by the adults around them.

By the time of the Victorian era, children and the protection of them was of growing social importance. Victoria herself had nine children and was often depicted surrounded by them, and families in general tended to be large. Poor living and working conditions created by the increasing migration to cities during the industrial revolution led to social reform, with a number of laws aimed at protecting the welfare of children passed from the 1830s onwards. The novels of Charles Dickens from this time display the interest in the lives of children that was developing, sometimes described as 'the cult of the child' (Dowson, 1889). The increasing expectation was that children should live a life of protected innocence. Romanticism in the arts also idealized childhood as a time of virtuousness that would provide creative inspiration for a lifetime (Heywood, 2013).

Today in European cultures we generally associate childhood with the traits of innocence, vulnerability and asexuality. Twenty-first century ideals portray childhood as a happy, carefree time of life. However, as can be seen from the above discussion, this is a relatively new development in concepts of childhood. It does not exist uniformly across cultures even in the twenty-first century (Heywood, 2013), and tends to co-exist within a single culture alongside stark contradictions. In the Victorian era for example, the ideal of childhood as a time of protected innocence existed alongside a thriving trade in child erotica and pornography (Heins, 2001). Similar contradictions exist in our time. While modern day parents may view it as important to shield their children from media content that portrays violence or sexual conduct, conflicting social trends see a flourishing child fashion industry that promotes the sexualization of even pre-school aged children through the use of make-up and provocative clothing. Although legislation is growing to control pedophilia and education programs to inform both children and parents about the dangers of pedophilia are increasing, children are in many ways being increasingly treated as young adults, for example, being increasingly expected to spend extensive periods of time in structured lessons as early as 3 or 4 years of age.

How are these changing concepts of childhood displayed in children's songs across the centuries? While there was nothing unusual about bawdy jokes, strong language and references to alcohol or violence in children's songs from the sixteenth century, those that are still used today tend to have been 'whitewashed' to suit modern concepts of appropriateness for children. This has happened gradually over time as songs texts have changed or their original meanings have become less apparent. Those regarded as less suitable for children's ears have presumably, been gradually lost from the popular repertoire that parents sing to their children. The main difference in lyrics between traditional and contemporary songs displayed in the sample we have discussed in this chapter, relate to the use of time-specific imagery such as agricultural scenarios in traditional songs from less-industrialized time periods, and frequent reference to mechanical objects in modern songs.

However, even in the small sample of songs analyzed in depth in this chapter, some further differences are apparent. Themes of innocence, cleanness and fun associated with childhood were found primarily in contemporary songs. It is understood in the modern age that children are a product of both genetics and their environment, and that the relationship between children and parents is in fact bidirectional with parents both influencing and being influenced by their children. However, the idea that children are born innocent and are shaped largely by parental influence remains strong. In modern times, we are used to happy endings, with advertising, film and other media promoting the myth that life should be all fun and joy, living 'happily ever after'. This idea is reflected in children's songs that portray a life of carefree play as the ideal for children today. Although playfulness is intrinsic to humans and animals alike, in earlier centuries and parts of the world today where living conditions are much harder on children and the age of working and childbearing is much younger, it is likely that the concept of 'fun' was less a part of childhood than it often is in Western cultures today.

Functions of Singing to Children

De Vries (2004) argues that lullabies developed from simple musical sounds such as humming or 'lulling' that were created to put babies to sleep, to an increasingly complex genre that may include additional layers of metaphor and satire which address an audience over the head of the baby. Our modern sample revealed that irony and humour were a part of both contemporary songs and traditional songs still in use today, whether for sleep-time or play-time. However, our analysis does tend to confirm the idea that the humour and irony found in sleep-songs is intended to be more for the benefit of the adult than that of the child. The fact that our modern day participants were more likely to choose popular music for sleep-songs than for play songs and the fact that sleep songs tended to use more complex language than play songs, suggests that in the case of sleep songs, the content is often chosen for the entertainment or personal expression of the singer than for the child. Play songs, however, are generally intended for older infants and children and may even begin to engage them in the song production, and therefore tend to involve styles and themes more likely to entertain a child. Therefore, lullabies are more than just songs to make a child sleep. They express the fears and frustrations of the carer, recording social practice and ritual, and strengthening the bonds between the child and its carer.

While several of the sleep songs and play songs nominated by our sample contained adult themes or strong language, the use of 'protest songs' are perhaps less evident in our modern day sample than in the cross-cultural examples discussed earlier in this chapter. It could be argued that this is because in modern Western societies women are less trapped by marriage and motherhood than in the cultural contexts discussed above. However, psychic conflict is still a large part of parenting in Western lands today. A parent may feel torn between his or her sense of love and responsibility for the child, and feelings of resentment for the sleep deprivation and encroachment upon one's lifestyle that having a child entails. In fact, as discussed in Chap. 7, women may be more isolated in caring for children in the modern day, since children are generally raised in the environment of a nuclear family rather than extended family or village situations in which tribal cultures of the past and today may raise their children. However, there appears to be a code of silence around the difficulties of parenthood among many women today, with mothers fearing being labeled as bad parents or as suffering post-natal depression if they speak up about the difficulties they experience (Walker, 2014). Thus, the less overt use of sleep songs as an expression of the frustrations of parenthood in our sample may be largely attributable to a reluctance to voice these frustrations. It is evident however, that even in this modern day sample, carers are able to use music as a form of personal expression, often choosing music to soothe children that was not specifically written for them, and that likely reflects the taste of the parent.

The arousal potential of the music was also a primary consideration in both sleep songs and play songs, with lullabies demonstrating neutral valences, low arousal levels and a prevalence of words about sleep, and play songs displaying positive valences, high arousal levels and higher rates of words about action and motion than sleep songs. Participants also described their desire to either soothe, or entertain the child as being the principal considerations reflected in their choices.

The fact that some participants selected songs because they had been sung to them in their childhood, suggests that for some the nostalgic value, or the passing on of family values and customs is an important consideration when singing to children. The case study also illustrated how songs can become symbolic of relationships. This is often described as the 'darling, they're playing our song' phenomenon when discussed in the context of romantic relationships (Davies, 1978; Kivy, 1989). However, our study shows that music can take on the same symbolic functions in parent-child relationships as well, further tending to confirm the importance of social bonding as a primary function of music. Particular songs may develop psychological associations with a period in our lives in which we felt cared for, loved and nurtured, and these sentimental connections become strengthened when we become parents ourselves, making the songs that become deeply encoded in our memories as children take on even greater significance when we use them with our own children.

Thus, it is clear that aside from discussions about the intellectual or academic benefits of musical engagement, the songs that we hear in childhood shape and are shaped by relationships with our parents and other carers, and the wider community. An examination of children's songs also throws an interesting light on our social history and changing attitudes towards childhood and parenting, adding further to our argument that musical choices are influenced by a complex interaction of historical, cultural, social and personal variables.

REFERENCES

Anglicus, B. (13th Century). *De Proprietatibus Rerum*. Project Gutenberg.

Archard, D. (2004). *Children' Rights and Childhood*. New York: Routledge.

Cooper, M. (1744). *Tommy Thumb's Pretty Song Book*. London: Cooper.

Cryer, M. (2010). *Love Me Tender: The Stories Behind the World's Favourite Songs*. Retrieved from ReadHowYouWant.com

Davies, J. B. (1978). *Psychology of Music*. California: Hutchinson.

de Vries, A. (2004). The Beginning of All Poetry: Some Observations About Lullabies from Oral Traditions. In T. V. d. Walt, F. Fairer-Wessels, & J. Inggs (Eds.), *Change and Renewal in Children's Literature* (pp. 159–170). Greenwood Publishing Group.

Del Giudice, L. (1988). *Ninna-nanna*-Nonsense? Fears, Dreams, and Falling in the Italian Lullaby. *Oral Tradition, 3*(3), 270–293.

Dissanayake, E. (2008). If Music Is the Food of Love, What About Survival and Reproductive Success? *Musicae Scientiae, 12*(Special Issue), 169–195.

Dowson, E. (1889, August 17). The Cult of the Child. *The Critic, 17*, 433–435.

Farber, W. (1990). Magic at the Cradle: Babylonian and Assyrian Lullabies. *Anthropos, 85*(1), 139–148.

Finnegan, R. H. (1970). *Oral Literature in Africa*. Clarendon, P.

Garrido, S. (2014). Childhood Cognition. In W. Thompson (Ed.), *Music in the Social and Behavioral Sciences: An Encyclopedia*. SAGE Reference.

Gibson, M. (1972). *The Vikings*. London: Wayland.

Gitanjai, B. (1998). Effect of the Karnatic Music Raga "Neelambari" on Sleep Architecture. *Indian Journal of Physiological Pharmacology, 42*(1), 119–122.

Halliwell, J. O. (1849). *Popular Rhymes and Nursery Tales: A Sequel to the Nursery Rhymes of England*. London: John Russell Smith.

Hannon, E. E., & Johnson, S. P. (2005). Infants Use Meter to Categorize Rhythms and Melodies: Implications for Musical Structure Learning. *Cognitive Psychology, 50*, 354–377.

Heins, M. (2001). Not in Front of the Children: "Indecency". *Censorship and the Innocence of Youth*. Hill & Wang.

Heywood, C. (2013). *A History of Childhood: Children and Childhood in the West from Medieval to Modern Times.* John Wiley & Sons.

James, A., & Prout, A. (Eds.). (1997). *Constructing and Reconstructing Childhood: Contemporary Issues in the Sociological Study of Childhood.* London: RoutledgeFalmer.

Kivy, P. (1989). *Sound Sentiment.* Princeton University Press.

Klymasz, R. B. (1968). Social and Cultural Motifs in Canadian Ukrainian Lullabies. *The Slavic and East European Journal, 12*(2), 176–183.

Mackinlay, E. (1999). Music for Dreaming: Aboriginal Lullabies in the Yanyuwa Community at Borroloola, Northern Territory. *British Journal of Ethnomusicology, 8*(1), 97–111.

Malloch, S., & Trevarthen, C. (2009). Musicality: Communicating the Vitality and Interests of Life. In S. Malloch & C. Trevarthen (Eds.), *Communicative Musicality: Exploring the Basis of Human Companionship* (pp. 1–15). New York: Oxford University Press.

Masuyama, E. E. (1989). Desire and Discontent in Japanese Lullabies. *Western Folklore, 48*(2), 144–148.

Neuberg, V. E. (1969). *The Penny Histories: A Study of Chapbooks for Young Readers Over Two Centuries.* New York: Harcourt, Brace & World.

Opie, I., & Opie, P. (1988). *The Singing Game.* Oxford: Oxford University Press.

Opie, I., & Opie, P. (1997). *The Oxford Dictionary of Nursery Rhymes.* Oxford: Oxford University Press.

Orme, N. (2003). *Medieval Children.* Yale University Press.

Phillips-Silver, J., & Trainor, L. (2005). Feeling the Beat: Movement Influences Infant Rhythm Perception. *Science, 308,* 1430.

Rock, A. M. L., Trainor, L. J., & Addison, T. L. (1999). Distinctive Messages in Infant-Directed Lullabies and Play Songs. *Developmental Psychology, 35*(2), 527–534.

Schubert, E., & McPherson, G. E. (2006). The Perception of Emotion in Music. In G. E. McPherson (Ed.), *The Child as Musician: A Handbook of Musical Development* (pp. 193–212). Oxford: Oxford University Press.

Shenfield, T., Trehub, S., & Nakata, T. (2003). Maternal Singing Modulates Infant Arousal. *Psychology of Music, 31*(4), 365–375. https://doi.org/10.1177/03057356030314002

Trainor, L. (2005). Are There Critical Periods for Musical Development? *Developmental Psychobiology, 46*(3), 262–278.

Trainor, L., & Heinmiller, B. M. (1998). The Development of Evaluative Responses to Music: Infants Prefer to Listen to Consonance Over Dissonance. *Infant Behavioral Development, 21,* 77–88.

Trehub, S., & Prince, R. (2010). Lullabies and Other Women's Songs in a Turkish Village of Akçaeniş. *UNESCO Observatory, Faculty of Architecture, Building and Planning, The University of Melbourne Refereed E-Journal, 2*(1). Retrieved from https://www.utm.utoronto.ca/infant-child-centre/sites/files/infant-childcentre/public/users/ldhotson/TrehubPrinceUNESCOobservatoryEjournal2010.pdf

Trehub, S., Schellenberg, E. G., & Kamenetsky, S. B. (1999). Infants' and Adults' Perception of Scale Structure. *Journal of Experimental Psychology: Human Perception and Performance, 25,* 965–975.

Trehub, S., & Trainor, L. (1998). Singing to Infants: Lullabies and Play Songs. In L. P. Lipsitt, C. K. Tovee-Collier, & H. Hayne (Eds.), *Advances in Infancy Research* (Vol. 12, pp. 43–78). Greenwood Publishing Group.

Tucker, A. N. (1933). Children's Games and Songs in the Southern Sudan. *The Journal of the Royal Anthropological Institute of Great Britain and Ireland, 63,* 165–187.

Unyk, A. M., Trehub, S., Trainor, L., & Schellenberg, E. G. (1992). Lullabies and Simplicity: A Cross-Cultural Perspective. *Psychology of Music, 20,* 15–28.

Vahman, F., & Asatrian, G. (1995). *Poetry of the Baxtiārīs: Love Poems, Wedding Songs, Lullabies, Laments.* Det Kongelige Danske Videnskabernes Selskab.

Walker, E. (2014). What No One Tells You About Motherhood. *Women's Agenda.* Retrieved from https://womensagenda.com.au/latest/what-no-one-tells-you-about-motherhood/

Warner, M. (2011). *No Go the Bogeyman: Scaring, Lulling and Making Mock.* Random House.

Yopp, H. K., & Yopp, R. H. (2000). Supporting Phonemic Awareness in the Classroom. *The Reading Teacher, 54*(2), 130–143.

CHAPTER 9

Coming of Age and Birthdays

Historical and Cross-Cultural Practices

Coming of age, in which an individual passes from childhood to adolescence or adulthood, is argued by some to be the 'rite of passage' that is subject to the greatest cultural variability. While other rituals such as those surrounding birth, marriage and death include important commonalities across cultures, those attending the passage from childhood into adolescence or adulthood are considerably mutable from culture to culture (Roscoe, 1995). In fact, as discussed in the previous chapter, defining childhood and the age in which a person is considered to have reached adulthood is itself changeable according to context. In many tribal societies and in some Medieval European settings, adolescence was largely nonexistent. In some cultural contexts, an individual was considered to have reached marriageable age upon reaching sexual maturity and was expected to take on adult responsibilities at that point.

Thus in many tribal societies coming of age rites are often performed when a young person reaches puberty. They may involve being separated from the community for a period, giving proof of one's maturity by undergoing grueling physical or mental ordeals, receiving special instruction from tribal elders, and then being ceremonially welcomed back into the village community with a new status (Delaney, 1995). Such ceremonies and their associated traditions help the individual to adjust psychologically to the changes they are going through, making them aware of the

© The Author(s) 2019
S. Garrido, J. W. Davidson, *Music, Nostalgia and Memory*, Palgrave Macmillan Memory Studies,
https://doi.org/10.1007/978-3-030-02556-4_9

expectations surrounding them in their new role within the community as well as notifying the community of their new status (Kroger, 2006). It has also been argued that these rituals enable a society to: avoid the harmful effects of such changes on the community and the individual (Van Gennep, 1960), to maintain male dominance over females (Read, 1952), to legitimate the continuing social order (La Fontaine, 1986), and to symbolically sever a male from the world of females (Whiting, Kluckhohn, & Anthony, 1958). In addition, the performance of such community rites contributes to the stability of a society by offering clear definitions of self and encouraging resolution of fear and uncertainty by adhering to communally accepted beliefs and authority systems (Dunham, Kidwell, & Wilson, 1986).

Music, song and dance are often an integral part of these ceremonies in many parts of the world, frequently being believed to hold almost magical powers. For example, young girls aged 14–16 in the Okrika tribe of Africa are taught by the elderly women of the tribe to sing traditional songs during their coming of age rites. Traditionally, the girls must go to the riverbank at dawn for several days to sing the songs, which are believed to help the girls to free themselves from romantic attachments to water spirits so that they are ready to receive human suitors (Gleason & Ibubuya, 1991). Similarly, within the Tukuna people of the Northwest Amazon, when a young girl begins to menstruate she will be secluded from the rest of the tribe for 4–12 weeks during which period she is believed to be in the underworld. At the end of the period of seclusion the young girl emerges from her shelter and dances with her family until dawn in a ceremony believed to break the power of demons over her, allowing her to enter womanhood (Lincoln, 1991).

In other cultural settings the songs serve more educational purposes. For example, the Venda of southern Africa traditionally held a cycle of initiation involving several ceremonies and educational periods for girls over a period of one to four years (Blacking, 1985). Songs and dances accompanied every part of the rites and were designed to express symbolic relationships with the natural environment as well as to be sensuous physical experiences for the initiates. Similarly, among the Kamba people of Kenya songs are used during circumcision ceremonies lasting from 6–10 days to educate young people about local customs and traditions, gender roles and sexual knowledge (Naomi, 2014).

For other cultures the songs signify the youth's acceptance into the adult world by allowing them to participate in a sacred world in which they have previously not been able to take part. For example, in the Jewish culture, 'bar mitzvah' (for boys) or 'bat mitzvah' (for girls) is held when the child reaches 12 or 13 years of age. Chanting of the *haftarah* text from the prophets such as Jeremiah is an integral part of the ceremony. These chants are well known to Jewish people, also forming part of their regular worship services. However, at this coming of age ceremony the child joins in the chanting for the first time, symbolizing their initiation into Jewish traditions (Edelman, 2003). Similarly, in India, Hindu families celebrate a 'thread ceremony' or 'Upanayana' on a child's twelfth or thirteenth birthday. In this ceremony the child is given a sacred thread to wear, symbolizing his coming of age and induction into Vedic traditions. An important part of the ceremony is the chanting of the Gayatri mantra, a three-line verse from the hymns of the ancient Hindu text, the Rig Veda. This is the first occasion on which the child will hear these sacred chants, indicating the attainment of an age in which they are entrusted with the ancient texts and will begin further instruction in the Hindu faith.

In other contexts, the music may serve an altogether different function. Among the Mitsogho people of Gabon in West Africa, initiation ceremonies involve near-death experiences induced by the use of a drug known as Iboga. The ceremony is accompanied by continuous polyrhythmic music played on the mouth bow, the harp, percussion instruments and singing (Maas & Strubelt, 2003). German researchers Uwe Maas and Süster Strubelt, who themselves participated in the ceremonies in the course of their research, report that the polyrhythms of the music are crucial in inducing the trance-like states and visions that are an integral part of the ceremony, as well as serving so as to improve the mental and physical well-being of the initiate throughout. Today, the ceremony is seldom held to mark the transition to puberty but more often to address illness or for spiritual or personal development.

Many of the traditional rituals discussed above are changing, although not disappearing altogether. Their significance is also changing with the times. In many cultures, although such ceremonies are still performed, they may no longer be required in order to be viewed as having attained the status of adulthood (Gleason & Ibubuya, 1991). In other settings, their performance may no longer indicate marriageability or that the child is ready to accept adult responsibilities. This loss of significance as a major marker of the transition to adulthood means that in modern times such ceremonies are decreasing in popularity in some cultures except as tourist attractions, and tend to have to work around other factors such as school routines (Blacking, 1985). For example, Naomi (2014) reports that although circumcision ceremonies are still performed among the Kamba people of Kenya today, the content of the songs have changed to reflect more modern views of gender roles and of the behavioural expectations of youths after their circumcision.

English customs, particularly those for girls, were used in the past to signal marriageability to the wider community. Queen Elizabeth I introduced the custom of having young women presented to her at court during the latter half of the sixteenth century (Escales, 1993), a ceremony that was further developed by Queen Victoria. Being presented at court for a young woman in the Victorian age symbolized the attainment of an age at which courtship and marriage were considered appropriate, and women of the nobility typically attended a 'season' of balls and dinners in which they would have the opportunity to meet eligible bachelors subsequent to their 'coming out'. A similar tradition was followed in the U.S. among wealthier families beginning in the late nineteenth century, known as a 'debutante' ball (in French 'leading off'). On both sides of the Atlantic, the ritual became an expression of wealth, status and family lineage. The practice is still followed today although it seldom represents any real changes to a young woman's status or life. Despite this loss of ritual significance, the practice has been growing in popularity since the 1980s (Escales, 1993). Although more about socializing and raising money for charity than about attaining marriageable age, the Queen Charlotte's Ball in London for example, is still regarded by many as one of the most prestigious society events to which only a small number of hand-picked young women are invited (Jones & Webb, 2013).

Among Mexican-Americans, a modern day coming of age celebration is commonly held for young girls when they reach the age of 15, a ritual that has its origins in both European and indigenous traditions that signaled fertility as well as the transition from childhood to adulthood (Cantu, 2002). While the ritual was popular among Mexican-Americans in the early part of the twentieth century, they dwindled in frequency in the 60s and 70s, experiencing a resurgence in popularity in the last decade of the century (Cantu, 2002). An essential part of the celebration is a dance, which may at times be a waltz with the young girl's father or a choreographed dance.

As globalization gains pace and traditional coming of age ceremonies are losing their significance, in some contexts formal coming of age ceremonies are often being replaced by birthday celebrations in the Western style. In effect, celebrations of significant key birthdays such as 'sweet sixteen', turning 18, or a twenty-first birthday celebration, have become the new coming of age rituals of the modern age. Twenty-first birthday celebrations in particular, have become renowned for excessive alcohol consumption and risky behavior in young people (Glassman, Dodd, Kenzik, Miller, & Sheu, 2010).

The twenty-first birthday has been a significant life moment for many years, likely due to the fact that it was the age of majority in many Western countries for some time. In medieval times the age of twenty-one was the age at which a male or unmarried female could inherit property (Hanawalt, 1995). Although in Australia, the UK and England the official age at which a majority is attained became 18 years around the 1970s, the twenty-first birthday is often still seen as a significant marker of maturity in many countries.

As in so many important rituals throughout the life cycle, music remains a recognizably important part of the celebration. According to the 1998 Guinness Book of Records, "Happy Birthday to You" is the most recognized song in the English language and has been translated into many other languages. Originating in the U.S. in the mid-nineteenth century, 'Happy Birthday' can be heard in most parts of the world even in countries where English is not the first language. As we will see in the next section, this song is still a popular choice for celebrating birthdays in the twenty-first century.

MODERN DAY PLAYLISTS

In order to explore how music plays a role in modern day celebrations of coming of age, we asked 740 participants on the MLAP website what music they would choose to celebrate a key birthday such as their twenty-first and why. The participants included 223 males, 507 females (6 participants selected 'other' and 4 participants did not answer the question), with a mean age of 36 (SD = 15.7, range 12–83 years).

The most frequently chosen song was the traditional tune "Happy Birthday", which was selected by 54 participants (7%), nearly half of whom were from non-English speaking backgrounds. Other popular songs included Stevie Wonder's "Happy Birthday", (n = 10), "22" by Taylor Swift (n = 5), "Forever Young" by Youth Group[1] (n = 5), "Celebration"

---

[1] Track 55: Forever Young, Youth Group.

by Kool & The Gang (n = 5), and "Bohemian Rhapsody" and "Don't stop me now" by Queen (n = 4 respectively). A total of 18 different songs had the word birthday in the title, including songs by 50 cent, Kings of Leon, New Kids on the Block, Katy Perry, Concrete Blonde, Altered Images, and Mental as Anything, and covering genres from Motown to rap, punk rock, and alternative rock from Taiwan and Iceland. The music selected was usually quite celebratory in style, with both valence and arousal ratings of the selected songs being relatively high (M = 4.2 and 4.1 respectively).[2]

When asked why they would select their nominated song for their key birthday celebration, the most commonly selected reason for the choice was that they liked elements of the music such as the rhythm, the instruments or the singer's voice (n = 166). Another commonly selected reason was that it was a 'good party song' (n = 106), which included songs such as "You Say Its Your Birthday"[3] by the Beatles (n = 9). Songs in this category had significantly higher valence scores, suggesting a 'happier' tone to the music than music selected for other reasons. Also common was that the participant had a 'history' with the music making it particularly significant to them (n = 99); or that it brought back some favourite memories (n = 91). Some participants chose music that expressed something about them personally (n = 61), such as Frank Sinatra's "My Way". Other people chose music because it was from an era that they particularly liked (n = 46), usually songs from the 50s, 60s or 70s such as "Blue Suede Shoes", "It's My Party and I'll Cry If I Want To", or "Dancing Queen". Participants who selected music for this reason tended to have high scores in nostalgia proneness on the Batcho Nostalgia inventory. Nineteen people chose music purely because it was a traditional birthday song. All of these people except for two who nominated traditional songs from their non-English speaking home countries, chose the traditional "Happy Birthday" tune. Sixteen people said they didn't particularly like birthdays and selected a song that reflected that (n = 16) such as "Don't Fight It" by The Panics, "Come as You Are" by Nirvana, or "Roar" by Katy Perry.

The lyrics of the songs nominated by participants in this study were analyzed using both Linguistic Inquiry and Word Count (LIWC,

---

[2] The range of possible scores was 1–5 where 3 would equal a neutral score. See Chap. 7 for a further explanation of valence and arousal ratings.

[3] Track 56: You Say It's Your Birthday, The Beatles.

Table 9.1   Top 15 most frequently used words in birthday lyrics

Stem word	Word count in lyric files
Like	905
Birthday	890
Love	869
Know	804
Time	767
Come	703
Get	622
Got	606
Let	573
Now	555
Dance	486
Good	484
Days	470
Feels	469
Make	465

Pennebaker, Booth, & Francis, 2007) and the qualitative analysis software NVIVO. We firstly ran word frequency analyses in NVIVO in order to identify the most frequently used words in the lyrics. The results are displayed in Table 9.1 This sample of words that appeared most frequently in the texts demonstrates the high emphasis on pleasure and parties in the songs chosen. The word "like" which was the most frequently used word, was used both as a verb in relation to activities such as dancing, as in the line "I would like you to dance" in the Beatles' "So You Say Its Your Birthday", or within a metaphorical statement such as "Like a bat out of hell" in the song of that name by Meatloaf. Words such as "let's" or "come" were also frequently used in relation to dancing or partying, such as in the line "Let's get a party going" in Andrew W. K.'s "Party Hard". "Time" frequently referred to similar concepts as in "having the time of your life" in ABBA's "Dancing Queen". Where the word "love" was used, this most frequently referred to romantic love and included both songs in which the singer declared his or her love for someone, or in laments and songs telling a story of heartbreak.

Since the words used here seemed to have strong thematic content relating to parties, dancing and fun, we decided to see how this compared to a random sample of songs from similar genres which were not specifically about birthdays. A sample of 480 songs was selected from a list of song standards. Linguistic analysis was performed on the lyrics of both this selection of standards and on the birthday songs and independent samples t-tests performed to detect whether there were any significant differences between the two song samples.

The results indicated that the birthday songs contained significantly less use of the word "I" than the sample of standards,[4] with many of the songs in the birthday song sample being written in the second-person (i.e. using the word "you") rather than in the first person. This may reflect the fact that birthday celebrations are usually highly social, an occasion on which an individual is acknowledged by a group of other people, rather than being something one celebrates for oneself. One notable exception to that was the song "Happy Birthday to Me" by punk rock band The Vandals. The lyrics to that song are very self-oriented, such as in the lines "Its my birthday and I'll do what I want to" and "Its not your birthday, so do what I say". In keeping with the punk rock genre, they express a great deal of anger, particularly at having one's birthday forgotten: "Fuck you for forgetting my birthday". While this song was more self-referential than most nominated songs, the text here again emphasizes the importance to individuals of having their birthday acknowledged by other people.

The birthday song sample also contained significantly fewer verbs, particularly those in the present tense. As the NVIVO analysis suggests, where verbs were used, these often related to suggesting a future event, such as in 'let's party', or 'come and dance'. The birthday sample similarly contained more positive emotion words and less negative emotion words than the standard sample. However, they used fewer words indicative of cognitively complex thinking, more words relating to time, e.g. "let's have a good time", and more words relating to leisure. There were no significant differences between the standard song sample and the birthday song sample in words relating to family, money, work or achievement, among other things. Thus, the linguistic analysis highlights the focus on socializing and celebrating in the birthday songs nominated by participants.

After nominating their own choice for a song to be played at a key birthday celebration, participants were played an excerpt from Stevie Wonder's "Happy Birthday", a single released in 1981. The song was written by Stevie Wonder as part of a campaign for the birthday of Martin

[4]All results reported in this paragraph had $p < 0.001$ and Cohen's $d > 0.3$.

Luther King Jr. to become a national holiday in the U.S., a campaign which was ultimately successful in 1983. Martin Luther King Jr., was a humanitarian and a leader in the African-American civil rights movement who promoted non-violent methods for achieving social change. This is reflected in the text of the song which declares that the whole world should set aside time to celebrate the life of a man who "died for good", and who stood for peace and unity.

Ten people had already chosen this song in the previous question about their choice of a birthday song. The most prevalent reason for choice of this song as a personal selection was that it was 'a good party song' ($n = 6$). Other reasons given were that the participant had a history with the song, they loved the era of the song, or that they enjoyed the musical features of the song. None mentioned the historical significance of the song or the political and social message contained in it. In response to the excerpt, 263 people (35.5%) also said this would be a song they would use at their own birthday celebration. The most frequent reasons given were that the song had 'a birthday vibe' ($n = 99$), that it had appealing musical features ($n = 45$) or that they were a fan of the artist ($n = 31$). Only 26 participants selected the reason that it was 'historically written for a birthday' and only 13 mentioned the political and social message in the song. The majority 64.5% ($n = 477$) said they would not use it for their birthday, primarily because it had no personal meaning for them ($n = 141$); was of a genre that was not their style ($n = 76$) or that they didn't find the music itself appealing ($n = 52$).

Overall these results suggest that for many people in the twenty-first century, birthdays are about celebrating with friends and family. The music selected tended to be positive in valence and high in arousal with lyrics that placed a high emphasis on fun and parties. The lyrical analysis also suggested the social nature of the event, as did the reasons participants gave for their selections. In order to illustrate how people use music to celebrate their birthdays, we now turn to a case study example of a fortieth birthday celebration.

Case Study: Joy's Birthday

Joy's case illustrates our other findings, with one key twist: Joy was a professional musician, so her celebration included many of her friends performing songs for her. The evening was held in a hotel, with 120 guests sitting in groups of 8 at tables spread out around a dance floor. Musician friends and associates had been invited to play in an ad hoc dance band, formed and led by one of the guests. These players arrived and rehearsed a little in advance of the event.

The evening itself began with commercially available recorded popular music playing over a sound system in the background. Joy described its function as being to "get the party spirit happening as guests arrived." Among the pre-selected choices were many of Joy's own favourite tracks, selected for their upbeat tempi and positive lyrics, e.g., "You are the sunshine of my life" by Stevie Wonder and many salsa tracks. As guests slipped from the bar to the dining area, that music continued, one group of 10–15 younger people (20s–30s) getting up onto the dance floor to the salsa music, and more or less offering the on-looking group a dance demonstration.

As the meal got underway, each course was interspersed with friends offering solo songs and short anecdotes about Joy, all being relevant to her birthday. This included some lighthearted material and some more serious, classical music with offerings from a Kurt Weill cabaret song to a singer-song writer ballad. The topic was about the passage from youth to middle age, much of it done tongue-in-cheek, and all emphasizing Joy's own energetic and lively nature. Joy herself a singer, performed 3 songs across the evening: first, a humorous song mocking divas ("The Diva's Lament" by Betty Rowe); second, a George Gershwin song about what kind of music the singer should like ("By Strauss"); and finally, a cover of Madonna's "Material Girl", with a change of lyrics to fit Joy's own life and work. This final number then led into the dance band's performance and an ensuing dance floor party with people dancing the Conga, and generally having fun.

At Joy's birthday, music was the primary ingredient of the party: it provided a vehicle to channel the emotions of happiness that were spread through the group of 120, many who did not know one another. Through songs, fitting lyrics and sentiments were shared; through dance music, energetic physical action spread out from the band to the dance floor and on into the onlooking guests who could be seen clapping and tapping in time to the Conga beat. The presence of the live entertainment amplified the proximity and engagement of the audience with the sights and sounds of the music. While this was not a coming of age ritual, on this occasion, music formed a central part of the celebrations, marking a personally significant milestone in a way that reflected Joy's own identity as a musician, and illustrating the way music is inextricably entwined in the recognition of individual's arriving at key life moments in the twenty-first century.

The Trajectory from the Past to the Modern Day

In technologically advanced Western societies in the modern day, the demarcation between childhood and adulthood is often less formally marked than it was in the past. Indeed, children and adolescents today attain the various responsibilities of adulthood in gradual increments, perhaps reaching sexual maturity well before they reach the age of legal majority, drink alcohol, drive a car, or earn a living independently of their parents.

In fact, in Western countries, adolescence—a period between puberty and adulthood—is a relatively new 'discovery'. While puberty occurs in early adolescence, coming of age in modern day life in technologically advanced countries may occur in the late teens and early twenties. However, this has not always been the case. As noted in the previous chapter, youths typically began earning a living, got married and began to raise their own children at a much earlier age in previous centuries than they do today. Today, increased standards of living have meant that puberty typically occurs some four years earlier in youths than it did in the nineteenth century (Cote & Allahar, 1994), while economic independence tends to occur much later. 'Education inflation' means that young people typically need to spend much longer in education before entering the workforce in order to compete for available jobs. Quentin Schultze and colleagues (Schultze et al., 1991), for example, report that only 6% of young people aged 14–17 were still in school in the U.S. in 1890, compared to 90% in 1980. Thus adolescence is a relatively new phenomenon in some sense, with sexually mature individuals remaining dependent on their families for many years before taking on the responsibilities of adulthood that youths in centuries past would have been expected to incur many years earlier. This prolonged period of proximity to family is argued by some to be an important contributing factor to the stress and conflict that tends to characterize adolescence in the modern day (Cote & Allahar, 1994).

How, then, is coming of age marked in the twenty-first century? Since the beginning of puberty no longer coincides with the commencement of adult responsibilities, few formal rituals exist in technologically advanced countries to mark the transition from childhood to adolescence. However, even where people do not engage in such formal initiation rituals, coming of age may still be marked within smaller social units. Howe (2002) remarks, for example, that "a substantial number of family rituals appear to involve occasions for celebrating or marking major life transitions for one or more family members" (p. 439). He further argues that such celebrations are often accompanied by distinct changes in relationships between family members, including changing roles, responsibilities and levels of engagement in various aspects of family life. Whether or not such changes in family expectations precede or occur in response to the celebrations that mark these major life transitions is not completely understood.

Less formal rituals may also be marked in peer groups. New arrivals at a high school, for example, may undergo arduous ordeals of initiation that are reminiscent of those in tribal initiation ceremony, such as including 'hazing'—pranks or acts of humiliation or ridicule—or involvement in behaviours considered signifiers of maturity such as smoking, drinking, and dating. However, Cassandra Delaney (1995) argues that rituals in which a change in status is acknowledged only by peers rather than by societal elders, lacks the power of more traditional rituals:

> This, along with the lack of established structure, often diminishes the sense of legitimacy of these rites. Also, without the participation of elders, the initiates are not likely to experience a feeling of continuity. They are not afforded the wisdom of past generations and the empowerment to carry these on into the future. Thus, young people who must initiate themselves or each other do not have an opportunity to gain a view of themselves as part of a greater pattern. (p. 894)

More formalized rituals tend to be celebrated towards the end of adolescence, as young people move towards increasing independence and responsibility. In the twenty-first century, coming of age often coincides with graduation from high school and going to college or University which for many, involves moving away from the family home and experiencing a greater degree of freedom and autonomy than ever before (Dunham et al., 1986; Moffatt, 1989). Formalized observances here include graduations ceremonies, formal proms and dances that are often preceded by a lengthy period of tests and ordeals in order to reach this landmark stage. These stages in a young person's life tend to involve more public and adult acknowledgement of the individual's attainment, although many of them centre around activities with peers. However, for many individuals, they still do not necessarily represent a significant change in status, since a level of independence from parents may already have been achieved. For others, even graduation may not involve any great changes to their status or level of dependence on their parents. These rituals seldom involve any sharing of cultural knowledge or ancestral wisdom as have coming of age in traditional societies.

Given that coming of age is seldom marked with the level of ceremony today that it has been in the past or still is in less technologically advanced societies, birthday celebrations of a key age such as 'sweet sixteen', turning eighteen, or twenty-one, or even a fortieth birthday may represent a more significant way in which landmarks of personal development and achievement are marked in many parts of the world in the twenty-first century. Such celebrations may include both peers and important adults in the lives of a young person and may also mark the attainment of certain legal privileges, such as being able to learn to drive, or to legally drink. On the other hand, as illustrated by our case study, older adults may also mark the attainment of a particular age through similar celebrations as a testament to life achievements.

Evidence suggests that acknowledgement of the attainment of such milestones is psychologically valuable in the lives of young people. In fact, there is a strong argument for the fact that a lack of formal coming of age rituals can contribute to the tension that teenagers often experience in transitioning from childhood to adulthood. The teen years can be a period of intense conflict between parents and their children as both struggle to balance and adjust to the growing independence of the adolescent.

While we may tend to blame hormonal and biological changes for the difficulties of adolescence, some scholars suggest that this is of minimal impact (Brooks-Gunn & Warren, 1989). In fact, anthropological evidence confirms that adolescence is not accompanied by such difficulties in all cultures, tending to substantiate the idea that culture and community play an important role in shaping adolescent behavior during this period of transition (Cote & Allahar, 1994). Elkind (2001) argues that coming of age rituals provide some security from the struggle of adolescence, taking some of the confusion and ambiguity out of teenage transformations, since they provide a definitive landmark of the new phase of the youth's life. It likely influences adult behavior towards the youth as well, serving as a demarcation point beyond which adult expectations change.

The fact that rituals such as graduations, debutante balls, or spontaneous rituals that have developed around the attainment of a particular age, are regaining in popularity, is testimony to the psychological need that they can fill. Joy's fortieth birthday, referenced earlier, provides an example of this. However, such rites in technologically advanced nations tend to receive comparatively little attention compared to the ethnographic intercultural descriptions of exotic dances and ceremonies (Dunham et al., 1986).

Richard Dunham and colleagues (1986) argues that since non-traditional rites of passage often result only in nominally changed roles, their key importance lies in the social recognition of transitioning role boundaries that they provide. They call the more formal ceremonial occasion a "macro-rite" while arguing that macro-ties are both preceded and followed by numerous less formal and dramatic "micro-rites" which are also important in marking the transition (p. 150). Delaney (1995) similarly argues that while the forms of adolescent rites of passage can vary greatly, the key elements are the need for the involvement of elders, and a recognized change in status.

In summary, therefore, in technologically advanced nations in the twenty-first century we see a resurgence of interest in formal coming of age ceremonies such as graduations and debutante balls that had dwindled in the latter decades of the twentieth centuries. However, these seldom signal the same changes of status of coming of age that they may have in other time periods and cultural contexts.

These changes are broadly reflected in the music that people use to mark important coming of age birthdays. The role of the music itself has also changed greatly. In previous tempo-cultural contexts, music was used to protect young people from spirits, educate them about sex and gender roles, to initiate them into the cultural wisdom of their elders, or to signal their marriageability. However, the music used in modern-day coming of age rituals, whether in large social groups or smaller units such as families, has little to do with the passing on of knowledge or cultural traditions. In fact, few people in our modern-day sample selected music for either its message or its role in tradition. Even of those who nominated the well-known 'Happy Birthday' song, at least half did not come from an English-speaking background and therefore could not say that it represented tradition for them. In addition, the lyrical content of the songs revealed that complex ideas and thoughts, and thoughts about responsibility, adulthood or family roles were seldom the subject of these birthday songs. Rather they focused on themes of celebration. Even where a song with an important cultural and social message was a popular choice with Stevie Wonder's "Happy Birthday", few people seemed to be aware or interested in its political significance. This reflects a wider phenomenon, in that the growth of modern technology has increased the emphasis on individuality and made it easier for youths to shape their lives in ways very different to that of their parents or their own cultural heritage (Tinning & Fitzclarence, 1992).

Nevertheless, we see how the musical selections tend to confirm the importance of social acknowledgement of the individual's attainment, an aspect that seems to be a common factor in coming of age rituals from the traditional tribal societies of Africa to the modern cities of the twenty-first century. While individuals preferred musical selections that reflected their own characters or musical taste, the importance of the music providing the right 'vibe' for a social celebration was paramount to most participants. The lyrical analysis similarly revealed an emphasis on external recognition of the event. This reflects a common source of internal conflict in many societies in the twenty-first century, the fact that while individuality is increasingly emphasized, social acknowledgement, particularly of key life moments, is still a strong psychological need. Thus musical selections again provide an interesting reflection of broader social changes as well as playing important psychological functions in the celebration of key-life rituals cross-culturally and throughout the centuries.

REFERENCES

Blacking, J. (1985). Movement, Dance, Music and the Venda Girls Initiation Cycle. In P. Spencer (Ed.), *Society and Dance: The Social Anthropology of Process and Performance* (pp. 64–91). Cambridge, UK: Cambridge University Press.

Brooks-Gunn, J., & Warren, M. P. (1989). Biological and Social Contributions to Negative Affect in Young Adolescent Girls. *Child Development, 60*(1), 40–55.

Cantu, N. E. (2002). Chicana Life-Cycle Rituals. In N. E. Cantu & O. Najera-Ramirez (Eds.), *Chicana Traditions: Continuity and Change* (pp. 15–34). Illinois: University of Illinois Press.

Cote, J. E., & Allahar, A. (1994). *Generation on Hold: Coming of Age in the Late Twentieth Century.* New York: New York University Press.

Delaney, C. H. (1995). Rites of Passage in Adolescence. *Adolescence, 30*(120), 891–897.

Dunham, R. M., Kidwell, J. S., & Wilson, S. M. (1986). Rites of Passage at Adolescence: A Ritual Process Paradigm. *Journal of Adolescent Research, 1*(2), 139–154.

Edelman, M. B. (2003). *Discovering Jewish Music.* Jewish Publication Society.

Elkind, D. (2001). *The Hurried Child.* Cambridge, MA: Da Capo Press.

Escales, J. E. (1993). The Consumption of Insignificant Rituals: A Look at Debutante Balls. *Advances in Consumer Research, 20,* 709–716.

Glassman, T., Dodd, V., Kenzik, K., Miller, E. M., & Sheu, J. J. (2010). Social Norms vs. Risk Reduction Approaches to 21st Birthday Celebrations. *American Journal of Health Education, 41*(1), 38–45.

Gleason, J., & Ibubuya, A. (1991). My Year Reached, We Heard Ourselves Singing: Dawn Songs of Girls Becoming Women in Ogbogbo, Okrika, Rivers State, Nigeria. *Research in African Literatures, 22*, 135–147.

Hanawalt, B. A. (1995). *Growing Up in Medieval London: The Experience of Childhood in History.* Oxford: Oxford University Press.

Howe, G. W. (2002). Integrating Family Routines and Rituals with Other Family Research Paradigms: Comment on the Special Section. *Journal of Family Psychology, 16*(4), 437–440.

Jones, T., & Webb, S. (2013). Diamonds, Dance Classes and Dramas at the Debutante Ball: Behind-the-Scenes at London's Most Prestigious Society Event. *Daily Mail Online.* Retrieved from http://www.dailymail.co.uk/femail/article-2479511/Diamonds-dance-classes-dramas-debutante-ball-Behind-scenes-Londons-prestigious-society-event.html

Kroger, J. (2006). *Identity Development: Adolescence Through Adulthood.* SAGE Publications.

La Fontaine, J. S. (1986). *Initiation: Ritual Drama and Secret Knowledge Across the World.* Manchester: Manchester University Press.

Lincoln, B. (1991). *Emerging from the Chrysalis.* Cambridge: Harvard University Press.

Maas, U., & Strubelt, S. (2003). Music Is the Iboga Initiation Ceremony in Gabon: Polyrhythms Supporting a Pharmacotherapy. *Music Therapy Today, 4*(3).

Moffatt, M. (1989). *Coming of Age in New Jersey: College and American Culture.* New Jersey: Rutgers University Press.

Naomi, M. N. (2014). Evolutionary Changes in Thematic Lyrics in Songs with Reference to the Akamba Circumcision Songs in Kenya. *Mediterranean Journal of Social Sciences, 5*(5), 297–304.

Pennebaker, J. W., Booth, R. J., & Francis, M. E. (2007). *Linguistic Inquiry and Word Count: LIWC [Computer Software].* Austin, TX: LIWC.net.

Read, K. E. (1952). Nama Cult of the Central Highlands, New Guinea. *Oceania, 23*(1), 1–25.

Roscoe, P. B. (1995). Initiation in Cross-Cultural Perspective. In N. Lutkehaus & P. Roscoe (Eds.), *Gender Rituals: Female Initiation in Melanesia.* London: Routledge.

Schultze, Q. J., Anker, R. M., Bratt, J. D., Romanowski, W. D., Worst, J. W., & Zuidervaart, L. (1991). *Dancing in the Dark: Youth, Popular Culture, and the Electronic Media.* Michigan: Wm B. Eerdmans Publishing Co.

Tinning, R., & Fitzclarence, L. (1992). Postmodern Youth Culture and the Crisis in Australian Secondary School Physical Education. *Quest, 44*(3), 287–303.

Van Gennep, A. (1960). *The Rites of Passage* (Vol. 3). Routledge.

Whiting, J. W. M., Kluckhohn, R., & Anthony, A. (1958). The Function of Male Initiation Ceremonies at Puberty. In E. E. Maccoby, T. M. Newcomb, & E. L. Hartley (Eds.), *Readings in Social Psychology* (pp. 359–370). New York: Henry Holt & Co.

CHAPTER 10

Love and Heartbreak

HISTORICAL AND CROSS-CULTURAL PRACTICES

Love in Songs of Ancient Times

Romantic love appears to be a concept that is found in all cultures around the world and across time periods, albeit in differing forms and with varying degrees of importance (Jankowiak & Fischer, 1992). In fact, although some historians at times have proposed that the notion of romantic love was basically a European construct (see for e.g. Stone, 1988), others have argued that romantic love is a biological imperative. William Jankowiak and Edward Fischer (1992) define romantic love as an "intense attraction that involves the idealization of the other, within an erotic context, with the expectation of enduring for some time into the future" (p. 150). It is that longevity of connection which differentiates the drive to find romantic love from the sex drive. While the latter ensures human reproduction, romantic love motivates humans to attach themselves to a single mate, enabling them to create a stable environment in which to perform parenting duties (Fisher, Aron, & Brown, 2006).

Music has been intrinsically linked to romantic love throughout much of human history, and in fact, may be closely related to the very evolutionary function that music has served in human development. Charles Darwin himself proposed this, noting that for some bird species, song provides a similar function to the brightly coloured tail of the peacock—it helps them

S. Garrido, J. W. Davidson, *Music, Nostalgia and Memory*, Palgrave Macmillan Memory Studies,
https://doi.org/10.1007/978-3-030-02556-4_10

to attract mates. Although music has also served other evolutionary functions, song has likely played a role in mate selection and courtship since before pre-human times.

Of course fertility songs—performed to encourage procreation and abundance in humans, livestock and crops alike—are about as old as recorded human history. Some of the earliest recorded love songs come from Sumerian literature dating from around 2100–1800 BCE (Sefati, 1998). Rather than focusing on the love affairs of mortals, these songs deal with the love, courtship and sacred marriage of the Mesopotamian goddess of love and fertility Ishtar (Inanna). The songs form part of the fertility rituals of the ancient Sumerians, in which the king of Sumer had to marry the goddess Ishtar in order to ensure the prosperity of the Sumerian people (Kramer, 1962). The rituals were probably enacted with a priestess representing the bride, but the language of the songs paints love in terms of the sacred and transcendent, something that we are to see reappear in the love songs of other cultures and time periods.

Other early examples of loves songs come from ancient Egypt, such as those found on the Chester Beatty I Papyrus, and vase fragments in the Cairo Museum, dating to around 1300 BC (Ackerman, 1995). However, unlike the Sumerian examples, these Egyptian love songs deal very much with an earthly experience of love with all its frustration and thwarted desire. A frequently used image in the Egyptian songs is that of a lover outside his beloved's door who is lamenting his inability to gain access—an image that has become known as *paraklausithyron* (from the Greek meaning 'lament beside the door'). The very words for love song in ancient Egyptian texts *tekhm* and *tekhtekhw* are related to words meaning to drink or become drunk, leading some scholars to conclude that the Egyptians believed the behaviour of one who is in love to be akin to that of a drunkard (Badham, 2014). The texts often concern intimate descriptions of the beloved's person, using rich imagery that is a precursor to Solomon's Song of Songs and that is still found in love songs today.

Outside of Europe, ancient examples of romantic love can be found in song as well. In China, love songs from all over the empire were gathered together around the sixth century BC. These songs used scenes drawn from nature to illustrate romantic situations such as a bird calling to its mate to depict a man's longing for his loved one. However, as time progressed, Chinese attitudes towards sexual metaphor and imagery in literature and song became more repressive (Schimmelpenninck, 1997). While the peasant-class tended to continue to accept them, a large number of folk texts including songs were banned and destroyed between 213 and 210 BC (Gioia, 2015), with repression reaching a peak in the time of the neo-Confucianists from the ninth to eleventh centuries. In fact, religious and governmental censure of love songs seems a common and recurrent theme in many parts of the world at various times throughout history.

The Medieval and Early Modern Periods

The most comprehensive history of love songs that has been compiled to date is Ted Gioia's *Love Songs: The Hidden History* (2015). In it, Gioia traces the origins of many features of modern day love songs right back to antiquity, through the times of the troubadours and the jazz age of the early twentieth century. He argues that love songs have frequently been the force behind social change and have been subject to strident opposition. For example, in the early medieval period, the love song was the subject of ardent hostility by Christian religious leaders. The Council of Auxerre (651–65) prohibited *puellarum cantica* (songs of girls) that were commonly sung in villages in Spain because of their capacity to incite lust. Similarly, other sources from the eighth to tenth centuries contain condemnations of love songs, particularly during church festivities.

However, according to Gioia, while this repression continued in the Christian world, the conquering of the Iberian peninsula by Islamic forces meant that by the late medieval period, the mark of African music—and particularly songs created in Egypt by female slaves—could be found in the music of Europe. By the time of the troubadours, music would carry the evidence of both this Moorish influence and the idea of love as something mystical and supreme that was carried over from ancient Sumeria and from Christian influences.

These influences were apparent in the music of William IX, Duke of Aquitaine in southern France along with his contemporaries and successors, who created an idea of love that has come to be known as "courtly love". Several types of love songs have been preserved from the troubadour period: the *alba* (dawn) is set the morning after a clandestine lovers tryst when the lovers must part; the *pastorela*, a playful song in which a knight encounters a shepherdess; the *descort* (discord) speaks of love from the perspective of one who does not have it; the *retroncha*, a song form of 4 stanzas about the state to which love reduces you; and, the *canso* in which all 5 or 6 stanzas speak agreeably of love. A common theme in many of these songs was the unattainableness of the lady love, who was often the wife of another or a woman of superior rank (O'Neill, 2006). Thus Barolini (2006) states that at the heart of Italian troubadour poetry was the "unresolved tension between the poet-lover's allegiance to the lady and his allegiance to God" (p. 482). In the courtly love of the troubadours, the leitmotif of service or bondage to the beloved was also common, likely due to the influence of the music of Moorish slaves. Many troubadour lyrics are about thwarted love and unreciprocated love, using Christian imagery of pilgrimage, sacrifice and knightly devotion.[1]

However, one of the most important sources of medieval love songs today contains a number of songs that contrast quite starkly with the courtly love of the troubadours. The Carmina Burana is a thirteenth century manuscript which was seized by Baron Johann Cristoph von Aretin from the Benedictine monastery of Benediktbeuern in Bavaria. The manuscript includes around 130 love songs likely written by itinerant scholars and poets, some of which contain vivid depictions of sensuality (e.g. CB 76, 183), and others which describe love as military service (CB 60, 62, 166) in terms quite different to those of the troubadours. German composer Carl Orff famously used 24 of the original texts in his musical setting of the same name.

However, the legacy of the troubadours has arguably been more enduring. Their influence on love songs and poetry can be seen in Spain, Germany, Sicily, England and other parts of Europe. In thirteenth century Portugal, for example, the *cantigas de amor*, followed the model of the French troubadours. Other Portuguese love songs from this period include the *cantigas de amigo* (songs about a boyfriend), in which small objects take on talismanic significance in the lyrics. These songs were both more emotionally intense than the songs of the troubadours, and more grounded in the obstacles and heartbreaks of the real world. Similarly, in Germany we find the minnesingers who also sang songs of courtly love. These included the *Weschel*: a dialogue between lovers, sometimes by means of a messenger or intermediary; the *Tagelied*: a dawn song about the sadness of lovers parting when the sun rises; the *Kreuzlied*: again about the love and sorrow of parting; the *Liebesgruss*: a praise of the beloved; and, the *Frauenlied*: a woman's lament about an absent or unfaithful lover.

After the troubadours, the Church began to draw on the imagery of the troubadours love lyrics to revive commitments to the church, such as in St.

---

[1] Track 57: A Troubadour's Woe—Medieval and Renaissance Music Troup.

Francis of Assisi's 'Canticle of the Sun'.[2] In these religious songs 'the Lord' or Mary took the place of the beloved, with some even depicting erotic situations about her. This merging of the troubadour tradition with Christian doctrine "aimed to disarm Cupid and enlist him in the ranks of angels" (Gioia, 2015, p. 140).

In the meantime, in other parts of the world, a similar linking of love and the divine was occurring. In Persia, for example, thirteenth century Islamic philosopher and poet Jalal-al-Din Rumi was writing of love as mystical and spiritual. Similarly, in India, the Hindu deity Krishna was often depicted as a musician. His love affair with a cowherdess was the focus of the *Gira Govina*, a poem from the twelfth century by Jayadeva. These songs also provided a basis for future depictions of divine love. In fact, the love songs of Vidyapati more than 500 years ago are still performed at weddings in his native region.

However, in Europe, by the beginning of the Renaissance period, the concept of love as divine was again being replaced by more vivid depictions of carnal pleasures. Since the Catholic church was more tolerant than Protestantism, much of this movement in love songs came from the south of Europe during this period, such as the *canti carnascialeschi* (carnival songs) written by Lorenzo de Medici in the fifteenth century.

A popular form of Italian song during the fifteenth and sixteenth centuries was the *frottola*, songs for multiple voices or performed solo with lute accompaniment, which became an important precursor to the madrigal. Bartolomeo Tromboncino was one of the most celebrated masters of this form. He set to music the words of famous poets including Petrarch ('Che debbo' iofar? Che mi consigli, Amore?') and even Michelangelo ('Come harò donque ardire'). These songs often presented love in humorous and sardonic terms, at other times the lyrics seem deeply melancholy.

The madrigal—a descendent of the frottola—achieved more widespread popularity than its predecessor in the Renaissance and early Baroque periods. Even in Britain where the songs of the troubadours had never reached a high level of popularity, the refined way in which love was depicted in many madrigals ensured their acceptance. While evincing a delicacy that appealed to the sensibility of many, the madrigal did, however, have an intimacy about them, a 'confessional tone' as Gioia puts it (p. 151).

---

[2] Track 75: Canticle of the Sun, St Francis of Assisi, Schola Gregoriana Del Coro Pare.

Monteverdi, for example, wrote a book of madrigals in 1638 that he entitled *Madrigali guerrieri, et amorosi* (Madrigals of War and Love).[3] Each section of the book—War and Love—includes madrigals, a dramatic piece (*genere rappresentativo*) and a ballet. Despite falling within the War section of Monteverdi's volume, Il *Combattimento di Tancredi e Clorinda*[4] narrates the story of Tancredi, a soldier in the crusade who falls in love with Clorinda who is a Saracen. He ultimately kills her when she disguises herself as a male soldier in order to fight in the battle for her people. In actual fact, the entire eighth book as well as *Combattimento* itself, presents a continual juxtaposition of love and war. The texts that Monteverdi uses in both sections intertwine the themes repeatedly. In *Combattimento* Monteverdi alternates between passages that depict combat and those depicting the passion between Tancredi and Clorinda, and describes in his foreword that it was the opportunity to depict these contrasting 'affections' that motivated his choice of text.

In Monteverdi's time discourse about the expression of the 'passions' was a focus among music theorists, and composers were exploring techniques for expressing them. This coincided with a strong interest in the application of narrative and dramatic techniques to music, and was highly influenced by neo-Platonic beliefs in relation to the 'harmony of the spheres', the 'doctrine of the humours', and the 'ethos' of musical modes, particularly as described by Boethius.[5] These developments culminated in the birth of opera in Florence in 1600, and the development of a set of fixed 'musical gestures' and formulas intended to convey certain emotions that came to dominate music in the Baroque period. *Combattimento* falls within a broader style of composition described by Monteverdi as his *seconda pratica*, works in which the music is designed to enhance the emotional content of the text.

The text on which *Combattimento* is based—the twelfth book of Tasso's *Gerusalemme liberate* (1581)—uses language which also continually displays this tangle of love and violence. As the combat commences between Tacredi and Clorinda, Tasso describes them as fighting "like two fierce bulls provoked by love or rage", revealing Tasso's perception of them as closely linked, almost interchangeable. At the most tense moments of their

---

[3] For a more detailed discussion see Davidson, Kiernan, and Garrido (2017).

[4] Track 76: Combattimento di Tancredi e Clorinda, Monteverdi, Helsinki Baroque Orchestra.

[5] See Chap. 4 for more details.

battle, the combatants are described as being in a lover's embrace: "Three times his strong arms he folds around her waist".

Monteverdi highlights these contrasts by the use of agitated, tremolo strings to heighten the tension of the battle scenes, with the use of long, sustained notes in the more reflective scenes in which the dramatic action is paused. Monteverdi also uses contrasting keys and contrasts in vocal range to represent distinct emotions. For example, in the more neutral narrative passages, Monteverdi uses the mid-range tones. However, the agitated *concitato* sections tend to utilize the higher range of the narrator's voice. In contrast, when the combat has come to an end, the narrator sings: "In these languid words there resounds a note so tearful and soft\ that it touches his heart and stifles all anger\ and induces and compels his eyes to shed tears",[6] in the lower section of his range.

Interesting also in Tasso's text is the depiction of a woman fighting 'like a man': calling to mind both images of the heroism of the inspiring female martyrs during the crusades, as well as perhaps a sense that such behavior was somehow unfeminine, or even un-Christian. In fact, in the heat of battle, Clorinda reveals herself as unyielding and provocative, forcing Tancredi to relinquish his embrace of her and goading him to greater fury by recounting her military victories. In Monteverdi's setting, Clorinda is stripped of her femininity. She is dressed in her armoured disguise from the beginning of the tale. Monteverdi omits Tasso's descriptions of 'golden locks' or 'blazing eyes' in the selections of text he chooses to set. We are told from the outset that Tancredi believes Clorinda to be a man, and Clorinda in her demeanour and words does nothing to contradict this belief. However, in the moments before she dies, Clorinda is transformed. She becomes at that moment, both a converted Christian, and the very model of feminine piety. While Tasso's story continues, Monteverdi chooses this poignant moment to end *Combattimento*, the drama closing with Clorinda singing with her last breath in high-pitched, angelic tones: "Farewell, I die in peace". In both his selection of text, and his suppression of the femininity of Clorinda until the moment that she becomes converted, Monteverdi reconstructs Tasso's depiction of feminine fury, passion and courage, shifting the focus to the sacrifice, bravery and righteousness of the hero Tancredi. In Monteverdi's setting, we thus see love depicted as both pious and a source of suffering, as it has been throughout much of human history.

[6] English translations of Monteverdi's text are cited in Calagno (2012).

Songs of heartbreak are similarly found in cultures all over the world during this same period, such as the songs composed by the 6th Dalai Lama Tsangyan Gyatso in seventeenth century Tibet (Gyatso, 1993). In Japan during the Edo period (1603–1867), popular songs about love often contained depictions of 'love suicides', seen as the ultimate demonstration of love. According to Gioia, this theme seems particularly prevalent in societies in which there was minimal freedom to pursue romantic relationships.

After the Renaissance

The Middle Ages saw the ascendancy of the printing press and the rise of an urban middle class in Europe. The increased affordability of pianos and their popularity among this emerging middle class meant that salon-type songs were more in demand. As printing became more sophisticated greater dissemination of the popular songs of the peasantry also became possible, such as the collection of ballads amassed by Francis Child in the nineteenth century. In fact, Gioia found that around 67% of the songs from the Child ballads were about love, with more than 40% including both love and violence.

Interestingly, these ballads were often centuries old and had changed with the times, reflecting changing attitudes towards gender and love that took place throughout the centuries. One of the most fascinating examples of this is the song that has become known as 'Scarborough Fair/ Canticle', recorded by Paul Simon and Art Garfunkel in 1966 on their album *Parsley, Sage, Rosemary and Thyme*. However, the song actually belongs to a family of ballads that date back to at least the seventeenth century (Garrido & Davidson, 2016). The earliest documented version of this song-family is found in a black letter broadside from the collection of Samuel Pepys (1633–1703) held in the English Broadside Ballad Archive at the University of California (Magdalene College Pepys—Miscellaneous 358, EBBA ID: 32070). The song text consists of a dialogue between a female character and an 'elphin knight', in which the woman expresses a wish that the knight were in her bed. The two protagonists then go on to set each other a series of impossible tasks or riddles as a sort of love contest, including things such as the sewing of a shirt with no cuts or seams.

The text of this version is filled with sexual imagery, which is often expressed by the female character. The ballad was evidently originally intended to be a sort of humorous and playful courtship song that was used largely in rural contexts (Douglas, 2004). However, it seems likely that the idea that the male protagonist was an 'elphin knight' or some kind of supernatural 'fairy lover' crept into the text in an effort to make the ballad more closely reflect the social mores of the time. While medieval courtly literature portrayed the virtuous woman as remote and undesiring, the passive recipient of pursuit by an ardent lover (Burns, 2001), female sexual desire and initiative was often associated with harlotry and witch-craft during the seventeenth century (Gowing, 2003). Thus the originally humorous song was transformed into a moralistic tale that promoted the idea that female sexuality and agency were indicative of collusion with the devil or witchcraft.

By the Victorian era, in one version of the ballad—'Whittingham Fair'—the woman's role in the tale has been restricted even further. All reference to her sexuality and much of the sexual imagery is gone. In fact the male and female characters do not even communicate directly, but through an unnamed intermediary in much the same way that trouba-dour songs often involved the transmission of a lover's message to a far-off love by an envoy (Burns, 2001). Subtle changes in the tasks described in the ballad also reflect feminine economic dependency in the nine-teenth century.

By the time Simon and Garfunkel recorded their version, the 'hippie' counter-culture that stressed free love, freedom of speech and peace, was in full swing (Lund & Denisoff, 1971). Their version displays a simplicity of vocal style that puts it within the revival in interest in folk music that accompanied this era, suggesting an idealization of the simple pastoral life. Against a backdrop of the Vietnam war, Simon and Garfunkel also added to the traditional ballad a counter-melody drawn from an anti-war song called 'The Side of a Hill', which Simon had written some years earlier. In addition, the female protagonist in the original story never speaks at all in the text that Simon and Garfunkel used. Rather she is described perform-ing the tasks alone. The effect of these changes is to shift the focus of the song from one of courtship to the image of a lonely, heartsick soldier pin-ing for a distant love, while the women left at home must bear the load on the home front alone. In the context of the anti-war protests occurring at the time, the song thus depicts the pain and sense of futility that perme-ated public perceptions of the Vietnam war in many circles. In its transfor-mations, this ballad thus demonstrates the changing perspectives towards gender roles and love over time, metamorphosing from a humorous, bawdy courtship song, to a social commentary on female sexuality and a protest against war and social restriction.

The eighteenth and nineteenth centuries in Europe also saw the emergence of romanticism—a creative movement in which the expression of the passions was even more celebrated. In this period again, we see a great deal of focus on the pain and suffering of love, the yearning for the unattainable. Opera surpassed the madrigal in its capacity to depict love in dramatic ways, a factor which led to its strict censorship. Verdi's love scenes in *La Traviata* for example, are filled with tension, and his heroin, Violetta, makes the ultimate sacrifice of giving up her love and her own life for her beloved Alfredo. Wagner too imbued his operas with suffering, using highly disturbing chromatic harmony to depict the frustration of unconsummated love in *Tristan and Isolde*.

With the further advent of recording technologies in the twentieth and twenty-first centuries, love songs were able to be mass-produced, and thus entered the world of commerce. Nevertheless, music has continued to both shape and lend expression to social revolutions. Thus the twentieth century saw love songs move from the intimate tone of the crooners, to the 'free love' movement in the music of the Beatles and Simon and Garfunkel for example, through to the raw and deeply personal expression of the so-called 'indie' (independent) singer-songwriters of today.

Folk music from all over the world carries similar themes of love, both its pleasant side, and the pain of love gone wrong. It is to be found in the *min-yo* folk songs of Japan (Matsubara, 1946), in the lyric songs of Russia (Propp, 1993), and the *shan'ge* folk songs of China (Schimmelpenninck, 1997). In some cultures the link between courtship and music is particularly overt. For example, in southern Peru, the *charango*—a stringed instrument that looks much like a small guitar—is traditionally used as an integral part of courting rituals. Every young man will develop skills on the instrument and uses it in a series of elaborate rituals to signal his intentions to the object of his affections, and subsequently to signal the progress of the relationship to the community (Turino, 1983). In fact, the association between the *charango* and courtship is so strong that generally once married, a man will stop playing his *charango* altogether. In Japan, in the eleventh century music also played an important role in romance and courtship among the nobility because of the social limitations placed upon direct contact between the sexes (see for example, the *Tale of Genji* by Murasaki Shikibu).

However, in other cultures, notions of romance are less important. For example, among the Alawa tribe of northern Australia, an account from the 1960s demonstrates that men may sing magical love songs for help in securing a mate, but Western notions of courtship and romance play little part in this process (Lockwood, 1962). As Gioia puts it: "The quest for a suitable mate is itself a type of hunting and that the music that accompanies it is not just a passive soundtrack, rather a formidable tool that, in the hands of the skilled hunter, contributes to success in the chase" (p. 10). Similarly, the Flathead Indians of Western Montana believe that love songs are provided by guardian spirits, and can exert magical power over the beloved.

This review of love songs through history demonstrates that while themes of love have permeated the music of all cultures and time periods, this music both reflects and shapes the prevalent attitudes towards love and gender in every context. Historically, this seems to include frequent swings between a focus on the carnal and on the divine, with particular periods in history appearing to contain greater emphasis on the suffering of love than its joys. As we will see in the next section, music still plays a role in courtship and in coping with heartbreak today.

Modern-Day Playlists

Just as love has permeated song throughout history, it continues to do so in the modern age. Donald Horton (1957) found that 87.2% of the popular music in the 1950s in the U.S. was about love. In the 1960s this seemed to decrease slightly as political concerns became a topic for popular songs, but James Carey (1969) still found that in 1966 69.5% of the songs were about love. An informal survey of songs from the Billboard Hot 100 charts in 2015 seemed to indicate that love is back on the agenda, with four of the five songs examined being love songs (Temple, 2015).

While the prevalence of love songs does not appear to have radically changed over time, the ideals of love and the role of the individuals within them have changed greatly. Melvin Wilkinson (1976) looked at songs that were popular between 1954 and 1968 and found that the lyrics often echoed traditional sex-role expectations. However, some songs reflected concepts of gender that diverged from mainstream beliefs of the time. Wilkinson suggested that this demonstrated the desire for an equalizing in romantic love and provided an opportunity for men to express ideas generally considered un-masculine in Western society at the time. In this way they seemed to prefigure the social changes that were beginning to emerge during those decades. A similar study that looked at the 100 most popular songs between 1958 and 1998 (Dukes, Bisel, Borega, Lobato, & Owens, 2003), found that while the percentage of love songs did not change significantly over the period, the lyrical content did. The authors found that fewer love words were used over time, while references to sex, particularly by male singers, tended to increase. The authors attributed this change to the sexual revolution of the 1960s and 1970s.

What about in the twenty-first century? Does music still play a role in courtship, and if so, what kind of music do people most often use? How does music reflect current perspectives about love and gender? How do we use music to cope with heartbreak and what role does it play in our memories and nostalgia for past loves? On the MLAP website 668 participants (188 males, 475 females, and 5 unspecified) with a mean age of 33 years completed our survey. Participants were asked to nominate both a song that they would listen to in a romantic situation such as a first date and a song that they would listen to if they were feeling heartbroken.

Songs for Romance

The songs named by our participants that they would use for a first date came from a wide variety of genres. The majority were rock (31%) or pop songs (24%). However, even genres such as electronic (5%), hard rock and metal (2%), and classical/instrumental (6%) were represented. Participants rated these songs as being quite positive in valence ($m = 4.1$),[7] and slightly above neutral in arousal levels ($m = 3.5$). The vast majority of nominated songs had lyrics, most sung by male singers (72%), while 19% had female singers, 5% were instrumental and 3% were sung by a male and female duo. There were no significant differences in choice of singer between male and female participants. Some of the most popular songs nominated are shown in Table 10.1. The selections show a mixture of both slow and relatively fast tempos, but are almost exclusively in major keys. Other popularly noted artists and composers included Coldplay, Claude Debussy, Ed Sheeran, Norah Jones, Frank Sinatra and Taylor Swift.

These results differ somewhat from the results of Tia DeNora's interview with 52 women in *Music and Everyday Life* (2000) in which she

---

[7] Both valence and arousal were rated on scales of 1–5 with a neutral score being represented by 3.

Table 10.1   Frequently nominated songs for a first date

Artist	Song names	Genre	Approx tempo (bpm)	Key
Avril Lavigne (also Sixpence none the richer)	Kiss Me	Pop	100	Major
Beatles	I Want to Hold your Hand	Rock	148	Major
Blink 182	First date	Rock	200	Major
Bruno Mars	You can count on me	Pop	168	Major
	Just the way you are	Pop	104	Major
Christina Perri	A thousand years	Pop	48	Major
Falling Joys	Lock It	Rock	80	Major
Leonard Cohen	Suzanne	Folk	68	Major
Marvin Gaye	Let's Get It On	Soul	80	Major
Nick Cave	Into my arms	Rock	92	Major
Puccini	One Fine Day	Classical	52	Major
The Smiths	There is a light	Rock	142	Minor

states that none of the women nominated fast or loud music as something they would use as a prelude to intimacy. While we did not examine whether men and women selected music of different tempos, we did find that there were some differences in genre choices between the genders. Most genres were selected by an equal proportion of men and women, but women were more likely to select Soul music than men, while men were likely to select Hard Rock than women. These differences tend to support DeNora's findings to some degree. However, some genres such as hard rock, rap and hip-hop, which tend to have a tougher, more masculine sound, are liked by a number of women, and it cannot therefore be assumed that DeNora's findings apply to all women. In addition, our survey particularly asked people what they would use for a first date, rather than as a general prelude to intimacy. In general, the song selections nominated by our participants seem to be rather light-hearted and 'upbeat' rather than romantic. This may suggest the more casual tone that an individual might wish to achieve on a first date as compared to the more romantic tone that one might aim for as a relationship progresses.

The idea that many participants preferred to keep their music relatively non-romantic on a first date was borne out by the reasons participants gave for their selections. The most frequently cited reasons for choosing the selected piece was that the participant liked particular features of the music itself (58%) or was a fan of the artist or composer (41%).[8] Other reasons were that it expressed the participant's own ideals about love (32%), or it brought up special memories (26%). Only 32% of participants selected a song because it was 'romantic'. Other reasons reported were that it was good to dance to, that it has a happy or fun feel to it, that it made good background music, or to get a laugh. Others wanted to select songs that didn't have any clear messages or that wasn't 'too obvious', or wanted music that would make them feel relaxed. These selections may be reflective of both the newness of any relationship in a first date situation, as well as the casual approach taken to dating in a world where online dating and 'hook-ups' are the norm, particularly among younger age groups.

The songs nominated for a first date also differed depending on the coping style of the individual. People with high scores in rumination and other less healthy coping styles such as denial, emotion-focused coping and behavioural disengagement were most likely to rate the song they nominated as negatively valenced. This could reflect either a tendency to view the songs negatively or could reflect a generally negative perspective on love and hence a tendency to choose sadder songs in relation to love even outside of a situation of heartbreak.

Having conducted an extensive study of the predecessors of 'Scarborough Fair' as discussed above (Garrido & Davidson, 2016), we also wanted to find out how the modern day MLAP participants would respond to the Simon and Garfunkel version. Participants were able to listen to a recording of the song during the survey and were asked to describe any images or thoughts that were evoked by hearing the song. The majority of responses involved descriptions of some kind of pastoral or peasant-like imagery such as forests, villages, meadows of long grass or flowers, or 'long-haired, barefoot maidens'. Descriptions of personal memories evoked by the music were also numerous, particularly of family members such as parents, grandparents or siblings who had introduced them to the music. Frequent descriptions were also made of the emotions evoked by the music with the music being variously described as calm, soothing, eerie, peaceful, sad and whimsical.

Several participants also mentioned the concept of love in their descriptions, describing romantic scenarios such as carriage rides, dancing, or picnics in fields, while others commented on its association with courtly love and chivalry or a time when love was 'simpler'. Some participants

---

[8] Participants could select as many options as applied to them.

described the song as being a sad love song, about past love and loss. Others associated the music with medieval imagery such as knights, castles and troubadours. Only five participants appeared to know about the connection of this song with the anti-war movement, or anything to do with the historical origins of the music.

These results indicate that neither the original meanings of the songs (as far as we can understand them now), nor the emotional narrative created in Simon and Garfunkel's version were culturally available to the participants in our sample. Rather, the song had taken on a new meaning to listeners in the twenty-first century based on references far outside the narrative of the song. People who reported that they liked the song often did so because of its personal nostalgic connection to their youth or an idealized nostalgia for what they perceived to be a representation of chivalric love and a simple rustic lifestyle (see Chap. 2). Thus even a ballad that has held many historical meanings over the centuries is understood in the twenty-first century in the light of the idealized concepts of love that are current today. Such attraction to the concept of 'chivalry' and romance as they are perceived by many people today, perhaps represents a discomfort in some with the difficulties of negotiating gender roles in modern relationships. Thus on some level, the love songs of today often contain a note of mourning for an ideal of love that is rarely encountered in all the glory that in which it is depicted in fantasy and fiction.

Songs of Heartbreak

Our MLAP participants again nominated a wide range of genres reflecting personal tastes for the song they would listen to when feeling heartbroken. Pop and Rock again rated highly (24% each). However, a higher proportion of songs from the singer-songwriter and folk genre (27%) were nominated than for the song for a first date. These songs typically involve a single artist playing an acoustic instrument, and thus often convey a more intimate tone than larger bands or ensembles. Table 10.2 shows some of the most popular heartbreak song nominations. It is also obvious that these songs are considerably slower than many in the first date list. Other popular artists included Air Supply, Damien Rice, Nick Cave, and The Cure. Again, the songs selected were predominantly by male vocalists (61%) with a smaller proportion being by a female vocalist (34%), by a male and female duo (1%), or having no lyrics at all (3%). However, inter-

Table 10.2 Frequently nominated songs for heartbreak

Artist	Song names	Genre	Approx tempo (bpm)	Key
Adele	Someone Like You[a]	Pop	76	Major
Bon Iver (or Bonnie Raitt)	I Can't Make You Love Me	Folk	76	Major
Chicago	If You Leave Me Now	Rock	60	Major
Jeff Buckley (or Leonard Cohen)	Hallelujah	Rock	72	Major
John Mayer	Dreaming with a Broken Heart	Singer-songwriter	68	Major
Missy Higgins	Special Two	Singer-songwriter	76	Major
Passenger	Let Her Go	Folk	80	Major
Radiohead	Exit Music	Rock	60	Minor
Rod Stewart	I Don't Want to Talk About It	Pop	72	Major
Sinead O'Connor	Nothing Compares to You	Pop	60	Major
Taylor Swift	All Too Well	Country	92	Major
Yeah Yeah Yeahs	Maps	Rock	94	Major

[a]Track 77: Someone Like You, Adele

estingly this does represent a higher proportion of female singers than the first date selections.

A comparison of the top 10 words in the lyrics of the most highly rated songs for both a first date and when suffering heartbreak (Tables 10.1 and 10.2) revealed some interesting differences. Both categories of songs used the word 'love' frequently, but this was even more frequent in the heartbreak songs. The context of these words in the case of the first date songs was more positive, with phrases such as 'I'll love you for a thousand more', while the heartbreak songs used the word in the context of loss, pain or the absence of love, e.g. 'the love you don't feel'. The word 'when', signifying a time at which a particular action did or would occur, was also among the most frequently used words in each group of songs, occurring more frequently again in the heartbreak songs. Once again, the first date songs related to positive, ongoing events in phrases such as 'when you smile', while in the heartbreak songs the word often occurred in a context of remembering past events, such as in 'there was a time when'. Other words in the first date songs suggest hope such as the word 'forever', or attachment as in the word 'never' ("I'll never let go"), suggesting the optimism of new love and the idealization of the beloved. Other words used in the first date songs imply a desire to move the relationship forward such as in "let's" and "want", or a confidence in the beloved person, as in the word 'know' ("I know that you do too"). The word 'know' was also used in the heartbreak songs, but often related to knowing too late, "only know you love her when you let her go", or knowledge that the relationship is over "I know it's long gone".

The word "like" also features in both song lists. In the first date songs the word like was used both to express approval as in "I really like you" and in similes such as "sank beneath your wisdom like a stone". Similes used in the heartbreak songs express a hopelessness, such as in "like a bird without a song", "to break me like a promise". In the heartbreak songs the word 'cause' was generally used as a dialectical expression of 'because', and often expressed a searching for meaning in the lyrics of the song (e.g. "Cause you loved her too much"). Thus, while the lyrics of the first date songs seem to express hope, optimism, confidence, and future-oriented thinking, the lyrics of the heartbreak songs express the pain of loss, and a focus on past events and making sense of them.

First date songs	% of words	Heartbreak songs	% of words
Let's	2	Love	5
When	2	When	4
Want	2	Only	3
Love	2	Like	2
Know	2	Cause	2
Forever	2	All	2
Make	2	Know	2
Never	2	Say	2
Hand	2	Heart	2
Like	2	Go	2

Our analysis of the reported reasons for the nominated song choices revealed the ways that music was used to cope with heartbreak. The most frequently cited reason given for the selected song was that the song expressed how the person felt about their situation. Others said that the music enabled them to "wallow in '[their] heartbreak for a little longer" and to experience powerful memories of the beloved. Other frequently cited reasons were that it allowed them an outlet for their anger and disappointment as well as validating their feelings about the situation. Some participants also selected music that made them feel closer to the person they loved. Only 6% of participants chose music that they said gave them hope and cheered them up. Thus it appears that although some people are attracted to mood-improving music that can increase their hope, our strongest instinct in cases of heartbreak is to seek out music that reminds us of the beloved or times spent with them, and that allows us an outlet for our emotions.

That song choices for heartbreak are further related to coping style was confirmed by our further analysis of the lyrics of the heartbreak songs nominated by our participants. Patterns of word meanings in the heartbreak song group[9] revealed significant associations between the frequency of particular word groups in the lyrics of the chosen songs, and both personality traits and coping styles. Neuroticism from the Big Five Personality Inventory for example, was correlated with lyrical content containing words about the past, she/he words, and words about death. This suggests that people with high scores in neuroticism tended to select songs with a high level of focus on past events and the beloved 'other' who was the subject of their heartbreak. The comparatively high level of words about death suggests a tendency to extreme responses to their situation. These results are not surprising given the strong associations between neuroticism and depression or other unhealthy mental health outcomes, and further confirms that the songs selected by participants to cope with heartbreak strongly reflect their own thoughts and coping styles.

Associations between lyrics and other less helpful coping styles were also found. Mental disengagement, for example, was correlated with the use of words related to anger, as was emotion-focused coping. People who cope by suppressing actions—or choosing not to take certain actions—tended to select songs with lyrics that used a high number of words related to inhibition. Implicit mood measures also demonstrated that people who were feeling a sense of helplessness tended to select songs that used she/he words. The selection of songs like this likely expressed the participants' feelings of disempowerment in the situation. Helplessness is also associated with depression, since research indicates that when events are attributed to an external locus of control, the accompanying belief that one's

---

[9] Analysed using LIWC (Linguistic Inquiry and Word Count) software.

happiness is in the hands of another tends to increase depression (Abramson, Metalsky, & Alloy, 1989).

On the other hand, significant correlations were found between adaptive coping styles and word patterns in the lyrics of songs selected to cope with heartbreak. For example, people with high scores in extraversion tended to select music that expressed positive emotions and that contained a high number of personal pronouns, reflecting their people-oriented approach. Reflectiveness and active coping—which are both regarded as coping styles most likely to result in positive outcomes—were associated with words indicating a level of cognitive insight. Previous studies have found that the use of insight words suggests that a level of cognitive reframing or re-construal is occurring, processes that are themselves associated with positive health outcomes (Ayduk & Kross, 2010; Pennebaker, Mayne, & Francis, 1997). Active coping was also negatively correlated with the use of past-oriented words in our study.

These results confirm the strong relationship between personality and coping style and one's choice of music. Participants tended to select music to cope with heartbreak that reflected and expressed their own feelings. The lyrical content of the songs demonstrated a wide range of thoughts and emotions, with participants who scored highly on maladaptive coping styles or personality traits associated with mental health issues also tending to select songs that expressed a ruminative or past-oriented view of love experiences, as well as a sense of helplessness and inhibition. On the other hand, people with healthy personality traits such as extraversion or who scored highly on scores of adaptive coping styles such as reflectiveness or active coping, tended to either select music that expressed positive emotions and that gave them a sense of renewed hope, or songs that could help them to engage in processes of reappraisal and reconstruction so as to allow them to gain insight into events and their own emotions in response to them.

These findings tend to confirm the results of previous study we undertook to test whether people who listen to sad love songs would indulge in nostalgic remembrance of their own unhappy romantic experiences when listening to it (Davidson & Garrido, 2014). We also wanted to find out about the effect such memories would have on their mood. Data from this study came from a general questionnaire about music use in which we asked people to nominate a song that made them feel sad. Forty-seven participants nominated a love song that made them feel sad. We randomly selected a further 47 participants as a comparison group from among those who nominated a song that was *not* about love.

Participants who had selected a love-song as the song that made them feel sad scored significantly higher on the item indicating that the music made them remember past events. The same group also reported significantly higher scores in rumination and increases in depression scores after listening to their nominated song. Thus, despite the attraction to love-lamenting music in cases of heartbreak, these selections do not always seem to have a psychologically healthy effect for all listeners. This will be further illustrated in the following case study.

A Case Study: Peter

Peter[10] was a 46-year old male who had migrated to Australia as a teenager (Garrido & Schubert, 2011). Peter's preferred music was a particular love song genre that was popular in his country of origin. He described these songs as "romantic and melancholy … dark". Many of these songs concerned themes of unfulfilled love and troubled relationships. Peter had recently been diagnosed with clinical depression and anxiety, and he described himself as addicted to these songs despite the fact that listening to them didn't make him feel better. In fact, he stated that listening to those love songs made him feel worse, but that he felt almost "addicted" to the feeling the music gave him. In part, this strong connection to the music appeared to be due to the bond it had with his home country. The music triggered strong feelings of nostalgia in Peter, and enabled him to "revisit that space and time". However, Peter also seemed to believe himself "unlucky in love", and the songs allowed him to re-experience and express his feelings of frustration about the hardships he had experienced in his life. The music thus caused feelings of ambivalence in Peter in which he both felt an intense craving for the feelings it gave him, while at the same time stating that it made him feel blue and that a part of him would rather he didn't do it.

The word 'addiction' is one that is commonly heard in relation to love. Given the important biological function of romantic love, our brain is hardwired to provide powerful incentives to select a mate and remain attached to them. Neurological studies indicate that when people are in love, the areas of the brain that are responsible for critical thought become de-activated while the reward systems of the brain become activated

---

[10] Name has been changed.

(Bartels & Zeki, 2000). Thus falling in love can feel much like a natural drug high, producing brain chemicals such as dopamine and norepinephrine that are also produced during consumption of narcotics like cocaine.

Just as in cases of addiction to narcotics, when the cause of that dopamine rush is removed, the motivation to regain it becomes more powerful. Thus, in situations of rejection or loss of the object of our love, our desire to be with that individual only increases. Studies have shown that the parts of the brain that are associated with the calculating of gains and losses becomes active when heartbroken, suggesting that our willingness to take large risks to reclaim the object of our desire increases (Fisher et al., 2006). Helen Fisher and colleagues (2005) say that the brain patterns that are activated in rejected lovers demonstrate increases in "obsessive/compulsive behaviours, ruminating on the intentions and actions of the rejecter, evaluating options, and emotion regulation" (p. 9). Thus it seems that biologically, being in love is much like an addiction in that the craving to be with the person we love becomes even stronger in their absence. Music, in all its power to bring back vivid memories of a beloved individual and the feeling of being with them, may well be used in lieu of the individual themselves to induce a sense of connection with them.

The evidence also suggests that we are particularly attracted to 'love-lamenting' music when we are discontented with our own romantic relationships (Knobloch, Weisbach, & Zillmann, 2004). This appears to be especially true of men. In one study, women who were highly lonely demonstrated a preference for love-celebrating music, while lonely men preferred love-lamenting music (Gibson, Aust, & Zillmann, 2000), implying that individual differences in coping style play a role as well. It may be that for romantically disenchanted males hearing of the romantic successes of others increases distress (Zillmann & Gan, 1997), while some women may be able to enjoy a sense of romance vicariously through music, or to feel a renewed sense of hope in love through positive messages about love in the music. We also prefer to listen to love-lamenting music by performers of our own gender (Knobloch & Zillmann, 2003), perhaps deriving some sense of comfort from the knowledge that others of our sex have experienced similar frustrations. On the other hand, men and women who are in romantically satisfying relationships tend to prefer love-celebrating music.

Peter's addictive behavior towards tragic love songs is not altogether surprising, therefore, given his self-reported lack of success in finding love. However, people with depression also commonly report a sense of addiction to other behaviours although they may sometimes recognize that these behaviours tend to exacerbate their depression. In fact, depression and addictions of various kinds often co-occur in many people, with around one third of people with depression also reporting substance abuse (Davis, Uezato, Newell, & Frazier, 2008). Others describe depression itself as a type of addiction. For example, one anonymous blogger said "I am drawn towards my depression. I love listening to hyper-depressing songs, for how it makes me feel, it's like a friend visiting, a familiar feeling, a blanket that covers me. Intellectually I can see that its stupid, but it takes a lot not to return to the drinking fountains I use to feed by pain bodies" ("I feel drawn back into depression, is it like an addiction?," 2010). Thus, Peter's strong attraction to songs that 'feed' his depression may stem from a combination of the need to know that he is not alone in his suffering of heartbreak, the sense of nostalgia it gives him and connection to his home-land, an addiction to romance, and the fact that feeling depressed has become in some way familiar and comfortable. Peter's example highlights how music is used in complex ways to serve multiple functions in cases of heartbreak.

THE TRAJECTORY FROM THE PAST TO THE MODERN DAY

The above discussion demonstrates that romantic love is a universal emo-tion experienced by a majority of people, in various historical eras and in all the world's cultures, but it manifests itself in different ways based on the prevalent beliefs in society about love and appropriate behavior between lovers. In the earliest examples of music in love and courtship that we currently have available, music served a communal function in that it was part of the enactment of rituals designed to ensure successful pro-creation. Even in tribal societies in more modern times, music has contin-ued to serve the function of assisting in processes of mate selection and pairing, without the necessary involvement of romantic love. However, it is apparent that even from ancient times, music has also had a role in the expression of romantic love.

In the modern age, modern technology has enabled our use of music to become far more solitary and private than it has been in previous cen-turies. In some regards, music today can be used to feed private fantasies of an ideal love and to experience love vicariously in its absence or where the realities of relationships fall short of the ideal. Some scholars argue that much of the angst associated with love in modern-day contexts stems from the unrealistic fairy-tale-like concept of love that has been widely promoted by film and advertising in which the concept of an ideal mate—'the one'—has been advocated (Barker & Langdridge, 2010). As noted by other scholars, the concept of a lifelong partner fulfilling a multitude of personal needs is a relatively recent development in a historical record in which marriage and love have often been viewed as separate and marriage had more to do with economics and social connections than with satisfying individual emotional needs (Coontz, 2006). Studies have shown that even in the modern day people in non-Western cultures may be more likely to believe that romantic love is something temporary while marriage should be based on a more practical and enduring relationship (de Munck, Korotayev, de Munck, & Khaltourina, 2011). However, in less individualistic cultures or during time periods where group interests have prevailed over individual interests, love-based relationships have been seen to be disruptive, even dangerous because of their power to disturb the economic and social alliances on which marriages are otherwise based.

In Western cultures, the roots of the modern-day ideal of love go back to the time of courtly love and the troubadours. Some scholars argue that these ideals have created a tendency to dissatisfaction with relationships in Western cultures in the modern day. Thus, as marriage has become more closely associated with love, the belief that marriage should be a stable lifelong commitment has deteriorated. Many of our love songs therefore still contain images of an unattainable, idealized love—themes that inevitably engender a note of wistfulness and sadness in such music. In the words of Gioia: "today fantasy stands out as a key element in our love songs … enabling the listener to experience vicariously the passion and intense feelings only rarely granted by our quotidian routine" (p. 19). Modern-day love songs often echo the "fascination with romantic frustration" that Gioia noted in the love songs of ancient Egypt (p. 19).

The predominance of love songs in all cultures for centuries of human existence testifies to the strong biological urges that romantic love involves for humans. More than just an expression of the sex drive, romantic love motivates attachment to particular individuals, with the biological imperative to create a stable and protected environment in which to produce offspring. It still influences our perception of sexual attractiveness today. Love songs have thus had an important influence both on the development of music over the centuries, and on social beliefs about love and gender roles. Those who are in love celebrate their joy in music. Those who desire love experience it vicariously in song, while those who have lost love express their laments in songs of heartbreak.

These currents of sadness in many love songs appear to derive from two important historical influences on the development of the love song: the predominance of love songs from slaves and other oppressed individuals that became imbued with the sorrow of those who created them; and the religious influences that infused the love song with images of an unattainable love. There are however, powerful biological reasons that seem to pull us towards sad songs in times of heartbreak as well.

However, in much the same way as an addiction, when love is thwarted, our strongest instinct appears to be to listen to music that satisfies the craving for the beloved or for the sensations of love itself, turning to songs of love that both inspire and renew hope in love, and to songs that express the pain and hurt of heartbreak. Whether we choose to listen to love-celebrating music or love-lamenting music in turn depends on a number of variables including gender, personality and coping style. A number of people are able to use songs that express heartbreak as part of healthy psychological processes for working through their pain.

However, just as sad music generally can feed cycles of negative thinking in people with tendencies to depression, people with maladaptive coping styles also seem to turn to songs that express unhealthy viewpoints of love in times of heartbreak. Whether or not this has the effect of worsening their mood or helps them to recover and cope will require further testing in future studies. However, the studies reported here suggest that a highly past-oriented or emotion-focused approach to coping with heartbreak tends to be associated with negative mood outcomes in some people.

Nevertheless, as discussed above, the strong motivation we have to seek romantic love is biologically based, and the brain systems that are activated when in love provide powerful incentives to pursue love with energy and without regard for risk. Love songs, whether happy or sad, perhaps allow us a way to fill that need where real relationships are unsatisfying or unattainable. History and biology have come together to create an ideal of love that is often unreachable, a fact that often imbues our pursuit of love with some melancholy. Thus love songs, even sad love songs, stories, or films, resonate strongly with so many listeners around the globe.

Our study of modern day responses to the song "Scarborough Fair" demonstrated that in the modern age of speed dating, online dating and 'hook-ups', there is still a craving for the days of chivalry. However distorted our modern day concept of the realities of courtly love may be, music has played a role in contributing to our secret fantasies of ideal love.

In fact, as noted by Gioia, the very "fact that our modern romances bear so little resemblance to the traditions of courtly love merely heightens their allure" (p. 108). Thus the lyrics of some modern day love songs serve as a form of ideological expression and indulge our sense of historical nostalgia, in that they reflect longed-for ideals as well as realities (Frith, 1989). In addition, the dialogue between lovers that is often dramatized in love songs provides a language in which people can express the emotions associated with romance and heartbreak.

Furthermore, studies indicate that music is still the 'peacock tail' for many humans today. While women are mostly reluctant to accept the sexual overtures of an unknown male (Clark & Hatfield, 1989), one study of 300 young women in France found that women were more likely to comply when the male was carrying a guitar case (Guéguen, Meineri, & Fischer-Lokou, 2013). Thus it seems that musical ability does increase the chances of reproductive success even in humans in the twenty-first century.

It is further evident from the discussion in the current chapter that love songs are able to tell us a lot about relationships between men and women in the particular social and cultural climate in which the songs were created. Love songs have both mirrored and shaped the shifting societal views towards love and relationships throughout the centuries. The following chapter will consider how this has also occurred in the music associated with weddings throughout history.

REFERENCES

Abramson, L. Y., Metalsky, G. I., & Alloy, L. B. (1989). Hopelessness Depression: A Theory-Based Subtype of Depression. *Psychological Review, 96*(2), 358–372.

Ackerman, D. (1995). *A Natural History of Love.* New York: First Vintage Books.

Ayduk, O., & Kross, E. (2010). From a Distance: Implications of Spontaneous Self-Distancing for Adaptive Self-Reflection. *Journal of Personality and Social Psychology, 98*(5), 809–829.

Badham, B. P. (2014). *Ancient Egyptian Love Songs – With Commentary.* Lulu.

Barker, M., & Langdridge, D. (2010). *Understanding Non-Monogamies.* New York: Routledge.

Barolini, T. (2006). Literature, Italian. In M. Schaus (Ed.), *Women and Gender in Medieval Europe: An Encyclopedia.* New York and London: Routledge.

Bartels, A., & Zeki, S. (2000). The Neural Basis of Romantic Love. *NeuroReport, 11*(17), 3829–3834.

Burns, J. E. (2001). Courtly Love: Who Needs It? Recent Feminist Work in the Medieval French Tradition. *Signs, 27*(1), 23–57.

Calagno, M. (2012). *From Madrigal to Opera: Monteverdi's Staging of the Self.* Berkeley, CA: University of California Press.

Carey, J. T. (1969). Changing Courtship Patterns in the Popular Song. *American Journal of Sociology, 74*(6), 720–731.

Clark, R. D., & Hatfield, E. (1989). Gender Differences in Receptivity to Sexual Offers. *Journal of Psychology and Human Sexuality, 2*(1), 39–55.

Coontz, S. (2006). *Marriage, a History: How Love Conquered Marriage.* New York: Penguin.

Davidson, J. W., & Garrido, S. (2014). *My Life as a Playlist.* Perth: University of Western Australia Publishing.

Davidson, J. W., Kiernan, F., & Garrido, S. (2017). Introducing a Psycho-Historical Approach to the Study of Emotions in Music: The Case of Monteverdi's 'Ill Combattimento di Tancredi e Clorinda'. *Emotions: History, Culture, Society, 1*(1), 29–60.

Davis, L., Uezato, A., Newell, J. M., & Frazier, E. (2008). Major Depression and Comorbid Substance Use Disorders. *Current Opinion in Psychiatry, 21*(1), 14–18.

de Munck, V. C., Korotayev, A., de Munck, J., & Khaltourina, D. (2011). Cross-Cultural Analysis of Models of Romantic Love Among U.S. Residents, Russians and Lithuanians. *Cross-Cultural Research, 45*(2), 128–154.

DeNora, T. (2000). *Music in Everyday Life.* Cambridge: Cambridge University Press.

Douglas, S. (2004). Ballads and the Supernatural: Spells, Channs, Curses and Enchantments. *Studies in Scottish Literature, 33*(1), 349–365.

Dukes, R. L., Bisel, T. M., Borega, K. N., Lobato, E. A., & Owens, M. D. (2003). Expressions of Love, Sex, and Hurt in Popular Songs: A Content Analysis of All-Time Greatest Hits. *The Social Science Journal, 40*(4), 643–650.

Fisher, H., Aron, A., & Brown, L. L. (2005). Romantic Love: An fMRI Study of a Neural Mechanism for Mate Choice. *Journal of Comparative Neurology, 493*(1), 58–62.

Fisher, H., Aron, A., & Brown, L. L. (2006). Romantic Love: A Mammalian Brain System for Mate Choice. *Philosophical Transactions, B, 361*, 1476.

Frith, S. (1989). Why Do Songs Have Words? *Contemporary Music Review, 5*(1), 77–96.

Garrido, S., & Davidson, J. (2016). Emotional Regimes Reflected in a Popular Ballad: Perspectives on Gender, Love and Protest in 'Scarborough Fair'. *Musicology Australia, 38*(1), 65–78.

Garrido, S., & Schubert, E. (2011). Negative Emotion in Music: What Is the Attraction? A Qualitative Study. *Empirical Musicology Review, 6*(4), 214–230.

Gibson, R., Aust, C. F., & Zillmann, D. (2000). Loneliness of Adolescents and Their Choice and Enjoyment of Love-Celebrating Versus Love-Lamenting Popular Music. *Empirical Studies of the Arts, 18*(1), 43–48.

Gioia, T. (2015). *Love Songs: The Hidden History.* New York: Oxford University Press.

Gowing, L. (2003). *Common Bodies: Women, Touch and Power in Seventeenth-Century England.* New Haven and London: Yale University Press.

Guéguen, N., Meineri, S., & Fischer-Lokou, J. (2013). Men's Music Ability and Attractiveness to Women in a Real-Life Courtship Context. *Psychology of Music, 42*(4), 545–549.

Gyatso, T. (1993). *The Turquoise Bee: The Tantric Lovesongs of the Sixth Dalai Lama* (R. Fields & B. Cutillo, Trans.). New York: HarperOne.

Horton, D. (1957). The Dialogue of Courtship in Popular Songs. *American Journal of Sociology, 62*(6), 569–578.

I Feel Drawn Back into Depression, Is It Like an Addiction? (2010). Retrieved from http://ask.metafilter.com/153063/I-feel-drawn-back-into-depression-is-it-like-an-addiction

Jankowiak, W. R., & Fischer, E. F. (1992). Cross-Cultural Perspective on Romantic Love. *Ethnology, 31*(2), 149–155.

Knobloch, S., Weisbach, K., & Zillmann, D. (2004). Love Lamentation in Pop Songs: Music for Unhappy Lovers? *Zeitschrift fur Medienpsychologie, 16*(3), 116–124.

Knobloch, S., & Zillmann, D. (2003). Appeal of Love Themes in Popular Music. *Psychological Reports, 93*, 653–658.

Kramer, S. N. (1962). The Biblical 'Song of Songs' and the Sumerian Love Songs. *Expedition, 5*(1), 25.

Lockwood, D. (1962). *I, the Aboriginal.* Adelaide: Rigby Limited.

Lund, J., & Denisoff, R. S. (1971). The Folk Music Revival and the Counter Culture: Contributions and Contradictions. *The Journal of American Folklore, 84*(334), 394–405.

Matsubara, I. (1946). *Min-yo: Folk Songs of Japan.* Tokyo: Cosmo Publishing Company.

O'Neill, M. J. (2006). *Courtly Love of Medieval France: Transmission and Style in the Trouvere Repertoire.* Oxford: Oxford University Press.

Pennebaker, J. W., Mayne, T. J., & Francis, M. E. (1997). Linguistic Predictors of Adaptive Bereavement. *Journal of Personality and Social Psychology, 72*(4), 863–871.

Propp, V. (1993). *Russian Folk Lyrics* (R. Reeder, Trans. & R. Reeder, Ed.). Bloomington: Georgetown University Press.

Schimmelpenninck, A. (1997). *Chinese Folk Songs and Folk Singers: Shan'ge Traditions in Southern Jiangsu.* Leiden: Chime Foundation.

Sefati, Y. (1998). *Love Songs in Sumerian Literature*. Ramat Gan: Bar-Ilan University Press.

Stone, L. (1988). Passionate Attachments in the West in Historical Perspective. In W. Gaylin & E. Person (Eds.), *Passionate Attachments* (pp. 15–26). New York: Macmillan.

Temple, I. (2015). The Surprising, Nomadic History of Love Songs. *Flypaper*. Retrieved from http://flypaper.soundfly.com/features/the-surprising-nomadic-history-of-love-songs/

Turino, T. (1983). The Charango and the Sirena: Music, Magic and the Power of Love. *Latin American Music Review, 4*(1), 81–119.

Wilkinson, M. (1976). Romantic Love: The Great Equalizer? Sexism in Popular Music. *The Family Coordinator, 25*(2), 161–166.

Zillmann, D., & Gan, S. (1997). Musical Taste in Adolescence. In D. J. Hargreaves & A. C. North (Eds.), *The Social Psychology of Music* (pp. 161–187). Oxford: Oxford University Press.

CHAPTER 11

Weddings

HISTORICAL AND CROSS-CULTURAL PRACTICES

In many cultures, weddings are the most elaborately celebrated rites of passage. Among the Prespa of Albania, for example, a family will be looking ahead to a boy's wedding from the moment of his birth (Sugarman, 1997). Song dominates the days of wedding rituals to such an extent that conversation may be limited, and singing is the principal way in which the attendees participate in the wedding (Sugarman, 1997). In Bulgaria, music also features strongly in marriage rites, with the wedding being the only life-cycle ritual in which music plays such an important role (Rice, 1994).

Some cultures have dedicated musicians who are used to perform at weddings. For example, in Romania, Gypsy musicians called 'lăutari', a hereditary occupation dating from at least the fifteenth century, generally perform at weddings and other celebrations (Beissinger, 2005). Weddings are also the most commemorated among the ritual life events in Romanian society.

In modern times in Western cultures, many weddings still follow traditional patterns, often being conducted in churches and involving music and rituals that have been in existence for centuries. However, some things that people believe to be 'traditional' are actually relatively recent innovations (Koontz, 2006).

© The Author(s) 2019
S. Garrido, J. W. Davidson, *Music, Nostalgia and Memory*, Palgrave Macmillan Memory Studies,
https://doi.org/10.1007/978-3-030-02556-4_11

For example, it has not always been the case that marriages had to be sanctioned by church or state. In England, for instance, the marriage used to take place on the church porch rather than inside the church. Up until the seventeenth century, marriage was too closely linked to the concept of "carnal pleasures" to be held within the church, according to religious leaders (Koontz, 2006). Prior to the Reformation when there was a great deal of corruption in the clergy, it may also have been financial considerations that meant that the lower classes generally took their vows at the church doors. Thus, lavish church weddings were primarily the domain of the nobility. Lower class weddings were likely less formal, and often did not enjoy endorsement by either church or state. In fact, it wasn't until 1754 that English law required the marital parties to hold a state-endorsed marriage licence. Even then, marriage without it (and divorce without state sanction) was relatively common. Church weddings did not become the norm until around the nineteenth century.

The concept of marriage as being based on romantic love is also a relatively recent phenomenon. Until the eighteenth century marriages were seen as an important way to forge social, political and economic alliances for the benefit of the family, clan or even the nation (Koontz, 2006). Thus decisions as to one's marital partner were rarely left to the individuals involved, and were rarely based on an emotion as fickle and transient as love. The changes that took place in European cultures in which matches were based on love were fairly radical when looked at in the context of marriage throughout human history more broadly.

The 'tradition' of a white wedding dress is also relatively new. This custom was popularized by the wedding of Queen Victoria to Prince Albert in 1840. The event was described in the Sydney Gazette and New South Wales Advertiser of 23 June 1840: "She wore a brilliant tiara, and her train, which was of considerable length, was borne by twelve unmarried ladies! Her Majesty wore a white dress" (p. 2). The Sydney Herald of June 22, 1840 described the dress in some detail, saying "Her Majesty wore a magnificent lace robe and veil of the most exquisite workmanship … Her train was of white satin with a deep fringe of lace" (p. 2). Queen Victoria herself described the dress in her journal as "a white satin dress, with a deep flounce of Honiton lace" (Vol. 13, p. 345). Such details, publicized around the world to a degree that was unprecedented, created a big impact on the public imagination and set the standard to aspire to for weddings for decades afterwards.

Many of the earliest operas first appeared in conjunction with a wedding. For example, Giovanni de' Bardi's *Pellegrina*, was staged for the 1589 wedding of Ferdinando de' Medici and Christine de Lorraine. Similarly, the wedding of King Henri IV of France to Marie de' Medici in Florence in 1600 led to the debut of Guilio Caccini's *Il Rapimento di Cefalo*, and *Euridice* composed by Jacopo Peri with additional music by Caccini.

In England, music has been a part of wedding ceremonies for over 400 years. However, the form that is used in a traditional service today dates from the middle of the nineteenth century (Kerr, 1965). Royal weddings were again largely responsible for setting the trend that has lasted since the nineteenth century. There are numerous examples of lavish royal weddings in which music played a prominent role. For example, the Sydney Herald's description of Queen Victoria's wedding cited above also noted the use of a musical choir of 10 boys and 16 men. On occasion, new works would even be commissioned to celebrate the event, such as the *Festa Teatrala Acide* which Haydn composed for the wedding of Prince Esterhazy's oldest son in 1763.

Two of the most consistently popular choices of wedding music also came from a precedent set by a royal wedding. For example, a selection of Wagner's *Lohengrin* which includes the Bridal Chorus ("Here Comes the Bride")[1] was played at the marriage of Princess Victoria to the Crown Prince of Prussia in 1858, as was Mendelssohn's "Wedding March"[2] from *A Midsummer Night's Dream*. These two works have become almost globally known for their use in weddings.

While the nobility were striving to emulate the standards set by the royals, less wealthy people were more likely to have music performed by family and friends. However, one reason that the royal examples may have become so popular is because of the lack of any particular music written for weddings in general, particularly in Protestant England. Of course in the Catholic tradition, Orlando di Lassi wrote wedding masses. J. S. Bach—a Lutheran—also wrote several wedding cantatas: a number of sacred ones that incorporated hymns often associated with weddings and that would likely have been intended for more formal weddings at which a mass was performed, and three secular ones that may have been intended

---

[1] Track 78: Here Comes the Bride, Wagner, Czech Philharmonic.
[2] Track 79: Wedding March, Mendelssohn, Gewandhausorchester.

for use at the wedding breakfast following the ceremony (Hudson, 1968), or for non-church weddings.

It is the one generally referred to as the "Wedding Cantata" (BWV 202) *Weichet nur, betrübte Schatten*[3] which is the most celebrated of Bach's compositions for weddings. While it was likely written in the first decades of the eighteenth century, there is little available information about the circumstances of the creation of the Wedding Cantata. It is thought that the text on which it was based may have been written by Salomo Franck, a court poet in Weimar.

The text of the cantata makes no reference to religion, but rather to gods and goddesses from Roman mythology, such as the Roman fertility goddess Flora, the god Amor known as Eros to the Greeks and Cupid to the Romans, and to Phoebus also known as Apollo. The imagery of the text invokes that of the newness of Spring and the desire for love this inspires. The music is set for string trio (two violins and a viola) and continuo with solo parts being taken by the oboe and soprano voice. Nine short movements alternate recitative with aria, all but one of which are in major keys. The somewhat mournful opening using dissonant harmonies depicting the last strains of a cold winter are banished in favour of more cheerful harmonies and quickening tempos as spring arrives. The final recitative (the 8th movement) is a declamation of the hope that no unexpected accident will befall the couple to interrupt their love. This is followed by a joyful gavotte (the 9th movement)—a dance form which was often associated in Bach's works with the happiness of ascending to heaven—in which the soprano wishes the couple "a thousand bright and prosperous days".

Returning to nineteenth century England we do find an example of a song written particularly for English weddings later in the century in the form of a hymn by Dorothy F. Gurney. The text of the hymn entitled 'O Perfect Love' was written for her sister's wedding in 1883, but it was written to an already established tune ("Strength and Stay" by Dykes). It was sung to this tune at a royal wedding at Windsor in 1894. It was also set as an anthem by J. Barnby for the marriage of the Duke of Fife with the Princess Louise of Wales on July 27, 1889. Gurney was herself the daughter of an Anglican minister and her husband later became a minister too. The text that Gurney wrote asks God's blessings on those entering the marriage relationship, based on the ideal of the harmony between Christ

---

[3] Track 80: Wedding Cantata, J.S. Bach, Musica Antiqua New York.

and his followers. It was sung privately at many London weddings for a few years and then began making its way into hymnbooks.

Common Formats and Phases of Wedding Rituals

Weddings can form an important expression of social relationships such as gender roles, kinship, and the life-cycle. In many cultures the wedding marks the passage of the bride from her childhood home to her life as an adult in the home of her husband. In many cultures the groom and his entourage may come to the bride's house and after some ceremonial activities, bring her back to her new home with her husband and in-laws. Like many rituals, the wedding is therefore, frequently enacted in three distinct phases: there may be preparatory rituals or processions in which the leave-taking of the bride from her family is marked, a ceremonial phase in which the joining of the man and woman is performed, and rituals associated with leaving the ceremony or a post-ceremonial celebration of the new life being entered. Music often sets the tone and communicates the meaning of each part of the rituals.

These phases of a wedding can take place over many days. In Ancient Greece, for example, weddings could span up to 3 days, beginning with rites during which the bride prepares for the upcoming changes to her situation, a wedding feast hosted by the bride's father, and the departure to the bridegroom's home. Songs were a part of each of these stages (Hague, 1983). The sections below will outline some historical and cross-cultural examples of music as it is used in each of the stages of a wedding.

Processions and Preparations for the Marriage

Processions have a long history of involvement in weddings. In fact, in Biblical times, the procession bringing the bride to the groom's home was the crux of the wedding itself, with few additional rituals being involved. Other ancient literature also mentions processions and the use of music in them. In the *Iliad* for example, Homer mentions a wedding procession accompanied by bright torches, music, dancing and song (18.490–96). In fact, throughout Homer's works, song is frequently mentioned in relation to weddings. In traditional Hindu weddings also, the arrival of the grooms' party at the bride's residence often includes a formal procession with dancing and music.

Often in royal weddings of European cultures, historically, the bride would arrive accompanied by an entourage of servants to the city of her husband-to-be. These arrivals were often heralded with an air of military triumph. For example, in 1463, Margaret of Bavaria, bride of Federico I of Mantua, made her entrance to the city accompanied by 107 trombi, pifari, and trombone (Fenlon, 1980). Similarly, Eleonora of Toledo arrived at the gates of Florence in 1539 to marry Cosimo I de'Medici, she was greeted by the singing of 24 voices, four trombones and four cornets (Ferrai, 1882). In relation to the marriage of Queen Victoria to Prince Albert, The Sydney Herald article cited above described the use of drums and trumpets in the procession of the bridegroom which could be heard in the distance from within the cathedral where the wedding took place, signaling his approach.

Similarly, during the reign of Tsar Peter I (Peter the Great) in Russia during the seventeenth century, weddings among the nobility reached particularly epic proportions. Trumpeters often accompanied the procession to the church. For example, the Duke of Hostein's wedding procession to the church in 1725 involved a drummer and four trumpeters marching in pairs along with the Duke's servant (Sander, 2005). During this same period, Russian village weddings typically involved multiple non-Christian rituals including incantations of spells and lamenting, with the only Christian part of the proceedings being the actual church ceremony itself (Karlinsky, 1986).

As mentioned above, the Bridal Chorus from Wagner's *Lohengrin* was made popular by its use in the wedding of Princess Victoria to the Crown Prince of Prussia. It is still the most commonly used and recognized processional, used for the bride's procession down the aisle to the church altar. The portion of Wagner's music which is used comes from the overture to the first scene of Act III of the opera, the scene in which Elsa weds Lohengrin. The march style is particularly well suited to the procession of a bride down the aisle, and these days, so familiar is it, that the first few notes of the fanfare are enough to signal to all attendees that the bride has arrived and the wedding is commencing.

It has also been popular in royal weddings for the bride to enter to the singing of a hymn, and this custom has often been followed in private events as well. Handel has also been a popular choice at English weddings, including the Overture to *Esther*, the *Arrival of the Queen of Sheba*, selections from the *Water Music*, *Music for the Royal Fireworks* and *Messiah*. Other music that is popular here is Pachelbel's *Canon in D*, and Clarke's

Trumpet Voluntary, made popular by its use in the wedding of Lady Diana Spencer to Prince Charles.

In other cultures, preparatory rituals prior to the wedding take the place of a procession or may be conducted in addition to the procession in order to mark the separation of the bride from her family. In the sixteenth century during the reign of Ivan the Terrible in Russia, for example, music was used to announce the bride's awakening on the day of her wedding as well as to announce the arrive of the important male figures of the wedding parties at the bath houses where they would prepare for the wedding (Pouncy, 1994).

In Checha, a region that spans parts of Bulgaria and Greece, songs may be sung during several pre-wedding rituals as well, such as when shaving the groom's head, braiding the bride's hair and taking leave of the parents (Ilieva & Ivanov, 2013). In some parts of the region, sad songs about the grief of parting and the difficult life ahead for women are sung accompanied by ring dances by female companions outside the bride's house. Other villages have a custom where a group from the groom's party visit the bride's family home to negotiate the details of the wedding trousseau, a tradition involving ring dances and songs performed by the two groups.

In the Sephardic Jewish tradition, a primary pre-ceremonial ritual is the ceremonial bathing of the bride. A number of traditional songs may accompany this ritual, with a popular one being *Ya salio de la mar, la galena* ('The young beauty came out of the sea').[4]

Similarly, in Bulgaria, an important pre-ceremony ritual is the baking of bread by the female relations of the bride. Yeast is brought by representative of the groom to the bride's home and presented to her family, and then the female relations prepare the dough while singing specific songs (Rice, 1994). As described by Timothy Rice, these songs include themes relating to the reluctance of the bride to leave her family home, the preparations for the arrival of the bride at the groom's home, and the pending arrival of the groom (described as a dragon) to take the bride away.

In later stages of the pre-ceremonial rituals, the bride and groom are prepared in their respective homes: the bride may have her hair braided, while the groom's head is shaved. These grooming rituals are accompanied by songs again, with the bride's female relatives singing a melody comparing her hair to a grapevine. During the singing a contrasting melody in an unrelated key is played. The effect of these two simultaneously

[4] Track 81: Ya salio de la mar, la galena, Ofri Eliaz.

played tunes is a typical polyphonic sound known as 'gyurltiya' or 'joyous noise', an effect that is considered desirable for the celebratory occasion of a wedding.

The following day the groom comes to the bride's home in a procession that also is marked by music, with a song called 'Going for the Bride' contrasted against another song about the unity between the two families. In the meantime, the waiting bride is hearing songs about her duties to her new family. In her final moments in her parent's home, the bride is veiled, continually accompanied by the sound of songs comparing her to a grapevine that is to be uprooted and taken away by her new family and reiterating the harsh treatment she can expect from her mother-in-law.

Despite the fact that a wedding is generally viewed as a celebratory affair, the involvement of weeping and lament is actually not at all uncommon in pre-ceremony wedding rituals. In some parts of Europe such as Finland, Estonia and Russia, historically, pre-wedding rituals included a "wedding play", in which the meeting of the bride and groom and events of the courtship were re-enacted (Ling, 1997). These plays typically included songs both of lament and comedy, the former relating to the sorrow of the bride at leaving her parental home. The more joyful songs of the wedding play were often choral, with two choral groups representing the bride and groom's families who compare their wealth and status in a sort of vocal sparring session. Some scholars claim that in northern Russia particularly, the laments were of greater importance than the more light-hearted songs (Ling, 1997).

Similarly, in sixteenth century Russia, the bride typically sang lamentations prior to the commencement of the marriage rituals in anticipation of the miserable lives she was to lead under the domination of their mother-in-law (Pouncy, 1994). The singing of these lamentations was a skill that Russian women were often taught from childhood (Mazo, 1994). The laments could take place periodically as a marker between various key moments in the wedding preparations over a period of up to four weeks. Some of these key ritualistic moments include the covering of the bride-to-be with a shawl by her mother in order to conceal her from the spirits, or the handing over of the symbol of her virginity to a female companion.

Each lament was improvised, both the words and the melodies, although the poetic structures, verbal imagery, and vocal qualities in the singing were dictated by the traditions of the specific region. Margarita

Mazo describes the wedding lament ritual as inducing a "special psychological state" (p. 24) and triggering collectively experienced emotions. The skill level of the singer would be judged on the basis of how tearful they sounded. One particular feature of the singing style that was particularly utilized to invoke grief and lament was the gliding pitch contour. Other gestural devices add to the drama of the lament, such as the *khloyostan'e* in which the singer throws herself to the floor in between lines of song before rising and continuing her performance. The laments could be a solo, a duo including another female relative, or could have the addition of a female choral group. In the latter style the bride's lament continues on in free form while the chorus of women is more song-like and rhythmically structured. The two layers are improvised without reference to each other and with little alignment, while still being perceived as a unified performance. Mazo states that this is because of similar modal conditions between the layers and shared temporal organization.

Melancholy songs associated with weddings were also found in Gascony, an area in the southwest of France, with singers accompanying the couple to the notary and the church singing songs that were sometimes humorous and sometimes sad (Tiersot, 1889). In Sweden, we see examples of rituals surrounding the groom, such as the custom of 'singing out the bridegroom', in which the young men of the village would dance around the groom in a circle, taking turns to dance with the groom inside the circle, in a ritual symbolizing the groom coming to an end of his life as a single man (Ling, 1997).

In more modern times, non-European cultures still include music in pre-wedding rituals and processions. For example, in modern day Sumatra, Indonesia, pop songs about weddings, such as "Malam Bainai" are commonly played by hired musicians as the bridal party enters the location of the wedding (Fraser, 2011). These pop songs have become a "nostalgic articulation of Minangkabau identity, especially within migrant communities" (p. 201). Similarly, in non-Islamic weddings in Egypt there is a specific rhythm called the *zaffa* which can include drums, horns, bagpipes, and a belly dancer to lead the bride to the location of the ceremony. In a traditional Islamic wedding in Egypt, the procession to the church may include a group of musicians and dancing by the wedding guests including the bride and groom themselves, although the belly dancer will be omitted (van Nieuwkerk, 2012).

The Ceremony

The ceremony, in its various cultural forms, consecrates the change in status of the couple. In Romania, as mentioned above, the ceremony is framed by the veiling and unveiling of the bride, accompanied by particular ritual songs (Beissinger, 2005). Another ritual in which music is involved in Romanian weddings is that of the fir tree. The fir tree symbolizes fertility and the guests at the weddings dance around it. Following the ceremony, the fir tree is taken to the groom's house to symbolize the abundance of life that the couple will produce.

In European-style church weddings, much of the ceremony itself, of course, involves a talk by a minister or priest and the exchanging of vows. Music will most often not be played during this part of the ceremony. However, it was the fashion in English weddings for some time for a friend of the bride and groom to sing or play something during the signing of the Register (Kerr, 1965). The custom of playing music during the signing of the marriage documents is often still followed today.

In Somali weddings, the ceremony is performed by a Muslim sheikh, and can take place even in the absence of the bride and groom, as long as a family representative is present. Singing may be involved as a greeting to the groom's family as they arrive and may take place among the women of the family while the men finalize the marriage contract.

In some countries, an integral part of the ceremony is the arrival of the groom or bride at the home of the other party or at the place where the formalities associated with the marriage are to take place. Music can often be involved in this part of the ceremony too. Part of the ceremony in the Sudan, for example, is the *nyawer* in which the groom arrives outside the bride's house and the couple (or musicians hired to perform for them) sing couplets in which the groom asks permission to enter (Williams, 1998).

At Jewish weddings songs may accompany both the arrival of the groom and his family, and later of the bride. Blessings are also sung over the couple as part of the formal ceremony. Among Ashkenazi Jews, the groom signs the wedding contract and then is led with singing and dancing to his bride for the purpose of veiling her, both in order to verify her identity and to protect her modesty.

Recessional and Post-ceremonial Celebrations

At the conclusion of the ceremonial part of the marriage proceedings, European-style weddings will often include a recessional. This is when the married couple formally exit the space in which the ceremony has taken place. One of the most popular pieces of music used for this part of the proceedings is Mendelssohn's "Wedding March" from *A Midsummer Night's Dream*. As mentioned above, this was popularized after its use on January 25, 1858 for the marriage of Queen Victoria's eldest daughter (also named Victoria) to the Crown Prince of Prussia, later Frederick III. In the play itself, the wedding march is used for a processional in the scene of the Duke of Athens' wedding. However, the triumphant sounds of the music makes it seem particularly appropriate as the finale of a wedding ceremony. Other popular music used in recessional in traditional English weddings include Clarke's *Trumpet Voluntary*, Bach's *Wedding Cantata*, or some of the Toccatas and Preludes by Bach as well.

In some cultures, such as in Albania, the climax of the wedding is when the bride is taken to the house of the groom where she will now live (Sugarman, 1997). Similarly, in traditional Hindu weddings, ceremonies are held to welcome the bride to her new home after the wedding, with particular songs being associated with this phase of the rituals.

In ancient times, the *epithalamium* was a common part of weddings. These were songs sung to accompany the bride and groom to the nuptial chamber. The ancient Greek poet Sappho was a master of the form. She wrote songs that were apparently sung just before the marriage was consummated at the door of the room to which the couple would retire (Gioia, 2015). The tradition was carried out for many centuries, and would often be a mixture of blessings upon the newly married couple and erotic innuendo, leading to their condemnation by some religious leaders such as the bishop of Arles in the sixth century.

These songs at the door to the marital chamber are also found in other cultural settings. Amongst Spanish gypsies, for example, the *alboreás*, were typically sung to newly-weds at dawn after the wedding, often accompanied by a virginity test (Pohren, 2005). While typically it was believed that these songs should not be performed outside of a wedding, they have now been popularized as a flamenco dance form that is often performed for tourists (Ling, 1997).

In many cultures around the world, the end of the formal ceremonial aspects of the wedding will signal the beginning of feasting and banqueting, during which much singing and dancing will often take place. An early example of this is depicted in Homer's *The Odyssey*, in which a wedding feast involving a singer is held in the palace of Menelaus.

Numerous art works also demonstrate the involvement of music in wedding feasts. The "Peasant Wedding" (1567) by Pieter Bruegel the Elder, for example, depicts a sixteenth century rural Flemish wedding with bag-pipers entertaining the guests while they eat and drink. A more sumptuous wedding, that of Isabella of Parma to Joseph II at the Hofburg Palace in Vienna in 1760 is depicted by "Wedding Supper" by Martin van Meytens (1763) and shows galleries filled with musicians. Paolo Veronese's painting of the "Wedding Feast at Cana" (1563), while purporting to illustrate the occasion of a Biblical wedding at which Jesus turned water into wine, similarly depicts musical instruments typical of Venetian weddings in the sixteenth century. He in fact shows several groups of musicians and singers present at the same time, perhaps as a symbol of the harmony of marriage (Bassano, 1994).

In seventeenth century Russia among the nobility, ceremonial drinking at the wedding feast could be accompanied by trumpet fanfares which typically followed each toast, and ceremonial dancing (Sander, 2005). In Bulgaria ring dances will also be a big part of the wedding banquet (Ilieva & Ivanov, 2013). In Romania, the wedding banquet can take place all night and is accompanied by "virtually non-stop music and dancing" (Beissinger, 2005, p. 40). Traditionally this was often the *hora*—a circle dance often considered the Romanian national dance. Dancing of the *hora* was particularly regulated during the Ceausescu era in the 1980s. However, Romani's (or gypsies) often played their own Romani repertoire in a sort of underground musical-culture. Modern weddings are often dominated by the *menea*, a solo improvisatory dance with a more suggestive expressive style than was permitted in communist Romania, or another Romani dance form, the *lautra hora*, which is also a solo dance. These dance forms have become popular in non-Romani weddings in Romania as well, because of their association with the gypsy 'ideal', that of free-spirited passion and intensity (Beissinger, 2005). In Jewish weddings, music is an important part of the post-ceremonial celebrations as well, with the *horah* again featuring as a dance form similar to that found in Romania. In Jewish klezmer music the *horah* involves the married couple being held up on chairs while the guests dance around them to the accompaniment of Jewish traditional music such as *Hava Nagila*.

In typical Somali weddings, the celebrations may take place all in one location or separately for the women and men. They can occur over the course of several days, and can involve singing and dancing throughout the night. Music is of such importance at these weddings that dancing at someone's wedding is viewed as an important sign of respect for that person (Guerin, Elmi, & Guerin, 2006). The traditional wedding dance in which the female guests dance in a circle taking turns to dance in the middle is the *burambur*.

While church music and other traditional selections have dominated weddings for centuries, in modern times, wedding rituals are becoming more flexible, with couples often opting for more personalized music over traditional choices. However, many couples still choose to celebrate their cultural roots in their music selections, despite the wide options now available. This was a subject that we explored further in the MLAP research and will be discussed in more detail below.

Modern-Day Playlists

Our questionnaire about wedding music was completed by 518 people including 380 females, 132 males and 4 people who reported their gender as 'other', with an average age of 34 years. About half of the participants had some kind of tertiary education, and approximately half reported their nationality as 'Australian'. The majority were single (51%), while 30% were married, 14% living in a de facto relationship and 6% were divorced. The majority also had some level of musical experience (77%), with around 50% having had private music lessons, and with an average of 9 years of experience.

Participants were asked what their ultimate wedding song would be. The songs selected were from a variety of genres, most frequently rock (26%), pop (18%) and classical 15%. The most popular songs nominated are listed in order of popularity in Table 11.1. The most frequently nominated song was Mendelssohn's Wedding March. Several other classical pieces were also frequently nominated including Pachelbel's *Canon in D* and Handel's *Arrival of the Queen of Sheba*. Although participants were not asked to nominate a song for any particular part of the wedding ritual, these classical pieces are among those that have been used for the recessional (in the case of Mendelssohn) and for the processional (Pachelbel and Handel) for over a hundred years in Western cultures, as was discussed above. As can be seen in the Table, the most frequently nominated songs

Table 11.1 Frequently nominated songs for a wedding

Artist/composer	Song names	Genre	Approx tempo (bpm)	Key
Mendelssohn	Wedding March	Classical	72	Major
John Legend	All of Me	RNB	68	Major
Johann Pachelbel	Canon in D	Classical	56	Major
Nick Cave	Into My Arms	Rock	96	Major
Etta James	At Last	Soul	56	Major
Ben Harper	Forever	Singer-Songwriter	96	Major
Dolly Parton & Kenny Rogers	Islands in the Stream	Country	108	Major
INXS	Never Tear Us Apart	Rock	64	Major
Peter Gabriel	The Book of Love	Rock	56	Major
Handel	Arrival of the Queen of Sheba	Classical	116	Major
Christina Perri	A Thousand Years	Pop	52	Major
Billy Idol	White Wedding	Rock	148	Minor

were predominantly in slow tempos and almost exclusively in major keys. However, in European style weddings in modern contexts, the post-ceremonial celebrations will often include a live band or hired disc-jockey, and the common custom of the bridal 'waltz', in which the bride and groom take their symbolic first dance together as husband and wife. The slow and romantic style of several of these wedding song nominations would likely make them popular selections for the bridal waltz, despite the fact that only the songs "Never Tear Us Apart" by INXS and "At Last" by Etta James[5] are actually in waltz time (3/4). The trend to now use songs that are not in waltz tempo has led to the dance often being called the 'First Dance' rather than a Bridal Waltz. Other composers or artists who were frequently mentioned include J. S. Bach, The Beatles, Lamb, and Jason Mraz.

Participants rated their song choices as being positive in valence, (m = 4.3) and above neutral in terms of arousal (n = 3.4).[6] Interestingly, significant[7] differences were found on arousal ratings between the sexes, with women being more likely to have rated their song selection as of low

---

[5] Track 82: At Last, Etta James.

[6] Scores could range from 1 to 5 and a score of 3 would represent a neutral score.

[7] Significant at $p < 0.05$.

arousal than men. This may suggest that women prefer selections of a more slow and romantic nature than men, who may often prefer choices that are more celebratory or energetic. Valence ratings also differed depending on marital status, with people who were single or divorced tending to rate their song selections as less positive in valence than those who were married or living in a de facto relationship.

When asked for the reasons for their wedding song nomination, the majority of people said they had selected it because it was romantic and therefore perfect for two people declaring their love for each other (37%). Other popular reasons were that the music held some personal significance to the couple (19%) or that the participant liked particular features of the music itself ($n = 12$%).

In addition to asking about their own ultimate wedding songs, our participants were asked to listen to a recording of Elgar's *Serenade for Strings*, which had been composed in 1892, and had been played at the wedding of Kate Middleton to Prince William in 2011. The majority of participants stated that they had not heard it before (58%), but most were able to correctly determine which celebrity wedding it had recently been played at. The overwhelming majority said they would not choose it for their own wedding (82%), mostly because that music meant nothing to them or their partner personally (49%). Others reasons given were because it was not something the church congregation could sing along to, or that could be danced to, and that the mood it created was one of grandeur rather than celebration. Of those who said they would use it for their own wedding, the reasons given were primarily because they liked the music itself, because they thought it was romantic, or because they like the era of history it represented for them.

The descriptions that participants gave of what the music made them think about revealed similar patterns. The most frequently used word in the descriptions was "boring". A large number also mentioned royalty, aristocracy or the nobility, and many described the music as "grand", "pompous", "formal", or "conservative". In the words of one participant the music was most "suitable for a non-intimate royal wedding—impersonal". Another commented on how music of this sort was "too culturally embedded" to have much personal meaning, and several people also used the word "tradition" in their descriptions. A smaller number of people, however, described the music in a more positive light. Several mentioned its "calmness" and "serenity". Others described imagining a ball with "ladies in flouncy skirts", "powdered wigs", "marble halls" and "violins".

Ballet and Disney princesses, a setting from a Jane Austen novel, and pastoral scenes of the English countryside were also among the imagery conjured up by the music for some participants.

Traditional Versus Personal: Two Case Studies

Sam and Sura[8] were married in their mid-to late 20s. Both are of Middle Eastern origin. Sura was born in Iraq of Mandaean cultural background and migrated to Australia with her family 16 years ago. Sam is a third generation Australian of Assyrian origins. Mandaeans are a small religious group who describe themselves as followers of John the Baptist. Many escaped to Australia from Iraq because of religious persecution. Their religious rituals including weddings, closely involve ceremonies around water. However, in the case of this wedding, the groom's family was Catholic, and following the traditions of the Catholic church to which the groom and his family belonged was important for this couple. They were also strongly influenced by having been raised in Australia. They therefore selected the commonly used 'Here Comes the Bride' for their processional at the Assyrian-Catholic church where the wedding was held. Despite her Mandaean heritage, Sura says "since I was a little girl I always dreamed about walking down the aisle to this music". The wedding reception however, included many Arabic and Assyrian songs, since many of the guests were Arabic and Assyrian. Sura reports that this music was "a must for us and our guests in order to enjoy and celebrate our wedding", although several slow dance songs in English were also played. The couple described their wedding as traditional and reported that a wedding for them was "an important time to remember one's roots."

Thus this wedding demonstrated an interesting mix of cultural 'traditions'. A song that is commonly associated with church weddings was selected for the processional despite the fact that this music did not originate in the Catholic tradition in which weddings are generally incorporated into the normal ceremonies of the mass. However, the reception needed to cater to a wide variety of cultural groups. Assyrian weddings typically involve long periods of group dancing and these traditions are an important part of weddings for Assyrian people, allowing the two families to share the celebrations together and get to know each other better. However, for this wedding held in Australia at which many young people

---

[8] Names have been changed.

would have been present, the tradition of slow, romantic dancing which is common at Australian weddings, had also become incorporated into the plans.

In contrast to this more traditional wedding, is the wedding of Paul and Nikki.[9] Paul and Nikki were both in their early 30s when they got married. They had already been a couple since high school and decided to tie the knot when they felt ready to start a family. The beach had always figured highly in their lives. In fact Paul had proposed to Nikki on a beach in Fiji. Given their own personal love for the beach and the fact that they both wanted a more relaxed and intimate occasion rather than a big formal wedding, they chose a beach wedding. There was no formal walk down the aisle for this couple. They arrived at the wedding together and walked arm in arm between their guests to stand before the registrar conducting the formalities. A single classical guitarist played soft Latin-style music as the bride and groom arrived and greeted their guests. The bride wore a white dress but no veil, and the groom wore a white shirt without a tie with sand coloured trousers. Their vows had been written by them personally and expressed their own personal feelings about how their love had grown in the time they had been together and what they hoped their future years together would be like. The guests were also asked to make their own statements about how they viewed love and marriage and to write these on cards to be given to the bride and groom to look at later.

The use of a solo guitarist to provide the music in this wedding ceremony meant that the music was understated and very much in the background, serving to set a romantic atmosphere, but not overpowering the proceedings. When the wedding guests later retired to a nearby beachside venue for the reception, the music took on a more personal significance, but continued the relaxed, beachside atmosphere that the couple wanted to create. The songs played throughout the evening celebrations had been largely chosen specifically by the bride and groom themselves, and was mostly based on the type of atmosphere they wanted to create for their guests. They described that atmosphere as romantic and 'chilled'. Songs included Israel Kamakawiwo' Ole's version of "Somewhere Over the Rainbow", Bob Marley's "One Love", and various songs by the Beach Boys.

---

[9] Names have been changed

THE TRAJECTORY FROM THE PAST TO THE MODERN DAY

Ceremonies and rituals in which a marriage is formalized have been a part of human society since ancient times and across all cultures, albeit in differing forms. However, the significance of marriage ceremonies and the customs surrounding their celebration can vary widely from culture to culture and across time periods within a single cultural group. Music has been a dominant part of weddings, which may be among the most elaborate rituals celebrated in any particular culture.

Weddings among the nobility have, of course, always been more lavish than among the common people. However, there was a time period there where the British royal family really set the standard for weddings in many countries, and many traditions that were established in the weddings of the British royal family during the nineteenth century are still followed today in many parts of the globe. Examples of this include the tradition of the white wedding dress and the still common use of Mendelssohn and Wagner, customs now frequently observed even in non-European cultures such as Japan and Korea.

This holding to 'tradition'—albeit relatively new ones—is somewhat surprising given the changing significance of marriage in the twenty-first century. While weddings in the past may have sanctified the sexual union of the couple and signified the change from being single to being part of a couple, most people in modern day Australia will have already lived together as a couple for some time prior to their wedding. It is therefore interesting that so many people still want to formalize their unions. Furthermore, although the recent census in Australia revealed that the most dominant religion in Australia is now 'no religion', many people feel it is important to hold a church wedding (Wallis, 2002).

This continued emphasis on formal marriages and traditional ways of marking it for a surprising number of people may partly be due to the status symbol that a wedding provides. It can be seen by some as a natural progression through the social hierarchy and a milestone of independence from the parental family. It can also be a display of lifestyle and personal achievements (Cherlin, 2004). Some scholars argue that as traditional sources of identity such as class, religion and community have lost influence, one's personal relationships and marital status have become a more important form of self-identity (Beck & Beck-Gernsheim, 2002). Sharon Boden (2001) thus describes modern weddings as a 'cultural performance' rather than a genuinely religious celebration (p. 25).

Of course, shrewd marketing by the multi-billion dollar wedding industry also comes into it, as does the romantic ideal set in film of the 'fairy-tale' ending that any princess-at-heart must aspire to. In fact the twenty-first century has seen a trend towards expensive, lavish weddings. Vicki Howard (2006) states that in America in 2005 the average cost of a wedding was nearly $US30,000. She argues that much of this comes from business marketing strategies which have created an industry worth billions of dollars around "invented traditions or elaborations of older customs" (p. 2). Clever marketing strategies have managed to merge both the idea of tradition and modernism in order to incorporate the changing societal perspectives about marriage and gender roles in the modern age.

Penner (2004) argues that the increasing commercialization of weddings stems from the latter half of the nineteenth century, during which time lavish gift giving and extravagant celebrations began to be encouraged by urban businesses. Although Queen Victoria's wedding in 1840 had increased the popularity of a white wedding, for most people the marriage ceremony remained much simpler for quite some time. By the middle of the nineteenth century, weddings were more choreographed and lavish than that of previous decades in which a wedding might have been celebrated by means of a simple meal and a dance hosted at the home of the bride's parents. During the 1850s it became the practice to put the bridal gifts on display in a separate room in a way that mimicked a commercial display. The commercialization of the wedding became a full-scale business by the 1950s. Some of the mothers and grandmothers of today's brides may themselves have had their weddings during war-time. They were simple, brief registry-office weddings, dressed in their 'Sunday best' and returning straight to everyday duties the next day. Bridal gowns were not always white, and even if they were, were seldom meant to be worn on just this single occasion (Howard, 2006). However, in the post-war era of the 1950s, the white wedding emerged in part as a symbol of the economic and social triumph of capitalism (Howard, 2006). In short, romance has been used to sell consumer goods (Otnes & Pleck, 2003).

In fact, the concept of love has itself achieved a religion-like status (Beck & Beck-Gernsheim, 1995). As reflected in our results from MLAP the concept of 'romance' takes an even greater significance in how weddings are conducted in the twenty-first century than even the personal identities of the couple themselves. Thus music choices now, although still often based on what is believed to be traditional, are more often about the romantic ideal, even more than it is about the tastes and preferences of the bride and groom. Interestingly, our results also demonstrated that differing attitudes towards marriage may be reflected in song nominations, with single and divorced people tending to rate their song selections as of less positive valence than people in a committed relationships.

Otnes and Pleck (2003) also argue that the frequent inclusion of dancing and live bands in modern weddings is another sign of lavishness. From the 1980s in the U.S., they claim, DJs began to take on the role of master of ceremonies and to take responsibility for selecting music that would cater to both the individual tastes of the bride and groom as well as the inter-generationality of the wedding guests. The first song played at the reception would usually be something designed to create an atmosphere of romance and would often be something with personal significance to the bride and groom.

Thus, the way the British royal family may hold their weddings is too "impersonal" for most couples today. Rather than aspiring to follow the customs set by the aristocracy, many people prefer to put their own personal stamp on marriage ceremonies. As shown in our case study, weddings may be intentionally choreographed to reflect the individual tastes of the couple themselves. For some, the valuing of tradition and cultural roots itself reflects the personality and ideals of the bride and groom. This may be particularly so in cultural contexts in which collectivism is valued above individualism. Like many rite of passage celebrations, weddings are generally community events, and thus many of the customs surrounding weddings hold important social functions, such as increasing the sense of community bonds by communal singing during the wedding preparations, or to reinforce notions of social hierarchy or gender roles, or to enhance the cohesion of the two families being joined through group dancing. Even in modern European-style weddings, many celebrations often have communal dances, with some popular choices including "The Chicken dance", "The Conga", and the "Macarena". For migrant groups in particular, the use of traditional group singing, chanting or dancing, can serve as a nostalgic articulation of cultural identity.

A common theme among weddings across cultures and time periods is that they mark the passage to a new life for the bride and groom. For many women, this transition would often be a difficult one, and thus songs lamenting her separation from her parental home and the hardships of her life to come are found in many cultures. Other preparatory rituals included symbolic actions such as shaving the groom's head, ritual cleansing, the baking of bread as a symbol of fertility and prosperity, or the veiling of the bride. Other rituals celebrate the impending union of the bride and groom, and are designed to not only ensure the virginity of the bride, but also the fecundity of their marriage.

Increasingly, however, music choices for weddings are becoming more homogenized (Garrido, 2014). Culturally specific music may mostly be retained in the ceremonial parts of the marriage, alongside some Westernized customs, and may be even more absent in the post-ceremonial celebrations. In Japan, for example, the use of white wedding dresses and Mendelssohn's wedding march is commonly found alongside more traditional Shinto customs. Similarly, in Romania amplified instruments may now replace acoustic ones and popularized 'Gypsy' music is now heard rather than traditional Romanian songs (Beissinger, 2005).

Overall, the place of marriage in society and the relationship between the husband and wife has undergone dramatic transformations since the 1950s (Koontz, 2006). The balance between men and women in relationships has changed greatly, with couples tending to negotiate gender roles within a family in ways specific to their relationship rather than relying on social norms. These changes have in many cases meant positive changes for women, but they represent challenges as well. The negotiation of these changing dynamics between the sexes and changing relationship ideals are often reflected in new wedding practices that emerge alongside the traditional. As we have seen in this chapter and the previous one, music often seems to mirror these evolving ideals towards love, relationships and marriage. The following chapter will consider music's place in another central set of rituals marking a key rite of passage: funerals.

References

Bassano, P. (1994). A Second Miracle at Cana: Recent Musical Discoveries in Veronese's *Wedding Feast*. *Historic Brass Society Journal*, 11–23. Retrieved from http://historicbrass.org/Portals/0/Documents/Journal/1994/HBSJ_1994_JL01_002_Bassano.pdf

Beck, U., & Beck-Gernsheim, E. (1995). *The Normal Chaos of Love*. Cambridge: Polity Press.

Beck, U., & Beck-Gernsheim, E. (2002). *Individualization: Institutionalized Individualism and Its Social and Political Consequences*. London, Thousand Oaks, CA: SAGE.

Beissinger, M. H. (2005). Romani (Gypsy) Music-Making at Weddings in Post-Communist Romania: Political Transitions and Cultural Adaptations. *Folklorica*, *10*(1), 39–51.

Boden, S. (2001). 'Superbrides': Wedding Consumer Culture and the Construction of Bridal Identity. *Sociological Research Online, 6*(1). Retrieved from http://www.socresonline.org.uk/6/1/boden.html

Cherlin, A. J. (2004). The Deinstitutionalization of American Marriage. *Journal of Marriage and Family, 66,* 848–861.

Fenlon, I. (1980). *Music and Patronage in Sixteenth-Century Mantua.* New York: Cambridge University Press.

Ferrai, L. A. (1882). *Cosimo De' Medici: Duca di Firenze.* Bologna: Nicola Zanichelli.

Fraser, J. (2011). Pop Song as Custom: Weddings, Ethnicity and Entrepreneurs in West Sumatra. *Ethnomusicology, 55*(2), 200–228.

Garrido, S. (2014). Weddings. In W. Thompson (Ed.), *Music in the Social and Behavioral Sciences: An Encyclopedia.* Thousand Oaks, CA: SAGE.

Gioia, T. (2015). *Love Songs: The Hidden History.* New York: Oxford University Press.

Guerin, P., Elmi, F. H., & Guerin, B. (2006). Weddings and Parties: Cultural Healing in One Community of Somali Women. *Australian e-Journal for the Advancement of Mental Health, 5*(2), 105–112.

Hague, R. H. (1983). Ancient Greek Wedding Songs: The Tradition of Praise. *Journal of Folklore Research, 20*(2/3), 131–143.

Howard, V. (2006). *Brides Inc: American Weddings and the Business of Tradition.* Philadelphia: University of Pennsylvania Press.

Hudson, F. (1968). Bach's Wedding Music. *Current Musicology, 7,* 111–120.

Ilieva, L., & Ivanov, D. (2013). The People, the Customs, the Costumes, the Music. *Music and Dances in Checha.* European Territorial Cooperation Programme Greece-Bulgaria 2007–2013.

Karlinsky, S. (1986). Igor Stravinsky and Russian Preliterate Theater. In J. Pasler (Ed.), *Confronting Stravinsky: Man, Musician and Modernist* (pp. 3–15). Berkeley: University of California Press.

Kerr, J. M. (1965). English Wedding Music. *The Musical Times, 106*(1463), 53–55.

Koontz, S. (2006). *Marriage, a History: How Love Conquered Marriage.* New York: Viking.

Ling, J. (1997). *A History of European Folk Music.* Rochester, NY: University Rochester Press.

Mazo, M. (1994). Wedding Laments in North Russian Villages. In M. J. Kartomi & S. Blum (Eds.), *Music-Cultures in Contact: Convergences and Collisions.* Australia: Gordon & Breach.

Otnes, C. C., & Pleck, E. H. (2003). *Cinderella Dreams: The Allure of the Lavish Wedding.* Berkeley: University of California Press.

Penner, B. (2004). A Vision of Love and Luxury. *Winterthur Portfolio, 39*(1), 1–20.

Pohren, D. E. (2005). *The Art of Flamenco.* Westport: Bold Strummer.

Pouncy, C. (1994) *The Domostroi: Rules for Russian Households in the Time of Ivan the Terrible.* Ithaca, NY: Cornell University Press.

Rice, T. (1994). *May It Fill Your Soul: Experiencing Bulgarian Music.* Chicago: University of Chicago Press.

Sander, E. (2005). Music, Drinking and Dance at Aristocratic Russian Weddings. *Intersection, 26*(1), 34–61

Sugarman, J. C. (1997). *Engendering Song: Singing and Subjectivity at Prespa Albanian Weddings.* Chicago: University of Chicago Press.

Tiersot, J. (1889). *Histoire de La Chanson Populaire en France.* Paris: E. Plon, Nourrit.

van Nieuwkerk, K. (2012). Popularizing Islam or Islamizing Popular Music: New Developments in Egypt's Wedding Scene. *Contemporary Islam, 6*(3), 235–254.

Wallis, J. (2002). 'Loved the Wedding, Invite Me to the Marriage': The Secularisation of Weddings in Contemporary Britain. *Sociological Research Online, 7*(4). Retrieved from http://www.socresonline.org.uk/7/4/walliss.html

Williams, S. (1998). Constructing Gender in Sudanese Music. *Yearbook of Traditional Music, 30*, 74–84.

CHAPTER 12

Funerals and Mourning Rituals

Music has an association with the 'healing' of grief, which has been reported in human history since ancient times. Homer suggested that music could be used as an antidote to sorrow as early as the seventh or eighth centuries BC (Nelson & Weathers, 1998). Historical traditions reveal that while many rituals associated with grief and funerals seem not to have changed, many have adapted across time. This chapter draws distinctions between historical and modern funeral and mourning practices to illuminate the shifting role music has had for the individual and culture over time. Histories of funerals and mourning rituals from a range of cultural contexts are used to highlight the strong interaction between long-term oral cultural traditions or collective memories, and emergent individualized changes that have taken place in recent contexts.

This chapter briefly considers three historically persistent folk traditions: the role of the lament in Georgian funerals; the case of the 'cantos de ángeles' in Chile, used as a particular song form used for the funerals of very young children; and the jazz funeral from New Orleans in North America. These are then contrasted with the bell tolling practised in seventeenth century England to explore that historically specific context and how the function of the tolling bell has changed across a history of social and political landscapes. The chapter then focuses on the changing funerary practices across Australia's history, moving from settlement through to its current status as a richly multicultural society. The opinions and

© The Author(s) 2019
S. Garrido, J. W. Davidson, *Music, Nostalgia and Memory*, Palgrave Macmillan Memory Studies,
https://doi.org/10.1007/978-3-030-02556-4_12

practices of modern day Australians in relation to funerals and uses of music in mourning rituals is investigated though the MLAP data.

Without doubt music can provoke tears, and its use to deliver structured outpourings of grief vary in musical form according to contexts. In Western music, Mozart's *Lacrimosa* from his Requiem of 1791[1] is one such example, where the halting string figure literally mirrors the physical action of sobbing, as the choir sings about the mournful day, full of tears, when judgement is to be passed on a guilty man who is risen from the ashes. The text asks for mercy and requests that Jesus grants eternal rest.

The physical externalization of feelings assists individuals with the expression of strong emotions, with tears being one manifestation of grief that is commonly associated with bereavement (Castle & Philips, 2003; Goss & Klass, 1997). The ritualised structures of funeral and mourning expressions seem to provide support for the expression of grief, while at the same time preventing people from becoming overwhelmed by their emotions. Within the funeral, music can offer a context for grief to be expressed where there is a structure for its delimitation (Romanoff & Terenzio, 1998). In fact, in the music used in death ceremonies across cultures there is often an identifiable music leader present to invoke and manage the mourners' grief response. It has been noted that in many contexts, these musicians are not part of the emotional experience themselves, but rather facilitate the grieving in others (Kotthoff, 2001).

Given the powerful associations that also exist between music and identity (Connell & Gibson, 2003; Hargreaves, Miell, & MacDonald, 2002; Ruud, 1997), and its capacity for triggering memories, the music played at a funeral can tell the story of the deceased and of those who mourn them within the cultural context—it facilitates remembering in a particular way, and joins the mourners in a common feeling towards to deceased (Cook & Walter, 2005). In modern contexts, music choices can be highly personalised, and so the music has the potential to become entwined within the narrative of the deceased's life and that of the mourners.

A belief in an afterlife is promoted in most religious funerals, whatever the faith, and music rituals can assist to create an atmosphere of sacredness. This is often a primary goal for a funeral—assisting to make the ceremony one of veneration of the decreased—even in secular settings (Palmer, 2006; Penman & Becker, 2009). Thus, aside from its association with the bereaved, music can imbue the occasion with a sense of the

---

[1] Track 83: Lacrimosa, Requiem, Mozart, London Philharmonic.

special, something which can make the bereaved feel that the death is being treated appropriately. Additionally, it has been shown that it is important for the bereaved to continue to have memory bonds with the deceased. These can be achieved through ephemera, images of the deceased, and music which can also offer a powerful and ongoing emotional association (Klass, Silverman, & Nickman, 1996). To explore these factors in more detail, we shall now explore our case studies in more detail.

HISTORICAL AND CROSS-CULTURAL PRACTICES

Georgian Laments

Lamenting is a musical grief ritual that seems to have existed across cultures and human history to express loss through use of the voice, which is either wailed, chanted, sung or spoken, the latter being most typically in some sort of poetic form. Laments form an important part of a wake or vigil, enabling a sense of sharing the loss within the community (Kotthoff, 2001), thus strengthening social ties as well as making the bereaved feel less alone in their loss. In some cultural contexts, this genre of music is also used with the aim of stirring the spirit world (Schechter, 1994).

There are many examples of laments, but one example notable is in Georgia (Kotthoff, 2001). Located on the border of Asia and Europe, Georgia contains a blending of different cultural practices. The most distinctive feature of the Georgian lament is that it is polyphonic (containing several melodies sung at once) (Emsheimer, 1967). It was traditionally believed that this use of the voices progressed the soul of the dead person towards its final state (Nakashidze, 2002).

Georgian laments are typically performed by female members and neighbours of the decreased. Drawing on a specific format, the women gather around the coffin and lament, reflecting on personal memories of the deceased and speaking to the deceased's soul directly (Kotthoff, 2006). This improvisatory element results in the laments being partly sung and partly spoken, and so the lamenters interact, progressing their stories and memories of the deceased. The quality of the lament is judged on whether or not it stirs the mourners, and the mourner is expected to express appropriate feelings of grief, as signified, for example, by tears (Kotthoff, 2006).

Little Angels

In contrast to the concept of the musical process being entwined with wailing, the use of music to rejoice at funerals is also found in some cultures. A particularly interesting example of this kind of practice is the 'cantos de ángeles' (songs of angels), which appears in parts of Latin America. This specific song form is associated with the funerals of infants. It originated in Spain, with Jesuit missionaries taking the song form to the South American sub-continent in the 1500s. The Latin American variations are common, especially in Chile (Schechter, 1983).

The Chilean 'angelitos' (little angels) traditions have often been reported by onlookers as celebratory rather than sombre events. Without doubt these traditions mix European settler, Christian, and local indigenous belief systems. While it is evident that the celebratory and cathartic elements of singing and dancing are not primarily associated with Catholic mourning, the combination of Christian and Indigenous cultural practices has produced a deep emotional outpouring that accompanies the celebratory mood with much consumption of alcohol (Schechter, 1994).

Coming to grips with the impact of the loss of a child involves great emotional and psychological challenges. In the 'angelitos' ritual, the child's death is 'celebrated' as it is believed the child's innocence at death exalts them to the status of an angel (Schechter, 1994). Perhaps to account for the tragedy of the loss in the extreme poverty facing most of the populace, the Chilean belief in the transcendence of the child to the status of an angel offers the family an intercessor in heaven, so that when the parents and siblings die, they can also reach heaven. In these traditional contexts, superstition prohibits the singing of the angelitos songs at any other time, for it is felt that if the songs are heard out of context, another child will die (Orellana, 1990).

In the 'angelitos' ceremonies, which are now found almost exclusively in rural communities in Chile, singers are hired to perform the specialized songs, and in different geographical areas customs vary as to whether the singers enter the house of the decreased or not. The deceased child is made-up, dressed in a white tunic with angel wings attached, and seated on a chair, which is typically placed high in a corner of a room, looking down on the mourners. The songs feature incantations to stir the spirit world and take the child from the state of death to the spirit realm. It is believed that if this ceremony does not take place, the child may be left in limbo (Orellana, 1990).

During the actual wake, the choristers sing greetings to the 'angelito', and this is typically followed by dancing music of a more general nature (Dannemann, 2007; Schechter, 1983). Before the infant is taken to the cemetery, other songs are sung that take the perspective of the child as angel. For Chileans, these greeting and farewell verses are critical to the transformation of the child to a state of an angel.

It has been stated that the fiesta (party) atmosphere creates an illusion of normality which seeks to "entrap particularly the mother and the god-parents in a net of emphatic joy, thus saving them from the freedom to grieve" (Schechter, 1983, p. 52). At the same time, the "the emotions are already aroused [and] supercharge[ed]" (p. 55), the music giving direction to the outpouring of these emotions.

While the tradition is a fascinating hybrid of cultures, it has been susceptible to historical changes. One of the most interesting historical twists is that some of the songs themselves are being appropriated by modern popular folk artists and recorded in their own right, independent of the mourning ritual, which radically changes the song's meaning and impact on the listeners (Dannemann, 2007).[2] Such cultural shifts are part of historical evolution, but show quite simply how the underlying emotional meaning is being transposed to a different genre for a different kind of public consumption.

The Jazz Funeral

As the previous examples reveal, sending the soul to an afterlife is often a primary goal of the music used in the funerals of many cultures. In African-American communities in regions of the United States, the jazz funeral serves precisely this function again (Collins & Doolittle, 2006). In this practice, which was first associated with male members of the community, the musicians are present and play at a wake that takes place before the funeral. They also play during the funeral procession from the deceased home to the church and then on to the cemetery. This music typically includes hymns played in the jazz idiom. The mourners follow the marching musicians, so as the procession moves to the burial site (Sakakeeny, 2011). During this procession, the band often begins to play more upbeat music. This shift in tempo and meaning is referred to as "turning or cutting the body loose" (Secundy, 1989, p. 101), and often leads the

---

[2] Track 84: Rin Del Angelito, Violeta Parra.

mourners into dancing as they process. Mixed with a combination of Christian and long-held beliefs stemming back to the African ancestral past, it seems that this practice is undertaken to enable the deceased person to cross over to the next life. This celebration embodies the idea that the deceased has been liberated from the pain of life into a better condition (Secundy, 1989). Thus, the jazz funeral is often referred to as a "home-going celebration" (Collins & Doolittle, 2006, p. 959). Secundy (1989) reports that the funeral rituals of Afro-Americans of the jazz funeral tradition are "vitally important for helping blacks maintain mental health. They enhance self-acceptance, acceptance of others, and acceptance of nature ... The black church and black music, in or out of church, allow catharsis, survival, and coping..." (p. 100).

The jazz funeral tradition was at its height in the first half of the twentieth-century, and declined in popularity during the 1970s. This seems in part owing to the rise of other forms of music and the more personalized funerary preferences like personal ballad anthems and torch songs (see Davidson & Garrido, 2014). But today, intriguingly, a revival is underway, with modern African-American bands such as the Dirty Dozen Brass Band[3] bringing such marches back to the streets of New Orleans. Also, while the jazz funeral was historically generally for prominent Afro-American males, the revival of the practice now includes both men and women, with the emergent trend being to offer this type of funeral to those who have who have died tragically young (Sakakeeny, 2011). Clearly, the example reveals that tradition is not static, but rather evolving along with other societal changes. The newer practices seem to reflect an increasing trend for the personalized funeral and music.

The examples above have direct links to traditional customs and musics from ancient indigenous cultures. Western European cultures often also possess strong vestiges of pre-Christians customs, though these often become masked by strongly formal institutionalized practices such as the church and the state. Since Christianity and its complex history mingled with colonization, it is fitting that we now explore examples from England before shifting to Australia (once a colonial settlement). These examples consider the ways in which Christianity and subsequent modern day secularized cultural practices have emerged in relation to music and mourning rituals.

---

[3] Track 85: Just a Closer Walk with Thee, Dirty Dozen Brass Band.

Mourning, Bells and English Early Modern History

In Christianity, bells have been used as signals of death, symbols of respect for the dead, and also as devices through which to express feelings of sadness and loss. Paulinus of Nola (c. 354–June 22, AD 431), a Roman poet baptized as a Christian, who later became Bishop of Nola in Campania, Italy, is acknowledged as the first to introduce bells into Christian worship. By the early Middle Ages, bells were commonly incorporated into the church and cathedral buildings across Europe. As Christian symbols, bells have been described as examples of 'emotional communities', since parishioners were able to put a boundary on their expressive worlds by "isolating, categorizing, and classifying sounds while rejecting noises" (McKinnon, 2016, p. 31), the unique bell pitches and musical syntax being developed for particular emotional community outcomes.

While bells were used for a number of community functions, bell tolling for the dead was perhaps the most symbolically moving. Looking at Dolly McKinnon's (2016) detailed case studies of bell tolling in 16th and seventeenth-century England, we can begin to understand how parishioners may have responded to the sound of the bells they heard, and how their emotions and memories were stirred in particular ways. England was still going through a Reformation relating to religion and religious practices. Prior to the Reformation, praying for souls in purgatory—the state after death where some souls waited in suffering before their journey to either heaven or hell—was signalled by the tolling of bells. After the Reformation, Protestants abandoned the concept of purgatory, and some wished to eliminate bell tolling after death altogether. However, rather than giving up the practice completely, the tolling bell was used as a technology to memorialize the deceased and allow the mourner to reflect on their own spirituality. This change in Protestant religious practice in turn shifted the function of the death knell and the funeral bell, though people's memories and former associations would, of course, persist. Roman Catholics maintained their belief in purgatory and the tolling of bells was heard by them as a potential passage to heaven.

In her text, McKinnon refers to archival records from two seventeenth century deaths to illuminate differences between bell ringing practices used at the death of the Roman Catholic, Henry Howard, Lord Privy Seal for both James VI & I in Protestant London in 1614, and the Protestant cobbler, Christopher Ccurts, who died in Dagenham in Essex, 1606. It seems that in death, Henry Howard's Roman Catholicism could be heard, defiant of England's Protestant soundscape. On his deathbed, he paid to ensure that a bell be tolled ahead of his funeral. In the case of Christopher Courts, the cobbler, McKinnon cites records that he was buried within four hours of death, without any bell tolling or religious ceremony whatsoever. An analysis of the circumstances in which these significant cultural practices were overlooked reveals that there was evidence of other sudden deaths, which McKinnon attributes to the plague. Fear of plague would have doubtlessly have led to a swift burial, and the lack of an official funeral with associated bell tolling could have been a swift response to the evidence of plague—a silencing of potential fear associated with a death of this type.

This brief historical excursion shows that bell tolling for the dead, both united and divided English early modern Christian communities. It shows how different communities interpreted and responded to a single sonic symbol in quite distinct ways. If we turn to modern contexts, we can see that a significant historical change has taken place. Today, bells are not heard so often, in fact, bells are principally associated with large-scale memorial services, thus their function has become associated more with events involving many people, rather than individuals and families (Baldwin, Jackson, & Johnston, 2012). Yet the traditional Christian bell tolling practices discussed were observed until well into the 1960s.

Nowadays, people seem not to be so concerned with notifying or including local community in their grief. While there are many reasons for this, greater mobility means that families are often geographically dispersed and not living in the local neighbourhood. Also, friendships are now interest-based, rather derived from the neighbourhood in which someone lives. Here, we might also apply Rosenwein's (2002) idea of an 'emotional community'—albeit a much larger sense of 'emotional community' than expressed in the parish context of historical bell tolling—as we observe that in modern society people identify less with their immediate local community and parish but rather more with a secular system of belief and practice drawn from a more global sense of belonging and participating in the world. To direct our attention to these sorts of ideas, we now turn to a consideration of funerals across Australia and is transition from English colonial settlement to a diverse multicultural society.

Australian Mourning and Funerals Across the First Half of the Twentieth Century

A survey of newspapers at the founding of the Federation of Australia reveals that Mr. E. Crawford reviewed a volume of some 60 anthems suitable for performance at funeral services (TGR, 1910). The works were representative of the western art music canon including funerary pieces by Beethoven and the Funeral March by Chopin. All 60 items were reportedly included for their sorrow-evoking capacity. A couple of decades later, A. E. Floyd (1936) similarly describes the Dead March by Handel, funeral marches by Beethoven and Chopin, Guilmant's "Funeral March and Hymn of Seraphs" for organ, and Sullivan's "In Memoriam" overture.[4] These uses of specifically themed solemn works to memorialize the dead were the practices of the overwhelming numbers of European migrant settlers.

These trends were often so dominant that even those of different cultural and religious observance followed the practice. For example, the funerary requests left by Mr. Mahango Ram, as reported in *The Recorder* in 1933, stressed a desire for "suitable music" to be played ("Indian Hawker's Will: Suitable Music for Funeral," 1933). This man had worked as a hawker, and like many fellow Indian migrants, travelled to sell a range of goods to those living in regional areas, providing an essential service to remote communities (Joop, 2002). Of a non-Christian background, Mr. Ram may not have been personally familiar with music that would have been considered appropriate, but in his idea of what a socially respectable funeral would entail, the 'correct music' was clearly a vital element. His own cultural practices were set aside perhaps owing to a lack of critical mass of Hindus. In addition, however, he died a wealthy man, and this memorialization was surely, at least in part, a way of leaving a memory trace of someone who was successful and significant in the Australian social and political economy.

After the Second World War, and with the changing cultural landscape and rapidly growing migrant and refugee populations, the types of music selected for funerals in Australia were subject to more variation. For example, the burgeoning Italian communities who migrated in the 1940–1960s favoured not only high Catholic traditions, but also more popular music. While music had always featured heavily in the Italian Catholic funeral, through the organist or church choir, it became increasingly popular to

---

[4] Track 86: In Memoriam, Sullivan, BBC Philharmonic Orchestra.

hire a professional singer to lead the music at the funeral, someone able to deliver hymns, favourite popular songs and consult with the family to ensure a degree of familiarity and liking. Like the Georgian wailing, there had been a tradition of professional wailing in Italian communities, especially rural ones, and with migration, this tradition transformed itself to have a contemporary and contextual relevance (Co-operative Funeralcare, 2013; Hong, 2016).

As time has progressed, irrespective of cultural background, evolutionary changes to traditional music practices at funerals have been most clearly affected by the advent of pre-recorded music—"relayed music"—which enabled a cheap alternative to having to pay for an organ and organist or an ensemble of musicians. Also, as churches began losing business to the crematorium, a trend began towards giving funerals a less solemn and more of a celebratory atmosphere, with funeral dirges featuring less frequently (Parsons, 2012). But, it was not until there were major reforms in liturgy in all Christian denominations throughout the 1960s and 70s, that there was a clear movement to make funerals more personalised and less austere in format and music (Parsons, 2012).

In modern contexts sacred music often still plays a part of the Australian funeral service, but secular music is increasingly involved, even in church settings (Caswell, 2011–2012; Cook & Walter, 2005). In essence, within the Christian tradition alone, it is possible to see that in Australia, as elsewhere in the Western world, funeral music has gone from choices determined by custom or church ritual to where almost any music can be used and heard as being 'appropriate' if it was known to be of significance to the deceased.

Of course, the examples given thus far reveal complex histories, transformed by individual and collective negotiations and infused by culturally shaped memories of appropriate behaviour and music. For some people, as the example of Mr. Ram revealed, public perception motivated music choices for funerals. Even in the most seemingly individualized choices, other people inevitably feature, the funeral being a ritualized cultural expression of memorial for the dead (Adamson & Holloway, 2012).

Modern Day Playlists: Australian Funerals Today

It has been argued that, despite the relative decline of tradition underpinning funeral rituals in contemporary society, three elements have persisted over time: (1) the desire to re-assure loved ones that the deceased person is 'all right' even though dead; (2) the need to maintain a sense of ongoing connection to the deceased; and (3) the hope to keep alive an aspect of the deceased in us so that we can continue to show respect (Kastenbaum, 2004). This emphasis on memorialization might also be aptly described as a form of '*task-based coping*' (Corr, Nabe, Nabe, & Corr, 2008). By selecting music for the funeral the bereaved is actively engaged in a task that requires nostalgic reflection on the deceased and that ultimately assists them in processing their grief. When the deceased had selected the music themselves, this can be regarded as an engagement in communicating a message about themselves and their feelings for their loved ones. In this regard, the music can act as a symbol of the deceased. Given its emotive and reminiscence powers, the selection of music for a funeral therefore has the potential to be a highly effective tool for creating continuing bonds with the deceased—an ongoing sonic memorial—and forms one of many ways that an individual can deal with grief.

MLAP Funeral Studies

In the MLAP project, we investigated the extent to which music and tradition are still important to those making choices for funerals. In particular, we wanted to find out what kind of music people in modern day contexts choose to have played at their own funeral or at the funeral of a loved one as well as the primary motivations for such music choices. We were also interested in the extent to which historical tradition was important to people when making choices about music for funerals, and how various personality factors also influenced the music chosen.

In a first exploratory phase we conducted qualitative interviews with five people exploring the question of funeral music choice. Aged between 20 and 50 years, the interviewees choices were highly varied: Bach, classical, 'joyous', a 'graduation' song, and instrumental music. In fact, no one was able to nominate a specific piece of music. Rather, choices were somewhat generalized, and more about the overall ambience or message individuals desired for their funeral than about particular pieces of music. Those who chose classical and instrumental music felt the genre was an obvious choice because of its serious connotations, enabling mourners to grieve. The person who requested "joyous" music did so because it has been the genre that had stood out in her own life and represented the meaning she wanted her funeral to project. Her rationale was that the music should be things that had been significant in her own life and memories. The participant who nominated 'graduation' music had a light-hearted approach, with the intention of offering the mourners comfort, and signalling that she had moved on to a new phase of existence rather than ceased to exist.

After the exploratory interviews, a second phase of our research surveyed 227 undergraduate students from a university in Australia, many of whom were music students, mostly aged 18–25. In addition to being asked to pick music for their funeral and give a reason for the selection, they were also asked to rate the emotion of this music on a scale 1–5 (1 = a negative emotion like sadness or anger, 5 = a positive emotion like happiness or peacefulness). Not surprisingly, given the age and field of study of the students, the most popular choice of genre was pop music (39.6%), with classical music rated second most popular (27.4%). The majority selected music that they rated as having a positive emotion (67.8%). The music that was nominated for their own funeral largely equated with life review and personal taste: expressing the participant's ideals about life and death; reminding the participant of special times in their lives. In this survey, only 9.9% selected music because it was mournful, and less than 5% mentioned wanting a traditional or religious service with accompanying music.

The results of this second study phase reveal that following tradition in the twenty-first century in Australia is less valued than expressing personal meaning, despite the historical symbolism of traditional and religious serviced and music. Overall, the young people were concerned about leaving positive memories behind them. What is interesting, of course, it that they perceived music to be a powerful memorial, and something that would have enduring impact on the mourners.

In the third and final phase of the MLAP research we recruited 433 people from all ages and walks of life from the MLAP website. This included: 297 females, 131 males, 2 'others' and 3 people who did answer the question, who were aged 15–83 years (the mean age of participants was 35.6 years). We wished to explore whether particular personality traits were associated with the importance that an individual gave to people's choices of funeral music. Based on what we understood about nostalgia, we hypothesized that with a more diverse population and age range, some older people may value music of the past more than the young who tended to be understandably future-oriented. Additionally, since nostalgia concerns yearning for an ideal past which can be either past stages of an individual's own life (personal nostalgia) or for past history through which one has not necessarily lived (historical nostalgia) (Holbrook, 1993; Marchegiani & Phau, 2011), we also explored whether or not a proneness to personal or historical nostalgia could be related to selecting traditional music choices for one's own funeral music.

Another measure included in the study related to how people deal with issues like grief and death in their own lives. Measures of 'coping styles'—or how a person habitually responds to stressful events—were also included in this part of the MLAP data collection. As in the previous phase of the study, ratings of the selected funeral music were made. Additionally, participants were asked to listen to a brief excerpt from Mozart's Requiem, and were asked questions about whether they would consider playing this music at their funeral. The survey finished with a similar series of questions about the music they would choose for the funeral of another person.

The collected data was analysed, and the music being nominated for funerals was classified using 4 meta-clusters: Traditional/Sacred, Popular (including pop, rock, electronic etc.), Instrumental/Classical (which also included jazz), and Humorous. We also categorized items based on motivation for choices which included: Following Tradition, Personal Expression, Aesthetic Reasons, and Mood Creation.

Like previous phases of the study, popular music was the most frequently chosen genre for both one's own funeral and for the funeral of another, with Instrumental/Classical rating second highest, and Humorous and Traditional/Sacred choices being rated lowest. Analysis revealed that the genre of music selected for funerals was significantly different according to age, with the average age being 33.9 years for those who chose popular music and 42.2 years for those who selected Instrumental/Classical. Again, the music people chose was considered to predominantly express positive emotions of high energy such as joy or elation.

The main motivation reported for the specific music selection was Personal Expression, and similar choices were made when asked to select music for another person's funeral. When asked to listen to an excerpt of music from Mozart's Requiem and comment on its appropriateness for a funeral, the majority felt it was not music they would want at their own funeral (88.7%), since it did not mean anything to them personally, nor did it reflect their personality or beliefs. Of the minority said they would consider it, they said they liked it because it was appropriately mournful.

Exploring music choices in relation to personality, those who chose Traditional/Sacred music had significantly higher scores on the Religious

Coping subscale than people who chose popular music. People who selected Popular music scored higher on Coping by Humour subscale than those who had selected Traditional/Sacred music. Personal nostalgia was higher for those who selected music for Mood Creation than for those whose motivation was Personal Expression. The study also indicated that the choice of sad music was predominantly associated with people high in neuroticism while those choosing happy music were high in conscientiousness. These results indicate that even with changing overall approaches to the types of music use at funerals, both personality and individual coping styles motivate the types of music selected.

Case Studies: Exploring Real Music Choices

One limitation of the MLAP survey is that is participants were asked to think about what their music choices would be in the hypothetical situation or their own funeral or that of a loved one. While the connections found between music choices and coping styles indicate that selecting music for the funeral may contribute positively to the process of adjustment in situations of grief, the results reported here are not based on actual choices in many cases. To conclude this chapter, we therefore consider some real-life examples of funerals in the modern day. We begin with what was arguably the most viewed and discussed funeral of all time: that of Diana, Princess of Wales who was killed in a car crash at the age of 36. We then consider case studies of two recent Australian funerals: one of a 62-year-old woman, and another of 37-year-old man.

Diana, Princess of Wales (1 July 1961–31 August 1997)[5]

Diana became one of the most famous members of British royalty in history. Divorced from the heir to the British throne just a year before the car crash in which she was killed along with her new partner Dodi Fayed and their driver Henri Paul, Diana's death provoked an outpouring of public sorrow that swept across the Western world. The feelings expressed seemed to bring millions of people a temporary sense of community, these emotions providing a sense of equality for those sharing in the grief (Turner, 2004). Twenty years after that death, it is this shared emotional

[5] The section on *Diana, Princess of Wales* first appeared as a blog by the second author for the Australian Research Council's Centre of Excellence for the History of Emotions: www.historiesofemotion.com/2017/09/15/dianas-funeral-and-music/

community we can explore in considering her funeral, its music and the nostalgia recently experienced for that sad event.

It is important to contextualise that it was in part the deep loss expressed by the public that influenced how Diana's funeral was carried out. Queen Elizabeth II's lack of immediate and official acknowledgement of Diana's death resulted in public outrage. This in turn forced the Queen and her family to return to Buckingham Palace in London from their late summer retreat at Balmoral in Scotland. This wave of public grief also caused the Queen to take the unprecedented step of giving a state funeral to someone who had been distanced from the royal family. Reflecting on the funeral, several key elements made it deeply affecting for those who saw the ceremony on TV or in person: the images of millions of floral tributes laid outside Buckingham Palace; tens of thousands of people lining the route of the cortege, softly weeping, hushed in their respect; Diana's young sons following the coffin, evidently in deep shock; her brother's passionate and angry eulogy; and, perhaps most moving of all, the use of music in the service.

The funeral was viewed by 32.2 million people in Britain and more than one billion people internationally. It contained many traditional elements of the Protestant funeral ritual. As a state ceremony, the music was cleverly chosen to deliver different sorts of socio-cultural messages and provide a range of emotional impacts. Melancholy, solemnity, reverence and formality were achieved through the tolling of the tenor bell of Westminster Abbey. Organ music performed by Hubert Parry, Frank Bridge and Ralph Vaughan Williams generated a sense of Englishness. The service also included popular classical works like Johann Pachelbel's *Canon* and the *Adagio* for strings by Tomaso Albinoni, works known for their 'tearjerking' effect (Sloboda, 1991). Choral music in the form of the 'Libera me' from Giuseppe Verdi's *Requiem* and John Taverner's *Song for Anthene* also added to this special ambience, both works referencing the passage of the dead to heaven. But it was the inclusion of the song *Candle in the Wind* that gave the funeral service a popular reference and cemented Diana's reputation as 'the People's Princess' (*The Australian*, 3 August 2017). Considering the historical ritual of a state funeral, this popular song represented a real deviation from tradition, and in effect became the centerpiece of the service.

The impact of Sir Elton John's rendition of his 1973 hit *Candle in the Wind*,[6] with re-worked lyrics by Bernie Taupin, could not have been antic-

---

[6] Refer to Track 2.

ipated. According to *The Guinness World Records* (2017), after the funeral the song became the biggest selling single in the UK and US ever. The lyrics were adapted from the song's original reference to the tragic life and death of Norma Jean Mortenson (Marilyn Monroe) and applied to Princess Diana—'Goodbye England's Rose' as opposed to 'Goodbye Norma Jean'. For such a public ritual, the inclusion of this highly sentimental song signified much in the five minutes and seven seconds of its performance: the mass familiarity and resonance with the ritual of pop music performance; the tragedy of young beautiful lives being extinguished, blurring the boundaries between the celebrity of Norma Jean and Diana; the personal friendship between Sir Elton John and Princess Diana that clearly resulted in the song's performance at the funeral; and, perhaps above all other elements, the strong impact of the music on the emotions of all who engaged with the service.

Some post-hoc analyses have claimed that the tone and number of media reports in the week leading up to and including Diana's funeral has been overplayed, and that the level of mass grief has been romanticised. The second author, Jane Davidson, lived in England at the time of the funeral and can attest that the degree of sentiment expressed was phenomenal. Floral tributes were offered at churches and cathedrals across the country, and the number of people attending religious services in churches and cathedrals rose significantly.

On 6 September 2017, the exact 20th anniversary of Diana's funeral, Jane happened to be in her local village gift shop near Melbourne. As she browsed the stock, she gradually became aware that she was also listening to a radio playing in the background. It was an interview with Elton John, who was reflecting on how difficult it had been for him to hold together his own emotions in Westminster Abbey at Diana's funeral. Then, a snippet of his rendition of 'Goodbye England's Rose' poured out of the radio, and as Jane heard the opening chords she could feel tears welling up. To Jane, listening to that song was a very rare occurrence, but the socio-cultural associations and musical mechanisms the song elicits afforded a release of emotion, even if only for a few seconds. For many, in fact, Diana's funeral is distilled in its most intense form of nostalgia through the performance of *Candle in the Wind*. *Candle in the Wind* has subsequently become appropriated as an expression of loss for millions of people around the world. The nostalgia found in the music heard at Diana's funeral connects strongly with music's long-held historical function: to offer emotional expression and mood regulation, and to intensify memory. To recognise and reflect on the value of using music to 'have a good cry' and to express deeply held emotions is important—it is something that interfaces with our everyday experiences, not only our experience of significant historical events such as the state funeral of a princess.

No less significant, but far less publically celebrated were the lives of two of our dear friends who both tragically lost their lives to cancer. Unlike Diana, whose funeral music was as much a politically symbolic act as it was a mourning ritual, these funerals were very much shaped by their musical content and its symbolism in their lives.

Philippa Maddern (24 August 1952–17 June 2014)

Philippa, affectionately known as 'Pip', was a medieval historian and founding Director of the Australian Research Council's Centre of Excellence for the History of Emotions. She lived in Perth, Western Australia. She was also a devout Christian who enjoyed science fiction writing, cooking, and was a passionate musician. She lived with a diagnosis of bile duct cancer for three years. Though aware of her fatal illness, she did not plan for her funeral. Close friends and family made all funerary arrangements and decided to choose music that while respecting the funeral liturgy, was music that they knew Pip loved. Pip's funeral took place at Christ Church, Claremont, Western Australia.

Much of the music selected was closely connected with memories that friends and family had of Pip and the times they had spent together. The opening musical item for the funeral service, *Never Weather beaten Sail* by Thomas Campion (1567–1620), was selected by Pip's niece. This particular work was chosen as the opening music owing to the words 'O come quickly, sweetest lord, and take my soul to rest', reflecting the Christian convictions of an afterlife held by both Pip and many of her friends and family. It was also selected because of the personal significance the work had had to Pip, with family and friends having fond memories of performing it with Pip on a group holiday.

Another piece that was selected was *Si bona suscepimus*, by Orlande de Lassus (1532–1594). Matthew, a very close younger friend of Pip's, reported that Pip loved the piece. His last memory of the piece had been when he and his family had sung it with Pip just months before her death. Matthew also selected *O sacrum convivium* by Thomas Tallis (1505–1585), which he felt was an appropriate choice as a requiem mass. It was another piece that was associated with treasured memories of family and friends, as

Pip had sung the work with him and other friends at a party. Pip also loved the music of J.S. Bach. Thus, two of Bach's organ works were chosen to reflect this: the introit setting of the chorale *O Mensch bewein dein Sünde groß* and the Passacaglia in C Minor.

Due to Pip's Christian convictions, hymns necessarily made up an important part of the musical selections for her funeral. In fact, the week before Pip died, she had spent much of her final hours singing hymns in the hospital. The first hymn, *I know that my redeemer lives*, was chosen by Pip's sister to stress the hope of resurrection. The second hymn, *Deck thyself my soul with gladness* (Schmücke dich), was a hymn that Pip always asked for in hymn singing sessions. She had a fine alto voice, and loved harmony singing, this hymn lending itself to her vocal prowess. The final hymn, *The day thou Gavest, Lord, is ended*, was a family favourite and had been sung at Pip's mother's funeral, so had layers of association and memories.

Benjamin Patrick Leske (11 September 1980–7 March 2018)

Ben described himself as a community musician, a choral conductor and singer, and a researcher who explored community choral singing, sexuality and gender identity for young people. He completed his doctorate six months before he died. He used his music to promote gender equality, and in the six years that he lived with brain cancer, he also used vocal performance as a context to raise awareness and counter the stigma associated with the illness. Prior to full-time work as a community musician Ben was a civil servant. Ben was also a Christian of German heritage and loved all things German. Having discussed and planned for his own funeral, Ben wanted it to reflect his passion for music. His funeral took place in St Paul's Cathedral, Melbourne.

Before the service began, several pieces of music were played for the attendees. These selections represented Ben's broad musical tastes. For example, *Wachet auf!* by J.S. Bach (1685–1759), reflected his love of German culture. Another piece played before the service was *Piano Man* by Billy Joel (b. 1949). *Piano Man* had been a favourite song from Ben's youth that he would frequently play on the piano and at karaoke parties. Joel's lyrics also spoke to Ben's belief in the power of song, with its references to music's power to make us "feel alright".

Ben also selected hymns for his funeral, including *We know God is Love*, by Margaret Gunn (b. 1949), and *Set Our Spirits Free from All Fear*, by

Shirley Erena Murray, (b 1931). Both these hymns were composed by women and besides their fine melodies, their lyrics were sentiments Ben wishes to be projected at his service. Margaret's hymn was the winner of the 2015 St Paul's Cathedral Melbourne 125th Anniversary Hymn Competition.

Other musical pieces were played in between spoken tributes. These included *Thankful*, by Rumer (b. 1979), *Landslide*, by Fleetwood Mac, lyrics Stevie Nicks (b. 1948), *Sure on this Shining Night*, by Morten Lauridsen (b. 1943), and *Laura's Song*, a piece composed by Ben himself. The latter song was a work that particularly represented Ben's creative achievement and his pride in that. In fact, all of the songs selected held personal meaning for Ben. The first song comes from an album entitled *Seasons of My Soul* which contains several works with a common theme of reflecting on life. Ben was especially grateful for the present moment and his partner, Khang, recalls that the song *Thankful* had helped Ben to get through his darker days in his last six years with its lyrics that reflect gratitude for life. Similarly, *Landslide* was selected as a reflection on the changing phases of life. *Sure on this Shining Night* is a meditation on faith, wonder and nature, and is composition for choir that Ben had conducted when working with the Melbourne Gay and Lesbian Chorus.

For the committal, Ben selected *Abendlied (Evening Song)*, by Joseph Rheinberger, (1893–1901). This beautiful and demanding choral work was loved by Ben for its beautiful part writing. For the 'farewell' section of the service, Ben selected *Light of a Clear Blue Morning*, by Dolly Parton (b. 1946), *One Voice*, by The Wailin' Jennys (released 2004), *Two Step*, by the Dave Matthews Band (released 1996), and *Love at First Sight* and *Dancing*, by Kylie Minogue (b. 1968). All these songs had deep resonances for Ben, some because he had used them in choral contexts, others because he simply loved the performer, as was the case with Kylie Minogue. As a huge Kylie Minogue fan, Ben enjoyed the composition and upbeat arrangement of *Love at First Sight*, and *Dancing*[7] was selected as the final music of the funeral as a positive song about living life and going out with a bang. *Light of a Clear Blue Morning* was a piece Ben had intended to conduct with what was going to be his new choir, Newlands Choir. He identified with the lyrics, especially with his own journey with cancer, and the positive message of how things will be okay in spite of confronting circumstances. Similarly, *One Voice* was loved by Ben because it was about

[7] Track 87: Dancing, Kylie Minogue.

singing with others and singing with 'one voice'. Ben was a fan of the Dave Matthews Band during his university days and *Two Step* spoke to him about the temporary nature of life and the need to live in the now.

Of course, many of us have not experienced anything approaching the musically rich lives of Pip Maddern or Ben Leske, but we can see how the music, whether following the religious ritual or not, was selected with great care and love. Both cases facilitate understanding, sharing and expressions of remembrance, and also love of others. However, Pip did not select her own music, while Ben did. Pip's friends and family selected music that mostly reflected their memories of her rather than music that projects a particular message or atmosphere. With Ben, his aim was to create a cheerful atmosphere that celebrated his creative achievements. These 'real' funerals do strongly reflect the way the MLAP participants discussed the music they thought they would select. Some wanted to reflect tradition, reflect on the life of the deceased, as in Pip's case. Others, wanted something more joyous and celebratory, like Ben, who wanted to be remembered 'going out with a bang!'.

For people who are facing death (e.g. palliative care or the very elderly), funeral music choices might be a useful tool for dealing with anticipatory grief, as it did for Ben, who certainly spent a long time considering his funeral music and who should contribute both readings and eulogies. The selection of music in anticipation of a funeral can provide an opportunity for life review (Aldridge, 1999; Magee & Davidson, 2004). It also offers an opportunity to demonstrate concern for those who will be left behind, and this is perhaps why joy and laughter has been selected so frequently in the MLAP surveys. In fact, as we see in this chapter, the music used in funerals in recent years, along with the whole ceremony, has become more of a life-interpreting celebration, rather than a grief-focused event, and seems to reflect important changes in cultural approaches to life and death.

THE TRAJECTORY FROM THE PAST TO THE MODERN DAY

This chapter has shown that music is an important aspect of funeral practices and has been used to convey many different messages including the maintenance of tradition and social position. A consistent and enduring feature of the funeral has been to memorialize the deceased and also offer comfort and hope to the mourners. In some cultural and historical contexts, this comfort has been about giving hope that there is experience beyond death itself. Our recent enquires through the MLAP website reveal that while tradition was still important to some participants, for the majority, a desire to portray their own values in a funeral setting was of paramount importance, their music choice being a powerful way to achieve this goal.

This chapter has also shown that while music offers personal expression, there is a broader emotional community experience implied, as musical affect is capable of binding people in their shared feelings, whether they be purely in response to the music's structures or the social and political factors that otherwise shape its meaning. Arguably, the study of funerals and mourning rituals takes us to the heart of human culture, as it highlight beliefs about the meaning of existence (Jalland, 2006; Kotthoff, 2001). The role that music can play is clearly a subject for those seeking insight into the encounter we all must face with death.

REFERENCES

Adamson, S., & Holloway. M. (2012). A Sound Track of Your Life: Music in Contemporary UK Funerals. *OMEGA, 65*(1), 33–54.

Aldridge, D. (1999). *Music Therapy in Palliative Care: New Voices.* London: Jessica Kingsley Publishers.

Baldwin, J., Jackson, T., & Johnston, R. (2012). *Dove's Guide for Church Bell Ringers to the Rings of Bells of the World* (10th ed.). London: Central Council.

Castle, J., & Philips, W. L. (2003). Grief Rituals: Aspects that Facilitate Adjustment to Bereavement. *Journal of Loss and Trauma, 8*(1), 41–71.

Caswell, G. (2011–2012). Beyond Words: Some Uses of Music in the Funeral Setting. *OMEGA: Journal of Death and Dying, 64*(4), 319–334.

Collins, W. L., & Doolittle, A. (2006). Personal Reflections on Funeral Rituals and Spirituality in a Kentucky African American Family. *Death Studies, 30,* 957–969.

Connell, J., & Gibson, C. (2003). *Sound Tracks: Popular Music, Identity and Place.* London: Routledge.

Cook, G., & Walter, T. (2005). Rewritten Rites: Language and Social Relations in Traditional and Contemporary Funerals. *Discourse and Society, 16*(3), 365–391.

Corr, C. A., Nabe, C., Nabe, C. M., & Corr, D. M. (2008). *Death and Dying, Life and Living.* Belmont, CA: Cengage Learning.

Dannemann, M. (2007). *Cultura Folclorica de Chile.* Santiago, Chile: Editorial Universitaria.

Davidson, J., & Garrido, S. (2014). *My Life as a Playlist.* Perth: University of Western Australia Publishing.

Emsheimer, E. (1967). Georgian Folk Polyphony. *Journal of the International Folk Music Council, 19,* 54–57.

Floyd, A. E. (1936, May 2). Commemorative Music: Funeral Marches. *The Australasian*.

Funeralcare, C.-O. (2013). *Funeral Music*. Retrieved from http://www.co-operative.coop/funeralcare/arranging-a-funeral/your-guide-to-arranging-a-funeral/Funeral-Music/

Goss, R., & Klass, D. (1997). Tibetan Buddhism and the Resolution of Grief: The Bardo-Thodol for the Dying and the Grieving. *Death Studies, 21*(4), 377–395.

Hargreaves, D. J., Miell, D., & MacDonald, R. A. R. (2002). What Are Musical Identities and Why Are They Important? In R. A. R. MacDonald (Ed.), *Musical Identities* (pp. 1–20). Oxford: Oxford University Press.

Holbrook, M. B. (1993). Nostalgia and Consumption Preferences: Some Emerging Patterns of Consumer Tastes. *Journal of Consumer Research, 20*, 245–256.

Hong, J. (2016). *Theater of the Dead: A Social Turn in Chinese Funerary Art* (pp. 1000–1400). Honolulu: University of Hawai'i Press.

Indian Hawker's Will: Suitable Music for Funeral. (1933, November 8). Recorder, p. 3. Retrieved from http://nla.gov.au/nla.news-article96088248

Jalland, P. (2006). *Changing Ways of Death in Twentieth-Century Australia: War, Medicine and the Funeral Business*. Sydney: UNSW Press.

Jupp, J. (2002). *The Australian People: An Encyclopedia of the Nation, Its People and Their Origins*. Cambridge: Cambridge University Press.

Kastenbaum, R. (2004). Why Funerals? *Generations, 28*(2), 5–10.

Klass, D., Silverman, P. R., & Nickman, S. L. (1996). *Continuing Bonds: New Understandings of Grief*. Philadelphia, PA: Taylor & Francis.

Kotthoff, H. (2001). Verbal Art Across Cultures: The Aesthetics and Proto-Aesthetics of Communication. In H. Knobloch & H. Kotthoff (Eds.), *Aesthetic Dimensions of Georgian Grief Rituals: On the Artful Display of Emotions in Lamentation* (pp. 167–194). Tubingen: Gunter Narr Verlag.

Kotthoff, H. (2006). Communicating Affect in Intercultural Lamentations in Caucasian Georgia. In K. Buhrig & J. D. T. Thije (Eds.), *Beyond Misunderstanding: Linguistic Analyses of Intercultural Communication*. Amsterdam: John Benjamins Publishing.

Magee, W. L., & Davidson, J. W. (2004). Music Therapy in Multiple Sclerosis: Results of a Systematic Qualitative Analysis. *Music Therapy Perspectives, 27*, 39–51.

Marchegiani, C., & Phau, I. (2011). The Value of Historical Nostalgia for Marketing Management. *Marketing Intelligence and Planning, 29*(2), 108–122.

McKinnon, D. (2016). 'The Ceremony of Tolling the Bell at the Time of Death': Bell-Ringing and Mourning in England, c.1500–c.1700. In J. W. Davidson & S. Garrido (Eds.), *Music and Mourning* (pp. 31–39). Abingdon: Ashgate.

Nakashidze, K. (2002). *On Polyphony in Georgian Funeral Songs*. Paper presented at the First International Symposium on Traditional Polyphony, Tbilisi, Georgia.

Nelson, D., & Weathers, R. (1998). Necessary Angels: Music and Healing in Psychotherapy. *Journal of Humanistic Psychology, 38*, 101–108.

Orellana, M. (1990). *Versos por Angelito:* Poetry and Its Function at the Wake of a Peasant Child in Chile. *Journal of Folklore Research, 27*(3), 191–203.

Palmer, A. J. (2006). Music Education and Spirituality: Philosophical Exploration II. *Philosophy of Music Education Review, 14*(6), 143–158.

Parsons, B. (2012). Identifying Key Changes: The Progress of Cremation and Its Influence on Music at Funerals in England, 1874–2010. *Mortality, 17*(2), 130–144.

Penman, J., & Becker, J. (2009). Religious Ecstatics, 'Deep Listeners,' and Musical Emotion. *Empirical Musicology Review, 4*(2), 49–70.

Romanoff, B. D., & Terenzio, M. (1998). Rituals and the Grieving Process. *Death Studies, 22*(8), 697–711.

Rosenwein, B. H. (2002). Worrying About Emotions in History. *The American Historical Review, 107*(3), 821–845.

Ruud, E. (1997). Music and Identity. *Nordic Journal of Music Therapy, 6*(1), 3–13.

Sakakeeny, M. (2011). Jazz Funerals and Second Line Parades. In D. Johnson (Ed.), *KnowLA Encyclopedia of Louisiana*. Louisiana: Louisiana Endowment for the Humanities.

Schechter, J. M. (1983). Corona y Baile: Music in the Child's Wake of Ecuador and Hispanic South America. Past and Present. *Latin American Music Review/ Revista de Musica Latinoamericana, 4*(1), 1–80.

Schechter, J. M. (1994). Divergent Perspectives on the Velorio Del Angelito. *Journal of Ritual Studies, 8*(2), 43–84.

Secundy, M. G. (1989). Coping with Words and Song: The New Orleans Jazz Funeral. *Literature and Medicine, 8*, 100–105.

Sloboda, J. (1991). Music Structure and Emotional Response: Some Empirical Findings. *Psychology of Music, 19*, 110–120.

TGR. (1910). Music. *The Queenslander*, p. 20. Retrieved from http://nla.gov.au/nla.news-article21881817

Turner, G. (2004). *Understanding Celebrity*. London: SAGE.

CHAPTER 13

Towards a New Contextual Psychology of Music and Emotion

Linda Mitchell, Professor of Women and Gender studies at the University of Missouri states in her discussion of women in the medieval period: "All people are motivated by emotional responses and those responses are limited by our own chemistry: attraction, fear, hate, delight, love, lust, anxiety. … The differences lie in how these are expressed and repressed by culture. Medieval people lived in a culture that we could find alien, but they experienced emotions that we would recognize and with which we could empathize" (Mitchell, 2003, p. 5). This quote expresses well how the biological and the contextual intermingle in the evocation and expression of emotions. By extension, these factors and the emotional responses they create lay the foundation for memory and experiences of nostalgia, deeply encoding the details surrounding those emotional responses in our brains. Thus, while emotions are associated with physiological effects that have evolved biologically as part of a system of motivation and attraction that safeguarded the survival of *Homo sapiens* and our ancestors, emotional responses are also shaped by our individual experiences and the cultural and historical context in which they occur.

In the current volume, we have explored the question of how our cultural memory and historical nostalgia, as well as our personal memories, personality, and psychological states, influence our musical preferences. Linked to this, we have considered how music choices in the modern day reflect societal beliefs and values that have evolved over time. We have discussed the strong attraction of some people to music of the past despite

© The Author(s) 2019
S. Garrido, J. W. Davidson. *Music, Nostalgia and Memory*, Palgrave Macmillan Memory Studies,
https://doi.org/10.1007/978-3-030-02556-4_13

the vast transformations in our viewpoints and ways of life over the centuries.

These questions were examined in the present volume by examining both cultural and historical contexts, personal variables and situational variables. This body of work has drawn on the analysis of more than 300 texts, hundreds of musical works, and the responses of over 1000 people in modern-day empirical studies. We also conducted interviews and present individual cases that are illustrative of the trends we describe. In doing so, we have not only drawn together perspectives from multiple disciplines, but provided a model for research that incorporates historical and psychological perspectives—fields that are often considered disparate—and a medley of methodological tools.

In Part I of the volume, we discussed the personal and contextual variables that influence our music listening choices and the reasons why particular musical works take on significance in our memory. In fact, as discussed in Chap. 2, because of its emotional potency, music is one of the most powerful triggers of nostalgia, whether personal, historical or cultural. In addition, our individual propensity to nostalgia appears to influence the music to which we are most attracted, since it plays a role in determining the degree to which we are drawn to music that takes us back to the past. Indeed, this volume as a whole has demonstrated how the interaction between music, emotion and memory underpins a great deal of our music choices and preferences. Family history and upbringing also play a role (see Chap. 3), since our earliest musical experiences tend to occur in the family context and thus become entwined with memories of family and heritage. While other musical influences such as peers gradually take precedence for some, for those who experience disruptions or displacement within the family or cultural context, music can provide an ongoing link with these early memories, and help preserve an important sense of connection to the past.

These influence of these early formative experiences with music further interacts with our personality, education, gender and the cultural context in which we are placed in shaping musical preferences (see Chap. 4). Music serves both as an identity badge for the expression of our personality and the values we associate with it, and as a way to connect with other people of similar values, who in turn may further strengthen our connections to the music which the group identifies itself with. Our gender, and how we ourselves and the culture around us perceive the societal roles appropriate to our gender, further influence both the music to which we will be most exposed and that to which we are drawn.

A primary motivation for listening to music in the modern day, particularly in younger people, is for the purpose of regulating or modulating our affective states—our moods and emotions (see Chap. 5). Once again memory plays a key role in determining the effect particular pieces of music will have on our affective states. At a biological level, certain mechanisms appear to be involved in instinctive affective responses to musical cues. These responses are also moderated by cognitive processes, memories associated with particular music, and the social setting in which the music is heard. This is further influenced by our personality, and by the habitual coping styles we have developed for dealing with difficulties in life.

However, these regulatory strategies and coping styles may not always remain stable across the lifespan (see Chap. 6). While our strongest memories for music seem to come from what is often the peak emotional point our lives—our adolescence and early adulthood, known as the 'reminiscence bump'—other factors, including the changing physiology of the ear, maturing personalities, and ongoing life experiences, can exert an influence on our musical selections over the lifespan. Music can have a renewed place of importance in the lives of maturing adults, particularly the elderly and those facing issues of mortality, because of its capacity to reconnect us with powerful life moments from the past, serving as a form of life reflection and a means of redefining the narrative of one's life.

Overall, Part I of this volume demonstrated the vast array of variables including the personal and contextual that intermingle in shaping our music preferences and listening habits. The chapters in Part I made clear how music, emotion and memory work in a cycle—each reinforcing the connections with each other—in a constant way throughout the lifespan and in conjunction with the other variables discussed.

In Part II of this volume, we considered how the influences discussed in Part I interact to shape our musical choices at six peak life stages: birth, childhood, coming of age, falling in love and experiencing heartbreak, marriage and death. Within each of these topics we have traced a trajectory from the past to the modern day, depicting how cultural memory interfaces with individual variables to create our personal musical experiences. Real life examples in these chapters vividly demonstrated how this plays out in the lives of individuals in the twenty-first century.

Chapter 7 commenced this focus on key life moments with an in-depth consideration of the place of music in birth rituals throughout history and today. Both historically and in the twenty-first century across many cultures, music is found in three central events that surround the birth of the a child: labour and giving birth, announcing the birth or introducing the newborn to the community, and formal celebrations of the child's arrival such as a name-giving ceremony or the re-integration of the mother into the community. Traditionally, music during the birth itself has been used as a signal of solidarity between the women of a village or tribe and the birthing mother, a way to offer strength and support. Our modern day examples demonstrated that in the relatively disconnected and clinical birth settings of the twenty-first century, music selections can tend to suggest a desire for connection to the 'village' of feminine strength and communal solidarity as well. While the lives of many modern day working women do not allow for the same depth of ritual that has been traditionally found in tribal societies in relation to recovery from birth, music still provides a forum for personal expression by the parents, albeit a form of self-expression that is perhaps under-utilized in the context of birth in contemporary society. Thus this chapter demonstrated not only how the past influences our music choices today, but ways in which we have lost the potential for music to influence wellbeing in some modern day contexts.

Even after the birth and a period of readjustment to the new arrival for the family, music continues to have great significance throughout childhood, with biological developments ensuring that even small babies are equipped to discern important musical features (see Chap. 8). Singing provides an important means of communication and bonding between parents and infant, contributing to the child's overall cognitive and emotional development, as well as allowing the parent an outlet for personal expression of the joys and frustrations associated with caring for a child. Thus, childhood songs—both lullabies and more light-hearted play songs—are found in cultures all over the world throughout history. However, changing beliefs about childhood over time are reflected in the content of those songs. The innocence of childhood as is romanticized and valued in the twenty-first century, was less idealized and often short-lived in children of earlier centuries. Thus the lyrics of children's songs have tended to become more 'whitewashed' over time, demonstrating how music selections are strongly influenced by cultural memory and the emotional regime (Reddy, 2001) of particular societal and historical contexts. Childhood songs themselves become a strong source of nostalgic remembering, and are used to transmit family values and customs from generation to generation.

As children grow up, the role of music in marking important stages of development persists. While 'adolescence' as a concept is a largely modern, Western notion, implying the attainment of a stage between childhood and adulthood, ritualistic marking of the passage from childhood is found in many cultural settings and over many historical periods. In many settings young people were considered to have reached adulthood once they achieved puberty. However, traditionally, this point of transition formed a high point in the life of a young person and the community in which they resided. Chapter 9 considered how traditional coming of age rituals served important psychological functions in both the lives of the individuals they celebrated and those of the community as a whole. Music was often believed to hold important, even magical roles in the ceremonies of transition in many cultural settings. While the attainment of adulthood in modern day Western cultures is often more incremental than in the past, both families and peer groups have tended to develop their own rituals to celebrate major transitions along the path to adulthood. Music has taken on differing roles in these modern day rituals. Less about protecting young people from danger or educating them about societal roles, music in modern coming of age celebrations has less to do with the passing on of cultural traditions than with themes of 'partying' and enjoyment. However, as they have historically, modern day rituals still perform the function of providing social acknowledgement of the individual's attainment at any stage of their lives. Thus Chap. 9 demonstrated how music choices reflect broader societal changes while continuing to fulfill similar psychological functions across time and culture.

One of the most enduring subject matters that permeates the music of all cultures and time-periods is that of love and heartbreak. The subject of romantic love is found in the music of the ancient Sumerians from two thousand years before Christ, throughout the centuries and into the most popular song charts of the twenty-first century. However, Chap. 10 illustrates how music can both reflect the dominant emotional regimes of the societal contexts in which it is found and shape those beliefs, with the politics of love and lovers being manifested differently in song texts from different periods—even in a single song in the case of ballads that have remained in use over hundreds of years such as 'Scarborough Fair'. While the predominance of love songs in popular culture is testament to the strong biological imperative of romantic love, love songs have played a key role both in the development of music traditions and on modern-day ideals of love. The expression of heartbreak in music also finds its roots in powerful biological processes, as well as in the historical influences of the oppressed groups who often were the creators of love songs in times past. Thus this chapter provided some further insight into the complex interplay of history, biology and cultural climate in shaping our musical listening choices.

Weddings too, while demonstrating some basic commonalities across cultures and time periods, have changed greatly in cultural meaning (see Chap. 11). Music may dominate wedding rituals associated with the preparations for the big day, the ceremony itself, and the post-ceremonial celebrations. Nevertheless, modern day wedding rituals tend to reflect a level of tradition (albeit relatively new traditions) that is somewhat surprising, and that can at least in part be attributed to clever commercialization of the wedding industry and the 'fairy-tale ending' idealized in Hollywood films. Burgeoning communicative technologies in the nineteenth and twentieth centuries increased the degree to which wedding traditions, including the music used, have been influenced by the weddings of royalty and other celebrities. Thus, even in non-Western cultures, Wagner's Bridal Chorus and Mendelssohn's Wedding March have become globally recognized as symbolic of the wedding. Thus the music associated with weddings in the modern day tends to mirror both traditional elements and the changing significance that the ceremony holds in the twenty-first century. It seems likely that these choices are less reflective of a desire to emulate what is traditional than to project a romantic ideal. Thus Chap. 11 demonstrated how nostalgia, tradition, and history become mingled in their influence on our musical choices, with commerce, film and popular media each impacting on both the ideals portrayed and the social function of modern day weddings.

Chapter 12 considered end-of-life rituals and the spectrum of ways in which music is incorporated into funerals from expressing grief to celebrating life. Again, as in the other chapters, some features of these rituals appear to hold true across time and cultures, while others have metamorphosed with changing societal beliefs and perspectives. Increasing secularization of Western societies has meant that music's function is less to assist in the transformation of the deceased into spirit life or to express a belief in the afterlife than to join the mourners in common expressions of grief and to deliver a personal message of comfort from the deceased to those who survive. However, music still holds a spiritual role in funerals for many, both those who hold to religious convictions and those who do not, in its capacity to imbue an occasion with a sense of the sacred. Thus music continues to fulfill important psychological functions for grieving individuals, those anticipating their own death, and emotional communities as a whole.

Part II of this volume vividly depicted how the variables discussed in Part I merge to sculpt musical meaning and interactions in a variety of human contexts in the modern day. Nostalgia plays a vital connecting role here, with the capacity for music to invoke powerful memories acting as the force which draws together the strands of personal, historical and cultural influences. This merging in turn creates a response to music that is at once highly individual, while simultaneously being a result of biological and environmental influences that are experienced in common by human beings across time and cultures.

Figure 13.1 shows how this might occur. A cycle of music, the emotions it evokes and the memories encoded as a result, are subjected to the constant influence of a variety of forces including our age, our gender, our family, the culture in which we reside, the peers with which we associate, our personality—both genetic and as shaped by our environment, our

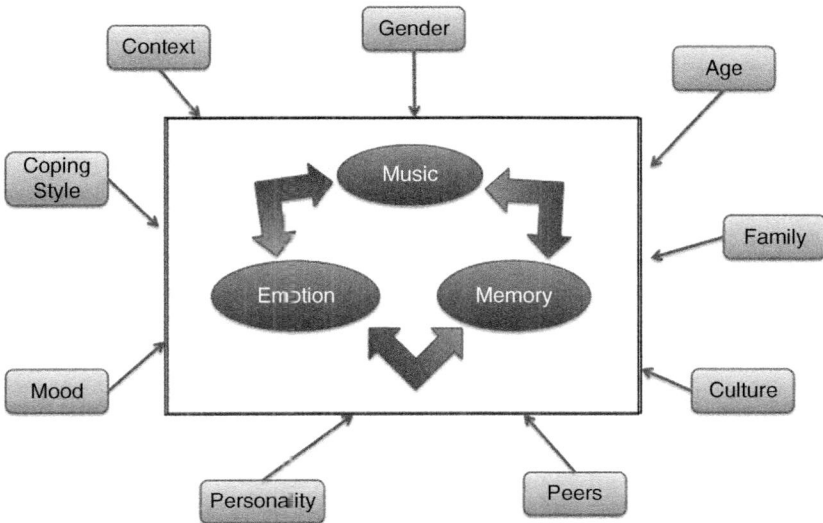

Fig. 13.1   Model of a contextual psychology of music and emotion

mood, the coping style we develop over time, and the physical and social context in which we hear the music. These influences impress their shape upon the development of music itself and the emotions we experience in response to them as well the memories that are encoded when we hear music and experience an affective response. However, the role of this cycle between music, emotions and memories remains central to the process and dictates the way other variables interact and mould our musical experiences. This way of understanding emotional responses to music can be described as a 'contextual psychology of music and emotion', a comprehensive model for investigating and comprehending musical preferences, choices, and interactions.

The interconnectivity and inseparableness of historical, cultural, contextual, and personal influences in creating our response to music and ways of using it, leads us to make the argument for a model of research which uses multiple perspectives and methodologies to gain a more complete picture of the role of the arts in modern day life than previous research has provided. Our understanding of how the arts influence our lives in contemporary society is incomplete without considering the contextual factors that have shaped our musical responses. Musical choices are influenced not only by the dominant social beliefs of the emotional regime in which we exist, but by the historical forces which have in turn moulded those beliefs. In addition, biological mechanisms underpin our response to music and the arts at the most basic level, and therefore, no consideration of historical factors can be complete without considering the biological basis of our response to external stimuli, and indeed the biological imperatives which drive the structures of human society. In fact, considering factors that appear to be held in common by societies across time and culture can help to reveal more about the demarcation between values that stem from a biological basis and those that are shaped by social processes.

Of course, while many different art forms (from story-telling to sculpture) stir an emotional response, modern evidence and history reveal that people often report stronger emotional reactions to music than to other art forms. However, these reactions to music can range from general moods via imprecise and seemingly undefinable feelings, to specific emotions. Attempts to understand these affective responses can be traced back for centuries. For example, the nineteenth century saw efforts among music scholars, theorists and composers to identify the exact source of expression in music, resulted in diffusing discourses on music and the arts.

In Western theory across the twentieth century, different types of engage-ment with music, dance, drama were discussed from within their own disciplines. It has only been in more recent time that interest in how disciplines can interact to advance understanding has been examined. As Wiebke Thormahlen (2019) argues, it was in fact as a consequence of the Second World War when people were subjected to the extremes of emo-tions (e.g. The horror of the Holocaust) that researchers really began to consider how to civilise emotions across disciplines by measuring, defin-ing, and formalizing them. In the study of music, this presents some incredible challenges that have made people explore the very psycho-social core of culture and society. That capacity for music to civilise or enact other powerful forms of behaviour has been discussed throughout this volume.

Indeed, rather than representing mutually exclusive viewpoints, mod-ern day psychological perspectives can add additional layers of understand-ing to the reconstruction of emotions in history of emotions research. Historical explorations similarly provide additional shades of insight into affective responses to music in the modern day, illuminating not only cross-cultural and inter-temporal commonalities in music use, but high-lighting ways in which the arts can be used to further improve well-being in the modern day as they have in the past. We thus, through this volume, demonstrate a multi-disciplinary, mixed methods approach to investigat-ing music and emotion, as depicted in Fig. 13.2.

The multi-disciplinary approach taken in this volume can prevent researchers from falling prey to criticisms by historians that psychologists tend for reductionism and fail to see the situatedness of their own disci-pline, its tools and processes. The current volume attempts to contribute to the interdisciplinary discourse about emotions, memory and responses to music. We suggest that any attempt at a comprehensive examination of music and emotion should incorporate a study of historical sources, con-sidering how music has been used in the past, the meaning of particular musical devices or musical works throughout history, and the emotional communities or emotional regimes in which they were created and heard. Furthermore, a study of the musical works themselves can consider ques-tions such as what the works and texts used suggest about the composer's own 'emotional community' (Rosenwein, 2002), or those of the context in which the work was composed. Analysis of the music can consider how the composer either expressed or avoided expressing particular emotions and how this reflects the values and beliefs of the cultural and temporal

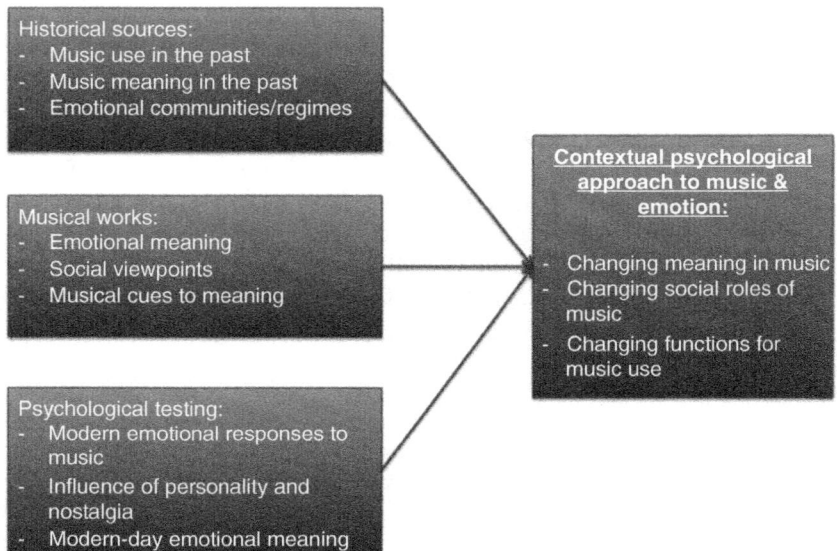

Fig. 13.2 A contextual psychological approach to music and emotion research

context of the music's creator. Particular musical devices used to express emotion can also reveal something of the biological underpinnings of our affective response to music in the way they mimic physiological changes that occur during emotional experiences (see for e.g., Davidson, Kiernan, & Garrido, 2017).

These historical and musical analyses can increase our comprehension of emotional responses to music, supplementing our understanding from empirical psychological research about how memory and nostalgia intertwine with modern-day values and meanings as well as our own personality and experiences to create our musical interactions in the modern day. A combination of approaches as illustrated in this volume can enable researchers to consider how the social and other functions of music as well as the meaning we draw from it have changed over time.

This volume has also illustrated how understandings of music perception, cognition and appreciation are limited by the focus that exists in much current research in the field on Western 'classical' music. We propose that the consideration of music from diverse genres, cultural settings, and time periods, can deeply enrich our understanding of the functions of music in human society and the processes by which it influences us. The research we have presented in this volume has considered the musical traditions of multiple cultures including those of African nations, Asia and a mixture of European nations, adding many shades to the picture of musical response and preferences. We have further included along with discussion of Western classical music, analysis of popular music traditions from Western cultures both past and present.

While it is our claim that a multitude of approaches, perspectives and methodologies is essential to providing a nuanced picture of musical responses and preferences, we acknowledge that such a broad brush approach has its limitations. Indeed, one could devote a lifetime to exploring one of the topics considered in this volume alone. In the current volume it has been impossible to explore each topic with the detail of scholars who have devoted their research careers to studying the works of Bach or the musical traditions of the Kikuya people of Kenya, for example. Nevertheless, we would argue that pulling together strands of research from a variety of sources as we have done in this volume, provides a unique and informative portrait of musical behaviours. Cross-disciplinary research provides an interesting avenue for future research in music psychology which will no doubt continue to further illuminate the complex processes by which we respond to music in human society.

REFERENCES

Davidson, J. W., Kiernan, F., & Garrido, S. (2017). Introducing a Psycho-Historical Approach to the Study of Emotions in Music: The Case of Monteverdi's 'Ill Combattimento di Tancredi e Clorinda'. *Emotions: History, Culture, Society, 1*(1), 29–50.

Mitchell, L. E. (2003). *Portraits of Medieval Women: Family, Marriage and Social Relationships in the Thirteenth Century.* New York: Palgrave Macmillan.

Reddy, W. M. (2001). *The Navigation of Feeling: A Framework for the History of Emotions.* Cambridge and New York: Cambridge University Press.

Rosenwein, B. H. (2002). Worrying About Emotions in History. *The American Historical Review, 107*(3), 821–845.

Thormahlen, W. (2019). Music and Dance. In J. W. Davidson & J. Damousi (Eds.), *Volume 6: 1920–2000s, A Cultural History of Emotions.* London: Bloomsbury.

Index[1]

A

ABBA, 179
Adele, 204
Adolescents, 50, 67, 71, 92, 102, 103,
     132, 183, 185, 186
Africa, 108, 130, 131, 174, 187
Age, 18, 29, 31, 33, 39, 43, 39, 91,
     101–103, 107, 109, 111–115,
     117, 129, 137, 139, 140, 152,
     159, 160, 163–167, 173–177,
     183, 185, 191, 199, 200, 202,
     210, 212, 229, 235, 252–254,
     271
Albinoni, Tomaso, 255
Anxiety, 35, 67, 129, 136, 143, 145,
     208, 265
Appraisal theory, 5
Aristotle, 83–85, 89
Armstrong, Louis, 103–105
Arousal, 52, 55, 66, 67, 69, 71, 137,
     137n4, 139, 140, 144, 145, 156,
     159, 159n2, 160, 168, 178,
     178n2, 181, 200, 200n7, 230, 231

Art Garfunkel, 37, 196
Australian Broadcasting Corporation
     (ABC), 17, 18

B

Bach, J. S., 14, 41, 141, 219, 220,
     227, 230, 251, 258, 275
Barber, Samuel, 42
The Beach Boys, 233
The Beatles, 99, 178, 179, 198, 230
Beethoven, Ludwig van, 249
Bells, 156, 162, 241, 247–248, 255
Beyonce, 54
Big Five personality
     extraversion, 67
     neuroticism, 31, 67, 206
Birth, 1, 11, 12, 21, 59, 100, 106,
     127–146, 194, 217, 267, 268
Blackletter broadsides, 154
Boethius, 83–88, 194
Brain stem reflexes, 79
Bruch, Max, 41

[1] Note: Page numbers followed by 'n' refer to notes.

© The Author(s) 2019
S. Garrido, J. W. Davidson, *Music, Nostalgia and Memory*, Palgrave
Macmillan Memory Studies,
https://doi.org/10.1007/978-3-030-02556-4

Bulgaria, 217, 223, 228
Burton, Robert, 90
Byrd, William, 14

C
Caccini, Guilio, 219
Cantos de angeles, 241, 244
Cappella, Martianus, 86
Cassiodorus, M.A., 84, 85
Cave, Nick, 203
Chapbooks, 153
Childhood, 7, 11, 17, 21, 50, 51,
    100–106, 113, 151–169, 173,
    176, 183, 185, 221, 224,
    267–269
Children, 29, 41, 49, 50, 52, 56–60,
    69, 81, 93, 102–105, 107–110,
    114, 127, 128, 130–138,
    140–142, 144, 145, 151–169,
    175, 183, 185, 196, 241, 244,
    245, 268, 269
Chile, 241, 244
Chinese opera, 57
Choirs, 86, 109–115, 117, 140, 219,
    242, 249, 259
Chopin, Frederic, 249
Churching, 134
Classical music, 18, 34, 40–42, 73, 92,
    159, 182, 252, 274, 275
Cognitive ecologies, 16
Coldplay, 200
Collectivist cultures, 50, 55–56, 60
Coming of age, 11, 21, 130, 173–187,
    267, 269
Communal music, 3
Conditioning, 80
Contextual psychology, 7, 265–275
Coping style, 18, 36, 43, 67, 67n1,
    69, 93, 94, 137, 138, 161, 202,
    206, 207, 209, 212, 253, 254,
    267, 272

Country music, 53
Cultural displacement, 34, 49,
    56–60
Culture, 4, 5, 8, 9, 21, 40, 43, 49, 50,
    52–61, 65, 68, 71, 72, 81, 82, 94,
    102–104, 107–110, 117, 127–135,
    140–145, 151–158, 165–168,
    173–175, 185, 189, 190, 196,
    198, 199, 210, 211, 217, 218,
    221–223, 225, 227–229, 234, 236,
    241–246, 258, 261, 265, 266,
    268–273, 275

D
da Foligno, Gentile, 87, 88
Dance music, 66, 68, 182
Dancing, 2, 57, 130, 132, 135, 142,
    155, 179, 182, 202, 221, 225,
    226, 228, 229, 232, 233, 236,
    244–246
Darwin, Charles, 189
de Pareja, Ramis, 88
Death, 1, 9, 32, 69, 127, 129, 173,
    206, 242–244, 247, 248,
    252–257, 260, 261, 267, 271
Debussy, Claude, 200
Dementia, 111, 114, 115
Depression, 31, 34–36, 68, 87, 90,
    91, 93, 112, 138, 144, 168,
    206–210, 212
Diana, Princess of Wales, 9, 20,
    254–257
Doctrine of ethos, 82, 85
Doctrine of humours, 86
Drive Reduction Theory, 6

E
Education, 9, 20, 30, 65–74, 103,
    105, 160, 166, 183, 229, 266
Electronic music, 51, 70, 101

Elgar, Edward, 135, 231
Elizabeth II, Queen, 135, 255
Elizabethan era, 88–89
Emotional communities, 14, 15, 17, 247, 248, 255, 261, 271, 273
Emotional contagion, 2, 79
Emotional regimes, 15, 17, 268, 269, 272, 273
Emotions, 2–6, 11, 13–17, 16n3, 29, 32, 34, 38, 42, 43, 52, 66–68, 70, 74, 79–84, 87, 89, 90, 92–95, 100, 107, 113, 115–118, 128, 137, 152, 160, 180, 182, 194, 195, 202, 206, 207, 209, 210, 213, 218, 225, 242, 245, 247, 252–254, 256, 257, 265–275
Entrainment, 79, 144
Enya, 136
Estonia, 224

F
Family, 4, 16, 20, 41, 43, 49–61, 65, 94, 100, 103, 108–110, 113, 114, 127, 128, 133–135, 140, 141, 145, 157, 158, 161–163, 165, 168, 174–176, 180, 181, 183, 184, 186, 196, 202, 217–219, 221, 223, 224, 226, 232–234, 236, 237, 244, 248, 250, 255, 257, 258, 250, 266, 268, 269, 271
Fertility songs, 190
Ficino, Marsilio, 88, 89
Fiji, 130, 233
Finland, 224
Folk music, 53, 139, 197, 198
Forli, Jacopo da, 87
Frottola, 193
Funerals, 11, 17, 18, 20, 21, 59, 134, 237, 241–261, 270

G
Gender, 20, 31, 39, 43, 61, 65–74, 94, 107, 117, 118, 174, 176, 186, 196, 197, 199–201, 203, 209, 211, 212, 221, 229, 235–237, 258, 265–267, 271
Georgia, 243
Globalization, 49, 55, 56, 176
Gospel music, 54
Grief, 5, 35, 114, 223, 225, 241–243, 248, 251, 253–256, 260, 270

H
Handel, George Frederic, 41, 141, 222, 229, 249
Harmony of spheres, 82, 86, 88, 194
Heartbreak, 11, 17, 21, 69, 74, 93, 179, 189–213, 267, 269, 270
Heavy metal, 6, 33–34, 43, 66, 70, 73
Hildegard of Bingen, 86, 129
Historical context, 4, 5, 7, 9, 10, 12, 16, 101, 158, 260, 265, 266, 268
Historical nostalgia, 10, 31, 43, 213, 253, 265
History of emotions, 11, 13, 14, 273
Homer, 82, 221, 228, 241
Hymns, 134, 135, 141, 175, 219, 220, 222, 245, 250, 258, 259

I
Iceland, 109–111, 178
India, 130, 132, 155, 175, 193
Individual differences, 6, 7, 10, 91, 209
Infants, 129, 132, 141, 151–153, 155–157, 165, 167, 244, 245, 268
Instrumental music, 34, 59, 71, 137, 251

J

Japan, 157, 196, 198, 234, 237
Jazz, 34, 35, 40, 43, 50, 53, 67, 71,
    73, 103, 104, 137, 191, 245, 253
Jazz funerals, 241, 245–246
Jewish culture, 175
Joel, Billy, 258
John, Elton, 9, 255, 256

L

Laments, 155, 179, 192, 211, 224,
    225, 241, 243
Latin music, 40, 59
Lennon, John, 39, 141
Love, 11, 15, 17, 21, 30, 37, 39, 90,
    103, 104, 106, 108, 114, 127,
    130, 139, 154, 157, 165, 167,
    179, 189–213, 218, 220, 231,
    233, 235, 237, 258, 260, 265,
    267, 269, 270
Lullabies, 135, 153–155, 157–160,
    167, 168, 268
Lyrics, 53, 69, 70, 93, 115, 139, 155,
    158, 160, 166, 178–182, 192,
    193, 199, 200, 203–207, 213,
    255, 256, 258, 259, 268

M

Madonna Louise Ciccone, 182
Marriage, 1, 86, 94, 129, 167, 173,
    176, 190, 211, 217–228,
    233–237, 267
Medieval period, 15, 41, 84–88, 164,
    165, 191, 265
Memory
    and emotion, 3, 10, 21, 32, 43, 65,
        79, 80, 100, 101, 107, 115,
        117–118, 256, 265–268, 271,
        272
    encoding, 3, 79, 100, 168, 265,
        271, 272

Mendelssohn, Felix, 94, 219, 227,
    229, 234, 237, 270
Mental health, 4, 89, 90, 207, 246
Migration, 56–58, 165, 250
Minor keys, 8, 92, 152
Mode, 15, 58, 82, 83, 85, 87, 88, 90,
    92, 194
Monteverdi, Claudio, 42, 89, 90, 194,
    195
Mood management, 7, 10
Mood management theory, 7
Mood regulation strategies, 7, 21, 67,
    70–71, 94, 256
Moods, 3, 4, 7, 8, 20, 31, 36, 37, 51,
    52, 66–69, 74, 79–95, 114, 115,
    163, 164, 206, 207, 212, 231,
    244, 267, 272
Mourning, *see* Grief
Mozart, Wolfgang Amadeus, 8, 18,
    154, 242, 253
Musical expectancy, 80
Musical identity, 58, 103, 107,
    113
Music preferences, 7–10, 18, 20, 33,
    35, 40, 43, 50, 53, 65–70, 95,
    100, 101, 267
My Life as a Playlist (MLAP), 17, 21,
    34, 39, 40, 51, 54, 59, 69, 71,
    73, 93, 101, 116, 127, 137, 142,
    159, 177, 200, 202, 203, 229,
    235, 242, 251–254, 260

N

New age music, 33, 136
North America, 130, 241
Nostalgia, 20, 43, 56, 60, 65, 109,
    110, 115, 178, 200, 203, 208,
    210, 213, 252–256, 265, 266,
    270, 271, 274
Nostalgia proneness, 32–34, 36, 43,
    178
Nursery rhymes, 153

O

Opera, 57, 68, 72, 89, 162, 194, 198, 219, 222
Orff, Carl, 192

P

Pachelbel, Johann, 222, 229, 255
Pain, 69, 128, 129, 136, 140, 143, 197, 198, 204, 205, 210, 212
Peers, 4, 74, 102, 104, 184, 185, 266, 269, 271
Perry, Katy, 178
Personality, 4, 7, 18, 20, 21, 35, 61, 65–74, 86, 94, 101, 116, 127, 206, 207, 212, 236, 251–254, 265–267, 271, 274
Plato, 1, 82, 84, 90, 91
Play songs, 153, 155–157, 159–162, 167, 168, 268
Pop music, 34, 35, 66, 70, 74, 117, 252, 256
Presley, Elvis, 39, 54, 116
Primary sources, 12
Psychology, 4–7, 11, 137, 255–275
Pythagoras, 82–85

R

Ramadan, 57
Rap/hip-hop, 6, 53–55, 67, 68, 70, 71, 73, 109, 178, 201
Reflection, 36, 69, 113, 187, 251, 259, 267
Rhythm, 58, 79, 83, 84, 87, 89, 109, 130, 136, 138, 139, 142, 144, 145, 152, 154, 155, 178, 225
Rite of passage, 127, 173, 236, 237
Rituals, 1, 2, 21, 55, 59, 96, 127, 128, 130, 132–134, 140, 143–145, 167, 173–177, 183–187, 190, 198, 210, 217, 221–227, 229,

232, 234, 236, 237, 241–261, 268–270
RNB, 34, 43, 55, 71, 101
Rock, 6, 34, 43, 53, 54, 58, 66, 67, 70, 71, 117, 137, 159, 178, 180, 200, 203, 229, 253
Romania, 217, 226, 228, 237
Rumination, 36, 93, 138, 202, 208
Russia, 38, 198, 222–224, 228

S

Secondary sources, 12, 13
Seeger, Pete, 53
Shakespeare, William, 165
Sheeran, Ed, 200
Shostakovich, Dmitri, 41
Siblings, 51, 52, 202, 244
Simon, Paul, 37, 196–198, 202, 203
Sinatra, Frank, 178, 200
Singer-songwriter, 136, 137, 198, 203
Singing, 50, 57, 71, 72, 104, 107, 109–113, 115, 130, 132, 134, 135, 139, 142, 143, 153, 156–159, 162–164, 167–169, 175, 195, 217, 222–226, 228, 229, 236, 244, 258, 260, 268
Social connections, 33, 211
Social interactions, 66, 115
Socrates, 82, 83, 85
Strauss, Richard, 42, 182
Swift, Taylor, 54, 177, 200

T

Technology, 2, 3, 16, 102, 186, 198, 210, 247, 270
Tradition, 10, 12, 31, 38, 41, 42, 50–53, 55–60, 133–135, 140, 144, 153, 154, 158, 173–176, 186, 193, 213, 218, 219, 223,

224, 227, 231–236, 241,
244–246, 249–252, 255, 260,
261, 269, 270, 275
Troubadours, 191–193, 197, 203,
211

V
Valence, 55, 69, 71, 73, 93, 137,
137n4, 159, 159n2, 160, 168,
178, 178n2, 181, 200, 200n7,
230, 231, 236
Vanilla Ice, 54
Venezuela, 132, 134
Verdi, Giuseppe, 198, 255

Victoria, Queen, 15, 165, 176, 218,
219, 222, 227, 235
Victorian England, 134–135
Visual imagery, 80, 136
Vivaldi, 141

W
Wagner, Richard, 42, 94, 198, 219,
222, 234, 270
Weddings, 11, 17, 21, 39, 58, 59, 94,
134, 193, 213, 217–237, 270
West, Kanye, 54
Wonder, Stevie, 177, 180, 182, 186
World music, 34, 40, 43, 59, 73, 74

Printed by Printforce, the Netherlands